Beyond the Five Whys

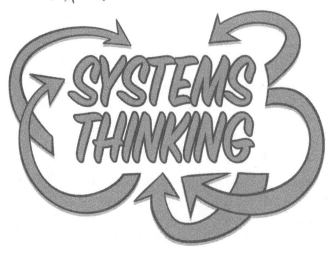

Beyond the Five Whys

Root Cause Analysis and Systems Thinking

James C. Paterson

WILEY

Registered Office(s)
John Wiley & Sons, Inc., 111 River Street, Hoboken, NJ 07030, USA, John Wiley & Sons Ltd, The Atrium, Southern Gate, Chichester, West Sussex, PO19 8SQ, UK

Editorial Office
The Atrium, Southern Gate, Chichester, West Sussex, PO19 8SQ, UK

For details of our global editorial offices, customer services and more information about Wiley products visit us at www.wiley.com.

Library of Congress Cataloguing-in-Publication Data is Available:

ISBN 9781394191055 (Hardback)
ISBN 9781394191062 (ePDF)
ISBN 9781394191079 (ePub)

Cover Design: Wiley
Cover Image: © Michael Rosskothen/Adobe Stock

SKY10057069_100523

To: Isabelle, for everything;

*To: Timothy, Claudie and Elodie; William;
Nicholas and Felicity – and all those near
and dear to the family;*

Contents

Introduction

'Don't Panic'.[1]

For the past 10 years, I have been working with clients in relation to root cause analysis and systems thinking, and it's time to provide an overview for a wider audience.

Why might this be of value?

1. To clarify why specific problems can be hard to fix and why surprises can come from 'out of the blue' despite lots of efforts to the contrary;

2. To help you think through, when things don't go to plan, how you might assess what any individuals involved did or did not do; put bluntly, should anyone take the blame?

3. To illustrate the benefits of moving beyond firefighting, addressing a few root causes now can head off many more problems in the future;

4. To give some suggestions to avoid things going off track in the first place.

From the start, I want to recognise how easy it is to misunderstand root causes. For example, the iceberg was not the root cause of the Titanic tragedy.[2]

Root cause analysis involves resisting the desire to blame someone or something immediately. Thus, neither Captain Edward Smith nor Lookout Frederick Fleet were the root causes of the Titanic disaster, nor were the number of lifeboats.[3] That said, I will illustrate the problems of a 'no-blame' mindset.

Root cause analysis helps us untangle the 'what, where, when, how and who' of a disaster or setback and helps us understand *why it happened.*

I will share numerous real-life accounts from executives and managers illustrating the 'hairline cracks' to look out for that can result in significant setbacks. Their stories challenge a lot of the received wisdom and urban myths about what separates success from failure.

This book gives an overview of the essentials of root cause analysis (RCA henceforth) and systems thinking that should be of practical value. The essence of what I am aiming for is summed up in Illustration 0.1.

The book has three main sections comprising 14 chapters and three optional appendices.

Illustration 0.1   Using Tools and Insights for the journey ahead

Section 1 provides a high-level overview of RCA and systems thinking.

Chapter 1 clarifies some critical points about RCA, including:

- What are root causes and how do these differ from other types of cause?
- Several ways to arrive at root causes, going beyond the popular 'five whys' approach.
- Can there be just one root cause or a primary root cause?

Chapter 2 explains the fishbone diagram and outlines eight ways to understand why things can go off track.

Chapter 3 introduces systems thinking and links this with RCA.

- The discussion also broadens to consider inquiries as well as RCA investigations.

Section 2 provides real-world examples of why things can slip through your fingers.

Chapters 4–11 focus on 'eight ways to understand why':

- With real-world accounts from board members, executives and others, to see how and why things didn't go as planned.
- Outlining what it means to say some problems are 'systemic' or 'cultural'.

Chapter 12 provides a fresh perspective on the Titanic tragedy of April 1912, offering parallels with contemporary setbacks.

Section 3 closes the discussion by looking at practical actions that might be taken so we can start to better understand and head off the 'wicked problems' we are increasingly faced with.

Chapter 13 explains how to encourage action after an RCA or inquiry.

- You can diagnose a disease through an RCA, or inquiry, but that doesn't mean the patient will take the medication needed.

Chapter 14 offers some further perspectives on how to address contemporary issues of importance.

Optional appendices providing further practical advice:

- Appendix A covers effective action planning.
- Appendix B offers advice for managers (including those working in quality, risk, and compliance roles etc.) including an overview of RCA and systems thinking techniques and useful links.
- Appendix C offers advice for those in audit, inspection or supervisory roles.

Overall, I hope to make the case that unless we can challenge old ways of thinking, we'll stay stuck in a 'Groundhog Day' of seeing the same old problems again, and again, and again.[4] As Einstein said, 'We can't solve problems by using the same kind of thinking we used when we created them'.[5]

Section 1

A High-Level Overview Of RCA and Systems Thinking

S ection 1 provides an introduction for those unfamiliar with root cause analysis (RCA) and systems thinking. It will also serve as a brief recap for those familiar with these topics.

Illustrations, diagrams and tables are included at intervals, recognising that sometimes 'a picture is worth a thousand words'.

Notes are available to provide references and to expand on specific points that may be of particular interest.

At the end of each chapter is a bullet point list of many of the key points covered. Thereafter are a few suggestions for those working in organisations that are looking for specific ideas to put into practice.

Section 1

A High-Level
Overview Of
RCA and Systems
Thinking

Chapter 1

Critical Points Concerning Root Cause Analysis (RCA)

'Addiction is finding a quick and dirty solution to the symptom of the problem, which prevents or distracts one from the harder and longer-term task of solving the real problem'.

– Donella H. Meadows[1]

Immediate, Contributing and Root Causes

If someone asks, 'Why did the Titanic sink?', the reply, 'Because it hit an iceberg', is a reasonable first answer. Specifically, *the immediate cause* that led to the sinking of the Titanic was that it hit an iceberg whilst travelling at around 20 knots on 14 April 1912.

However, an immediate cause is not the same as a root cause.

An immediate cause is the event or trigger that sets off a chain of events that results in an adverse outcome: think of a spark that might light a fire.

A contributing cause is something that 'sets the stage' for an immediate cause to create an adverse impact: think of dry tinder on a forest floor or the limited number of lifeboats on the Titanic.

So, beyond immediate and contributing causes, root causes are *the reasons why things didn't go as planned.*

Root cause analysis (RCA) describes a range of tools and techniques that examine what, when, where and how something happened, and who was involved, but ultimately seek to understand why something happened. It's about properly diagnosing an illness and – if we can – finding a cure, not just offering 'sticking plaster' solutions.[2] So, RCA can help you better understand what can be done to stop problems from arising in the first place, or if you can't prevent problems, be clear about what can be done to make any setbacks tolerable.

RCA Fundamentals: Facts, Timelines and Causality

The first cornerstone for an RCA, or inquiry, is gathering relevant facts and evidence in enough detail. Secondly, we need to establish a timeline of what happened; after all, one thing can't cause another without occurring before, or at the same time, as something else. And then we need to cross-check whether one thing is really causing the other or just loosely associated with it.[3]

Given that facts and evidence are central to an effective RCA or inquiry, *the root causes of a specific setback, or disaster, will always depend on the precise facts and circumstances at the time.* This is where forensic analysis comes in. And many of the crime and crash investigation programmes we can see on TV show us clearly how much can be involved to get to the truth. However, for this overview book, I want to concentrate on establishing root causes after this hard work has been done.

The Bowtie Diagram: Thinking through What Can Happen and What to Do about It

The Bowtie diagram was developed over 40 years ago in the chemical industry.[4] It sets out how you can picture an event that has gone wrong or might go wrong. It is a very useful way of helping you think through some of the most essential ideas in RCA. An example of a Bowtie is provided in Diagram 1.1:

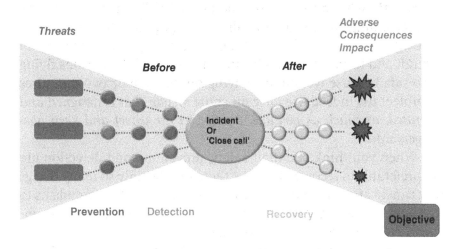

Diagram 1.1   Bowtie diagram (illustrative)

You read the diagram from left to right on the top row and then again on the bottom row, thinking about measures to ensure that incidents do not occur in the first place (e.g. through preventative and detective measures). Or, if they occur, they do not have significant adverse consequences (e.g. because of recovery measures that can be deployed after an incident).[5]

Let's consider travelling by air as a simple example. We can think about the ingredients that make up a Bowtie in this context:

- *A key objective* is to travel safely without damage to the plane or injury to any passengers or crew.
- *The threats* include the risk that an aircraft might hit something.
- *Preventative measures* to avoid encountering threats in the first place include flight plans for each aircraft, air traffic control with radar, a competent crew who can steer the aircraft away from danger, a plane that is capable of manoeuvring safely, etc.
- *Detective measures* to spot threats coming up include radar on aircraft, anti-collision devices, the crew who will look out for other aircraft, etc.

- *Recovery measures* include emergency procedures in case of an incident, trained crew capable of dealing with difficult events, air masks for passengers, etc.

Exactly what measures will be needed will depend on clearly understanding the threats the aircraft might face. But the overall message is that there should be, and are, multiple ways to keep an aircraft and its passengers safe, and this is one of the reasons flying is so safe because we are not relying on just one or two measures to protect us. Indeed, *we have an entire system that is designed and operated, as much as possible, to support air travel and keep passengers safe.*

When you think about air safety, prevention and detection are far preferable to recovery because there may be only so many things you can do after an incident occurs. Thus, the Bowtie reminds us to consider, in each context, the appropriate balance between prevention, detection and recovery measures.[6]

As well as using the Bowtie to think through aircraft and chemical plant safety, etc., it can be used for medical procedures and in a range of other domains.[7] Of course, in daily life we don't usually explicitly refer to preventative, detective or recovery measures, but much of what goes on in practice seeks to achieve those ends.

Prevention, Detection and Recovery Measures

With the Bowtie perspective, we can start the process of RCA if we fail to achieve an objective. We can 'unpack' causes, in a step-by-step way:

- First, was the objective we had *clear* and did we *understand the threats to achieving it?*
- Second, what measures were *planned, or designed*, to prevent and/or detect things from things going off track, or recover afterwards?
- Third, were the measures *implemented in practice* and working effectively?

Considering how things are planned or designed provides an illustration of how RCA techniques can be used to anticipate and engineer away potential problems before they occur, increasing our chances of success. This takes us to High-Reliability Organisations (HROs).

High-Reliability Organisations and RCA

HROs can be found in aviation, oil and gas, nuclear, the chemical industry and other areas with very high stakes.

Consider a chemical plant where a pipeline starts to leak. You would expect the operators to be able to detect a pressure drop and then organise a rapid response to look at the leak. After that, you would expect them to repair or replace the pipe and clean up any pollution. The mindset of identifying, planning for and fixing problems is sometimes called 'single-loop' learning, which can be summarised in Diagram 1.2.[8]

However, imagine that a few months later, there is another leak in a pipe and then another leak. It would likely become clear that a series of relatively quick-fix solutions aren't good enough; you need to go deeper into the underlying reasons why similar issues are arising. For example, is the pressure in the pipes too high? Or are the lines being damaged by external factors, for example, falling branches?

Thinking about why problems might be recurring takes us to what is called 'double-loop' learning, as illustrated in Diagram 1.3.

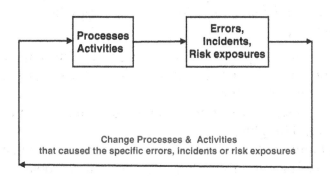

Diagram 1.2   Single-loop learning

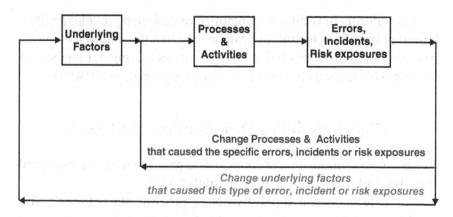

Diagram 1.3   Double-loop learning

'Quick fixes' have their place, but the smart thing to do is to recognise that seeing the same, or similar, problems repeatedly is likely to be a sign that we have missed some other factor that's causing problems. In the example given, maybe we missed opportunities to protect the pipeline adequately. Such a hypothesis could be investigated, and if it explained why the problem was recurring, you would work on this. And this way of thinking might encourage you to find even smarter ways to stop a leak in the first place. For example, you might reroute the pipeline or change the chemicals you are using.

So, HROs aim to maintain a high level of safety, quality, security, etc., over an extended period, *by continuously improving operational activities beyond quick fixes.* The key ingredients of an HRO are as follows:[9]

- A constant recognition that problems and failures might arise;
- Continuous monitoring and awareness of what is happening and what is changing;
- A reluctance to oversimplify things, meaning respect for expert views and insights;
- A commitment to resilience; designing 'layers of defence' that will stop or minimise the chances of minor problems turning into catastrophes.

An HRO perspective says, 'keep looking out for potential trouble' and 'it's better to be safe than sorry', even if there is an additional cost in the short term.

HROs have developed a range of tools and techniques to minimise the chances of problems arising by thinking about (i) design excellence, and (ii) excellence in operational delivery and monitoring, and (iii) carrying out rigorous RCAs if they encounter setbacks or 'near misses'.[10]

In an ideal world, you might hope that all organisations would want to aspire to be HROs. However, where risks seem lower or costs are constrained, this way of operating can seem too cautious, bureaucratic and wasteful. However, as the discussion about RCA and systems thinking progresses, I hope to show that an intelligent application of HRO practices can – in the right situations – significantly help organisations reduce the number of setbacks they experience.[11]

The 5 Whys (Five Whys) and More

One of the most well-known RCA techniques is called the Five Whys. Toyota developed it in quality circles in Japan and it has been used across the motor industry and beyond. It arose from a 'Lean manufacturing' approach, seeking to make things 'right first time'.

Thus, if things didn't turn out as expected on the production line, operators learned to ask why, why, etc., to diagnose the reasons for this, and as a result, to put in place solutions to fix problems over the long run. Other Lean techniques developed alongside the Five Whys include poke yoke (or mistake proofing) and a kaizen culture (of continuous improvement).

As you gain experience with why questions, it can become clear there are *different ways to focus these 'why' questions*. So, if something bad happens, you can ask:

- Why measures that might have *prevented* things from going wrong didn't work or work in time;

- Why measures that might have *detected* a threat before it went wrong didn't work or work in time;
- Why recovery measures that might have *reduced the impact of a problem* didn't work or work in time.

Thus, we arrive at the first RCA technique that goes beyond just asking why five times; it's called the 'three-way five whys', where we ask 'why' in relation to prevention, detection and recovery and recognise the need to go beyond looking for just one root cause. A template for the three-way five whys is provided in Diagram 1.4. It would be completed with answers to why something went off track, supported by appropriate evidence to underpin each of the conclusions so that they can be defended.

So, if a serious incident arises because of a leaking fuel pipe (say on an aircraft), it is quite possible it could arise because of all three of the following:

- A flaw in the fuel pipeline – which, if built with a better design, might have prevented the leak; and
- The absence of a fuel pressure monitor – which, if it was there, might have detected that fuel was leaking; and

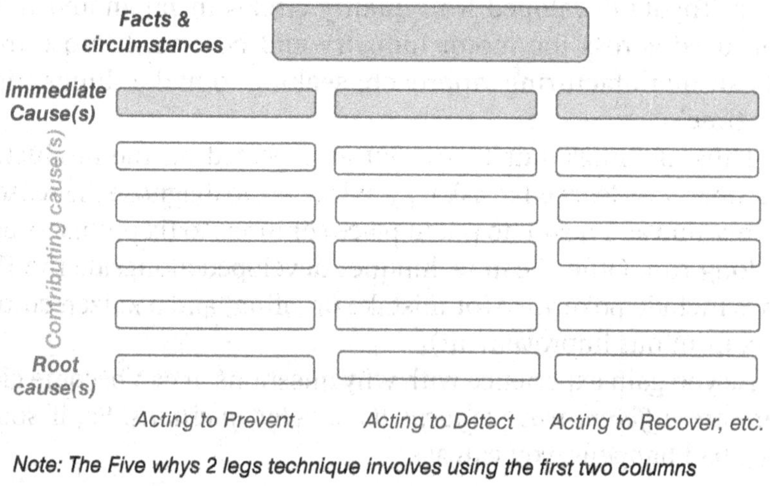

Note: The Five whys 2 legs technique involves using the first two columns

Diagram 1.4   Three-way five whys

- A missing secondary fuel pipeline – which might have been switched to if the first fuel pipeline failed.

All three of these factors are likely to be important, because if any one of the measures was working fully effectively, they might have stopped or reduced the impact of an incident in the first place.

Doing RCA using the three-way five whys can be likened to 'digging into' all the facts and looking for the important roots. Thus, the three-way five whys can also be depicted as a 'fault tree' using Diagram 1.5.

You can see how an analogy with the roots of a plant is useful. If you don't find and pull out all the roots, the plant grows back. If you remove all the roots, it won't grow back. So, suppose you see repeating issues or similar issues arising. In that case, there may still be root causes that have not been identified or addressed. It's a tool that can take us from 'single-loop' learning and quick fixes to 'double-loop' learning, where we aim to understand all the reasons why things went wrong to fix things for the long run.

The fault tree in Diagram 1.5 is one example of various 'tree' diagrams that can be used in RCA, e.g. issue trees, logic trees, etc. Tree diagrams are commonly used in oil and gas, aviation, and engineering environments, but can be used in a range of other contexts.

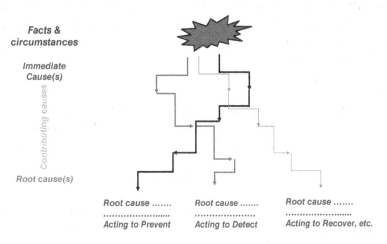

Diagram 1.5 Fault tree showing three-way five whys

They have power in the way that they can show how causes can 'split' (i.e. be the result of one thing as well as another). However, I am not going to cover 'tree' techniques further at this juncture since there are a range of other techniques that I want to look at, given the scope of this book. But more information about different tree approaches to RCA can be found in Appendix B.

Rare, If Ever, to Have Just One Root Cause: Beyond the Five Whys

As you become more familiar with RCA, you will discover it's rare, perhaps impossible, to find that there is just one root cause for a significant disaster or recurring problem. This is one of the reasons why this book is called '*Beyond the Five Whys*' because imagining you can just ask 'why' five times to get to the bottom of a problem can easily result in missing things.

The argument that there is no such thing as one root cause or no 'main' root cause can be hard to accept sometimes. I understand this, given that the term 'root cause analysis' seems to refer to a singular cause. If you are unsure about my assertion that there will normally be more than one root cause, I would ask you to keep an open mind for a little longer.[12] As I run through the real-life examples in this book and explain other RCA techniques beyond the five whys, I hope it will become clearer why it's useful and necessary to have this perspective.

In a nutshell:

> 'Everything should be made as simple as possible, but not simpler'.
> – *after Albert Einstein.*[13]

Summary

- It is crucial to distinguish between immediate, contributing and root causes.
- Root causes will always depend on the context and facts of the situation, so rigorous fact-finding techniques and the development of detailed timelines are standard in RCA investigations.

- Root causes are underlying reasons why something didn't go to plan.
- Identifying root causes should help you understand what might be done to stop things from going wrong or maximise the chances of tolerable setbacks.
- The Bowtie diagram is a useful tool when doing an RCA. It sets out objectives, threats, and then preventative, detective and recovery measures to keep things on track.
- It's always tempting to look at the people involved when things go wrong, but RCA encourages us to look beyond the who to understand the why.
- High-Reliability Organisations focus on putting in place a range of measures and controls to reduce to a minimum the chances of an adverse event.
- HROs apply 'double-loop' learning and avoid getting stuck in firefighting mode; this involves being able to question underlying assumptions.
- The '5 whys' is a well-known RCA technique. Still, it must be recognised that you can ask why in different ways – e.g. by looking at prevention, detection and recovery. This leads to the three-way five whys technique, recognising no such thing as one root cause.
- 'Fault trees' are commonplace in RCA. There are many different variations.
- There is rarely, if ever, a single root cause for a problem or near miss. Usually, there are hairline cracks concerning preventative, detective, and recovery measures.

Chapter 2

The Fishbone Diagram and Eight Ways of Understanding Why

'All the classifications man has ever devised are arbitrary, artificial, and false, but . . . reflection also shows that such classifications are useful, indispensable, and above all unavoidable since they accord with an innate aspect of our thinking'.

– Egon Friedell[1]

Can Root Cause Analysis Be Applied to Minor Defects? Insights from Lean Ways of Working

It should be self-evident that if something catastrophic happens or things show only a slight improvement over time (e.g. a pipe keeps leaking), this is a time to do a root cause analysis (RCA).

And, if there is a 'near miss' (where nothing bad has happened yet, but something bad nearly happened), this can also be a time to consider an RCA, because it may be the only warning you get before something much worse happens.

Over a period of time, Lean manufacturing insights highlighted that if you do something frequently, even the smallest defect might become a big deal (e.g. if you were to have a faulty air bag installed in thousands of cars) and so might merit an RCA, to avoid problems accumulating.

The Fishbone Diagram and Different Categories of Causes

While each RCA investigation, or inquiry, will be different, if you do RCA regularly enough or read enough inquiry reports, you start to see patterns

(i) in what happened or nearly went wrong (e.g. a project did not meet its deadline or keep to the agreed budget) and

(ii) in the underlying reasons things didn't go to plan (e.g. a failure to appreciate a project's risks, alongside insufficient contingency plans).

Those doing Lean manufacturing noticed the same thing; quality problems in car production were sometimes the result of similar root causes (e.g. poor maintenance of factory machines or poorly designed parts). So, quality engineer Kaoru Ishikawa developed a 'fishbone' diagram to set out cause and effect relationships for quality defects. This has evolved into one of the most well-known RCA tools.

The diagram takes an incident, a near miss or a risk of concern.[2] Then, it encourages us to look at the range of reasons (known as causal factors) why this has happened or why things might go off track. It is essentially a modification of a tree diagram, but it has more structure by emphasising certain key causal factors that you should check to make sure you haven't missed anything important when analysing the situation.

These causal factors also give you different ways to ask 'why' questions, taking you from immediate to contributing to root causes. You complete a fishbone diagram by asking why along the different 'bones' (in a similar manner to questions about prevention, detection and recovery) and – depending on the facts – you will likely establish several root causes for a given area of concern. An example of a fishbone diagram is provided in Diagram 2.1. Note that although there are six cause types listed in the diagram, there may only be two or three cause types present for a specific area of concern; it all depends on the facts.

Different versions of the fishbone diagram can be found. Popular root cause categories you might see include the following:

(I) In a manufacturing context: Manpower, Machines, Materials, Methods, Measurements and Environment (known as 5M+E);

(II) In a sales and marketing context: Price, Place, Promotion, People, Process, Performance, etc. (known as 8Ps).

And more generally:

(III) Strategy, Skills, Staff, Structure, Systems, etc., after the McKinsey 7S framework;[3]

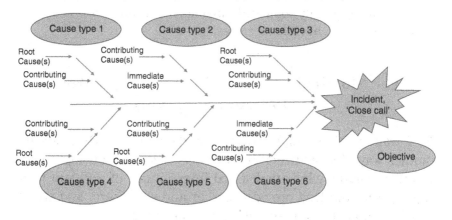

Diagram 2.1   Fishbone diagram

(IV) Strategy, Structure, Processes, People, etc., after the Galbraith Star Model;[4]

(V) Strategy and Objective Setting, Information and Communication, Governance and Culture, etc., after the COSO Model.[5]

Over the years of working with clients, I have noticed categories that seem to help people understand why things haven't been working, but also how easy it is to misunderstand some categories and, as a result, get confused about the root causes. Here are two example to illustrate the point:

- If you have 'People' or 'Staff' as an area to focus on, it is easy to focus on *who* was involved and *who, perhaps*, didn't get it right rather than *why these people did what they did.*
- Likewise, if you have 'Materials', 'Methods', 'Processes' or 'Systems' as lines for inquiry, you might focus on what and how rather than *why*.

Dr Mohammad Farhad Peerally (Associate Professor, University of Leicester) offers his perspective:

'I have studied the use of RCA in a medical context for several years. Over time, RCA practice has evolved and become more powerful. But there is no doubt that when you look at early attempts to analyze causes, the categories of "people" and "process" can be heavily populated. After all, many things come back to these factors, but this doesn't explain why.'

The Modified Fishbone Diagram: Eight Ways of Understanding Why

So, I want to share 'eight ways of understanding why', offering another way of structuring the fishbone diagram. The 'eight ways of understanding why' are distilled from a range of different techniques, from the lists provided earlier and elsewhere, and which have been effective in many situations and contexts.

The eight ways will be discussed in more detail, with practical examples, in Section 2, but in overview the eight ways focus on:

(I)   Whether strategies and goals were appropriately set, understanding key risks, and recognising what might be a tolerable setback;[6]

(II) Whether there was timely, accurate data, information and communications, to be able to see if things are going as planned or starting to go off track;

(III) Whether roles, responsibilities, accountabilities and authorities (R2A2) were set appropriately so there are no gaps in who does what and who makes decisions;

(IV) Whether there was a suitable design – of facilities, buildings, structures, equipment, systems, policies, protocols, procedures, reward and recognition, etc. – e.g. if you want to build a tall structure, you need a design, or a plan, that factors in the loads and stresses it will be subject to;

(V)   Whether external factors were identified and appropriately accommodated, recognising these might knock things off track;

(VI) Whether building, maintenance and change were effectively executed; this could be of structures, systems, policies, etc. Because even if a design is good, shoddy building, poor maintenance or repairs can be a precursor to problems;

(VII) Whether human factors were adequately considered; because if you want to fly to the moon, you need people with 'the right stuff', but even then, they will need to work as an effective team (both in the spacecraft and at ground control);

(VIII) Whether resources, priorities and dilemmas were properly understood and worked through.

The eight ways of understanding why can be set out in a 'modified fishbone diagram' – see Diagram 2.2.

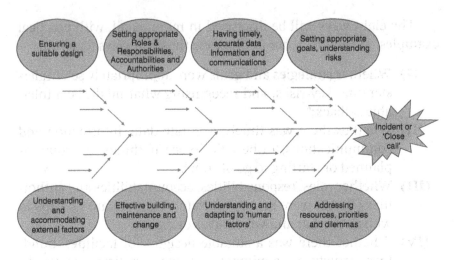

Diagram 2.2   Eight ways to understand why: a modified fishbone diagram

So, if a project isn't going to plan, we can ask 'why' in different ways: e.g. 'Is the project timeline and budget realistic?' and 'Are there adequate "early warning signs"?' or 'Are there issues with resourcing, etc.?' and, depending on the facts, start to unpick what has been going on and why.

The eight ways to understand why is not proposed as a definitive RCA framework. However, my experience working with clients has taught me that it usually helps to shift people's mindset on root causes. And as I walk through the 'eight ways of understanding why' with real-life examples from a range of contributors, it should become increasingly clear how and why one reason for a setback or recurring problem can be connected to another. To put it another way, it may become apparent how some challenges are 'systemic', which takes us to a discussion about systems thinking.

Summary

- Lean ways of working encourage a 'right first-time' mindset and use RCA to clarify why things may go off track.
- Lean techniques emphasise that RCA is not only for major issues or setbacks. Instead, relatively minor issues, defects, inefficiencies

or near misses may merit an RCA because when repeated they can become significant or they may be a warning of the risk of a much bigger adverse event.

- The fishbone (Ishikawa) diagram, developed through Lean ways of working, shows how different types of causes may have contributed to a problem or near miss. It automatically recognises there may be more than one root cause.
- The categories in the fishbone diagram can help you think about the common reasons why problems arise. They also act as a tool to help you head off problems before they appear.
- Categories in the fishbone can vary and should help you focus on why, not just who or what, etc.
- The modified fishbone provides 'eight ways of understanding why' things haven't gone to plan; the causal factors include: realistic goals; roles and responsibilities; addressing human factors; resources, priorities, and dilemmas.

Chapter 3
Systems Thinking and Eight Ways to Understand Why, with Connections

'A bad system will beat a good person every time'.
– W. Edwards Deming[1]

Systems Thinking – The Value of Stepping Back and Seeing the Bigger Picture

Gotthold Ephraim Lessing wrote, 'In nature everything is connected, everything is interwoven, everything changes with everything, everything merges from one into another'[2] as long ago as 1769. Over the years, biologists recognised again and again that it was hard to explain why the population of one animal species (e.g. lions) was declining without understanding the way it was affected by the presence or absence of other species (e.g. antelopes). And in turn, the population of antelopes depends on the availability of plants to eat, which depends on the terrain, the presence of water, the climate, etc. So, eventually the term 'the ecosystem' was coined by Arthur Tansley in the 1930s.

Fundamental to systems thinking is a recognition that some problems are *complex rather than complicated*. By way of an example:

- *Repairing a car is a complicated problem*: A car comprises many separate, discreet parts. If you identify something that is not working, parts that are faulty or broken can usually be repaired or replaced separately, in isolation. The parts can then be put back together again, and the car should work.
- *Improving transport links in a town or city is a complex problem*: Imagine that cyclists are looking for more traffic-free cycle lanes. If you do everything you can to solve their concerns, they might be happy; but you may create problems for other road users (driving cars and trucks), who might be (rightly or wrongly) unhappy about the impact this has on them.

So, a systems thinking approach recognises that for complex problems you cannot break down each bit of a problem into pieces, solve it separately and then put these solutions together and expect them to work. Indeed, systems thinking tells us that *thinking that you can solve a complex problem as if it was complicated (i.e. addressing issues as discreet, separate phenomena, in isolation) will very often create other 'spin-off' problems immediately or in the future.*

In business terms, if you take an organisation, you can consider its various activities (e.g. sales and marketing) as 'systems' that interact with and depend upon other internal 'systems' (e.g. procurement, finance and IT). Seen this way, the success or failure of an organisation can depend upon how well these systems (or elements) work together. And a classic term to describe poor working between parts of an organisation is to say there are 'silos'.

External factors such as customers, competitors, suppliers, regulators, the environment, etc., can also be regarded as systems, and how the organisation interacts with these can also explain how and why it succeeds or fails. So, not putting customer service as central to the way the organisation operates can result in problems.

Diagram 3.1 provides an example of how you see an organisation as a series of systems that interact with one another internally and are also impacted by external systems.

The ingredients detailed can be varied to suit each organisation and context, but the power of thinking in terms of systems is to 'step back and see the big picture'. Thus, if you are thinking about an objective you want to reach, or a problem you want to solve, a systems perspective can remind you of all the factors you need to consider. For example, we can ask: 'Do suitable systems and technology support our goals?', 'Do we have the right people and capabilities?' or 'Do we have suitable suppliers to give us what we need?', etc.

Thinking about business issues in systemic terms was first properly developed by Jay W Forrester.[3] In the late 1950s and early 1960s, he showed General Electric that highs and lows in its production of certain domestic appliances, which were thought to be due to external factors, could arise 'from entirely internally determined' elements of the organisation.[4] He was able to show that overly simplistic, linear thinking about business (i.e. thinking some problems were complicated rather than complex) could result in unexpected spin-off problems.[5] His concepts were applied across various industries and integrated with data analysis and computing.

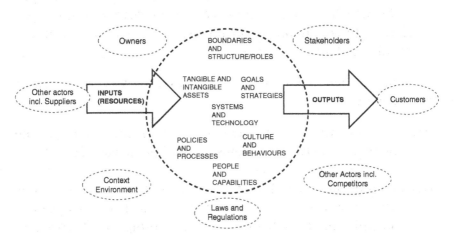

Diagram 3.1   An organisation as an open system (illustration)

It enabled him to create models for what might be happening and help decision-makers tackle even more complex challenges (e.g. urban planning, policy setting, etc.).

Since then, systems thinking has become of interest in certain contexts, but it is still not 'mainstream' in many domains.[6] However, there have been some popular books on systems thinking, such as

- Peter Senge's 'The Fifth Discipline' (1990) which highlights the benefits of looking at the big picture when trying to address challenges and the importance of a learning culture.
- Barry Oshry's 'Seeing Systems' (2007) which discusses some of the common interactions you see in organisations, including top/bottom and provider/customer, and the dysfunctional patterns ('dances') that can arise between different parts of an organisation.
- Donella Meadows' 'Thinking in Systems' (2008) (first written in the 1990s and emerging from work with Jay Forester at MIT) which explains systems analysis and feedback loops in a step-by-step way and illustrates how they can be applied to some of the global challenges we face.
- Derek and Laura Cabrera's 'Systems Thinking Made Simple' (2015) which provides a very accessible overview of the topic. They highlight, among other things, the importance of understanding different perspectives.

Common ingredients in a systems thinking approach include the following:

(i) Analysing systems into their sub-systems and looking at the interactions between systems to see how causes and effects work (i.e. systems analysis).[7]

(ii) Recognising that unless you understand causal connections and feedback loops within a system, and between systems, you will find yourself surprised when things don't work and surprised when new problems appear to come from 'out of the blue'.[8]

Illustrating the Power of Thinking in Systems – Causal Loop Analysis

Let's consider a simple example and see the power of systems thinking using causal loop analysis.

Suppose you consider sales of electric cars or vehicles (EVs henceforth). In that case, the number of positive customer experiences can generate good reviews and, in due course, positively impact sales. But, on the other hand, as more EVs are sold, there will be an impact on another system – the system for building and maintaining EV charging points (commonly called EV supply equipment or EVSE). So, if the number of available EVSEs cannot keep pace with the number of EVs on the road, more EV drivers will be waiting to charge their cars, especially at peak times and locations. And if this continues, it may generate dissatisfaction for some EV users, who will tell their friends and family, and which may eventually impact new sales to people who don't want to be 'caught out' without an available car charging point during an important journey.

These effects can be understood in terms of 'causal loops', with positive impacts called 'reinforcing loops' and negative impacts called 'balancing loops', set out in Diagram 3.2.

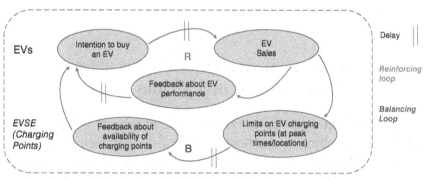

Outside of the chosen boundary, one could add:
Cost/benefit returns for those building EVSE etc.

Diagram 3.2   Electric vehicle sales, impact of charging points (causal loop diagram)

Although Diagram 3.2 repeats the written explanation, it does so with just a few simple symbols and highlights that *growth in EV numbers isn't only about how good the EVs are*. Instead, there are other factors upon which EV sales rely.[9] The diagram also contains a 'boundary' to highlight whether other factors, which may be relevant (such as the incentives for those building EVSEs, etc.), are included in any analysis or not.

From a simple causal loop diagram, you can build up the causes and effects of multiple elements, all potentially relevant to an area. Donella Meadows explained, 'Everything you know . . . is only a model. Get your model out . . . where it can be viewed. Invite others *to challenge your* assumptions and add their own'.[10]

So, causal loop diagrams can be used to:

(i) picture the critical elements involved in an area of interest,
(ii) clarify how they are related (e.g. directly or indirectly, and why),
(iii) find new ways to understand what the real challenges are (e.g. where constraints or dependencies may be impacting behaviour), and
(iv) consider different courses of action and their effects over different periods, e.g. 'If we do X, we should get Y, but might we see any spin-off problems?' And it can also help you think, 'If we see Z, what might be causing this, and what might we do about it?'

The Value of Stepping Back to See Patterns, Tipping Points and Vicious Circles

As you develop skills in 'unravelling the spaghetti' of causes and effects, it's possible to see how a factor in one system (e.g. building more charging points or ensuring that the charging points in use are working) might impact another system (e.g. the number of drivers waiting for a charging point) and then another (e.g. driver satisfaction with EVs), etc.

Systems thinking helps us see problems in new ways:

- It can help you recognise how things may appear fine now, but they may be approaching a tipping point.[11]
- It can also highlight when we might be trapped in a vicious circle and help us to 'unpack' what might be causing this and whether potential solutions are likely to work. Tackling inflation has been a hot topic in the United Kingdom and elsewhere in 2022 and 2023, and references to 'spiralling inflation' highlight the recognition of feedback loops, but this topic is crying out for more explicit systems analysis in the media and in public debate.[12]

Every System Is Perfectly Capable of Giving the Results it Currently Gives[13]

So, if you are seeing problems or getting results that are disappointing, the question becomes, 'What's going on in the system or other relevant systems, that is causing this?'.[14] Systems thinking encourages us to 'stand back' or 'zoom out' rather than the common tendency to 'zoom in'. It can give us fresh perspectives on why things might go off track, now or in the future.

Systems thinking helps you shift from single-loop learning to double-loop learning. You can consider how the whole game is being played so that you can play smarter, not just work harder.[15]

To provide a further real-world example of what I am talking about, Julian Amey (former VP of Global Supply Chain, AstraZeneca) explains how understanding the reasons for a problem became apparent after 'stepping back'.

> 'Years ago, I was involved in production planning in the US, working on secondment. This involved overseeing our own manufacturing facilities, as well as those of third parties who were doing contract manufacturing for us.
>
> We had a successful product where the manufacture was sourced from a third party in the Midwest under a contract

manufacturing arrangement. It was decided before I moved to the US that we would bring the manufacture in-house to our own facility on the East Coast. We had all the product and manufacturing intellectual property, and the decision to shift production was regarded as low risk. The product involved a sponge impregnated with liquid antiseptic, glued to a plastic scrub brush, with a nail pick, wrapped in a laminated silver foil package that was glued and sealed, and then boxed.

We built a line for in-house production, with equipment and layout like that used by the contract manufacturer. The plant performed successful commissioning trials, production trials and put material on stability testing. After building up some stocks and with everything considered "good to go," we switched over to our own supply.

We started shipping the product, and initially, everything was fine. But as we shipped the product across the US, we began to get reports of problems from the shippers. For some reason, shipments to California and the states west of the Rockies seemed to result in leaks from the packaging. There also appeared to be a problem when the product was sent by air freight when under time constraints to supply a replacement product.

Clearly, we were not happy to find these new problems, never seen before, with an important product, so a team was commissioned to understand the root causes of what was going on and put in place corrective measures. They looked at various issues and made various changes: they went to a thicker, heavier grade foil, amended the pressure on the sealing rollers and changed the sealing lacquer.

But all these changes didn't have any significant impact: the packages continued to leak when shipped to the West Coast. One evening, the US VP for Production talked to me about the supply issue and expressed his concern that we seemed to be getting nowhere in resolving the problem. He was very frustrated because it was an experienced team involved in the root cause analysis, and they had been looking at this for weeks and weeks. Despite trying all the things they had suggested, none of them was properly addressing the problem. He said he was now thinking he would need to reengage the contract manufacturing firm.

Now, at that time, I was still relatively young and was still in very much a "learning mode," so I asked a casual question: "Where is the contract manufacturer located, by the way?," to which I was told the name of a town. "Where's that?" I asked. "In Utah," came the reply. Although my knowledge of US geography was somewhat limited, I knew Utah was on the edge of the Rockies, so I next asked, "Do you know the altitude of the town?" I got a blank look, so we found an atlas, looked up the altitude and then did some quick calculations about air pressure.

And, then and there, we realised what the likely problem was. In Utah, the product was being packed at a high altitude, so it was almost like a vacuum pack effect. Whereas the production we had on the East Coast was close to sea level. The leaking problem was to do with expanding air in the antiseptic packs. It had nothing to do with any of the things the RCA team had been looking at – the solution to the problem involved, literally, thinking outside of the box. The RCA team had "zoomed in" on many of the details and technicalities they knew well but had not been able to step back.

In the end, we simply put a roller on the machine, which just compressed the foil package before it was sealed, removing the air, and subsequently, there were no more problems.

This is a good example of why you need a holistic, systemic approach to RCA, not just a narrow technical analysis. It made me realise how much even the best people can get "locked into a paradigm" that they don't realise they are trapped in. That team was focusing on the things they knew how to fix rather than beyond that.

It taught me how important it was to have a diversity of experiences and different ways of thinking when working on an important RCA investigation. Sometimes a non-technical perspective can offer a new angle, a new insight. Henceforth, I was always keen that we had cross-functional teams working on RCA investigations.'

Julian illustrates what it means to 'zoom out' and think about things that, at face value, appear to be either irrelevant or unimportant but are, in fact, at the core of what has been causing a problem.

Let me offer another example of how systems thinking, systems analysis and causal loop diagrams can help us understand things that might easily seem hard to grasp.

A Systems Perspective on the Financial Crisis of 2007–2008

Let's consider the 2007–2008 financial crisis and imagine we can talk to experts in the field. You could ask them to identify some of the main 'ingredients' involved in what happened. They might explain these were (1) the property market, (2) the availability of easy credit (via sub-prime loans/mortgages) and (3) how mortgages were turned into securities.

Then, you could then ask them to explain the links between these ingredients and add some others, such as (I) credit ratings standards, (II) the amount of capital to loans for each bank (i.e. 'leverage') and (III) processes used to assess any risks.

You could also ask the experts to explain the key risks that might arise from all these elements or systems. They might explain they were (i) the complexities of turning mortgages into securities, (ii) potential errors in risk assessments for liquidity, (iii) how the rules worked around bank balance sheets (e.g. the levels of 'leverage' allowed.), etc.

Already, you could easily feel overwhelmed; but when you start thinking about systems, I advocate avoiding getting drawn into an Alice in Wonderland world of complex explanations and words you may not understand. Instead, I recommend a KISS approach, where you see all the building blocks in play, but that doesn't mean you need to understand every one of these in detail.[16] And in the end, with the right help, you might get someone to draw out some of the key factors in the 2007–2008 crisis using a simple one-page diagram (see Diagram 3.3).[17]

Of course, the causal loop diagram does not contain every factor that influenced what happened, as denoted by the boundary chosen around the diagram. However, it is a 'starter for 10'.

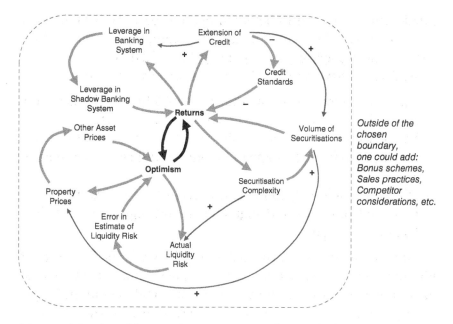

Diagram 3.3 Causal loop analysis – 2007–2008 financial crisis

And we might learn that during the early 2000s a whole host of elements, decades in the making, were on an upward, positive cycle, and any problems with the financial system were thought to be theoretical. But then there was an increase in interest rates, a fall in US property prices, resulting in a cascade of problems, one after the other, at breakneck speed. A former bank CEO, reflecting on what happened, said, 'We wondered if we broke the financial system'.[18]

For the purposes of this overview discussion it's not necessary to understand Diagram 3.3 in detail but rather note how a multi-faceted, complex set of causes and effects can be made relatively digestible when you think in terms of systems and use causal loops, revealing how 'one thing might lead to another'.

And while Diagram 3.3 was created after the 2007–2008 financial crisis, it could have been created beforehand, because there was a clear awareness of liquidity risks and the potential for a cascade of knock-on problems before the crisis. As Citibank's then-CEO

Chuck Prince said months before things fell apart: 'When the music stops, in terms of liquidity, things will be complicated. But, as long as the music is playing, you've got to get up and dance'.[19]

And so, we have a relatively straightforward illustration of

- why it's problematic to say the 2007–2008 financial crisis arose because of just one, or even two or three, root causes,
- how it would have been possible (and was possible) to predict much of what might happen before the full scale of problems arose[20] and
- why, after the crisis, so many aspects of financial services customs and practices and regulations, and regulatory oversight had to be changed?[21]

To reiterate, this book isn't a detailed 'how to' guide on systems thinking or causal loops. Instead, I hope I have illustrated that looking at things this way can provide a means to talk about and begin to grasp a complex problem in a way that reading a detailed 20-page, or 200-page, analysis with tables of numbers might not. Of course, the 20-page, or 200-page, analysis may be helpful and interesting for some people and in some circumstances, but the danger is that *too much complexity means most people can't engage with, contribute to, or challenge, what is being said and, perhaps most important of all, understand what is not being said.*

When to Stop and Boundary Diagrams

Given that a systems-based analysis involves 'stepping back', it's fair to ask how to ensure that such an approach doesn't lead to endless causes being uncovered. As Conrad Lorenz famously put it: 'If the flap of a butterfly's wings can be instrumental in generating a tornado, it can equally well be instrumental in preventing a tornado'.[22]

The question of when to stop can also be applied to root cause analysis (RCA). As leading Aviation Safety expert Sidney Dekker noted: 'What you call [the] root cause is simply the place where you stop looking any further'.[23]

Fortunately, there is a technique that bridges RCA and systems thinking that looks at the question of 'where to draw a line'. It is called the 'boundary diagram', used in an RCA technique called Failure Mode and Effects Analysis (FMEA). It provides a visual overview of different activities, processes, systems and other factors and can be used to help you make a conscious choice about the boundaries around any RCA investigation, inquiry or systems analysis so that you are clear about what you are and are not looking at.[24] I have already illustrated how you can draw a boundary in the causal loop diagrams for EVs (in Diagram 3.2) and the financial crisis of 2007–2008 (in Diagram 3.3).[25]

A boundary diagram is helpful because it highlights the choices you have when doing RCA or an inquiry, for example:

(I) focusing on a *specific area* (e.g. a department, project or system), or

(II) looking at *a wider set of activities* (e.g. an organisational process across several departments), or

(III) considering the *adverse outcome that you want to avoid* in the future (e.g. the boundary you would draw around the impacts in a Bowtie diagram),[26] or

(IV) looking at *a range of other organisations, or other external factors*, that may be 'in the mix' to fully understand what happened (which may include laws, regulations, regulatory and government bodies, etc.).[27]

If you carry out an RCA or inquiry with a broad scope, you will get a more holistic picture of what happened, but it may take longer to gather information and evidence and arrive at conclusions. Conversely, the narrower the scope of an inquiry, the easier and quicker it should be to complete, but the greater the chance all key root causes will be missed.

Diagram 3.4 provides an illustration of boundary choices for an RCA investigation in an organisation where a problem has arisen in a department (say, in Department 1). It shows some of the specific choices that can be made: (i) focus the investigation on

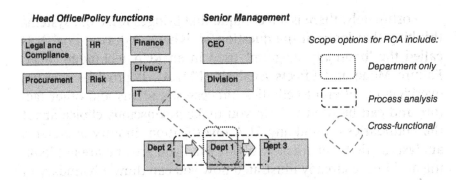

Diagram 3.4   Boundary diagram choices for RCA (illustration)

Department 1 or (ii) Departments 1, 2 and 3, which may be involved in a shared process, or (iii) include other functions as well (e.g. the IT department).

A boundary diagram doesn't answer the question of what you should look at in an RCA or inquiry, but it does show, in a clear and simple manner, the key choices you need to make. And fundamentally, systems thinking tells us that to properly understand the causes of a significant challenge properly, it is crucial to ensure that all the relevant parts of the system (or significant other factors interacting with it) are involved. Dr Mannie Sher (Principal Researcher and Consultant, Tavistock Institute) explains:

'We often work with senior executives who engage us to solve a problem or promote a development that is, for example, relevant in one area. The executives normally appreciate that a difficulty (or resistance to the development) in one area may be due to interactions with other areas in the organisation, which suggests that they are prepared to think systemically about what maybe is going on unconsciously. Normally, they would agree that we should work with several related departments that are involved, one way or another, in a problem (or development).

But the challenging bit comes when we ask, "What is the executive team's role in our review?" To which, often, we will hear, "The executive team will be here when you are finished; you can report your results when you have completed your work." And our response is invariably, "If you want challenges to be resolved over the long run, you will need to think about the executive team's role too, including your internal dynamics as a senior team, and be willing to change too."

Our message is that when you are looking for long-term, lasting improvements, you must have a commitment from all relevant parts of the system to participate in an inquiry into their roles into what has gone on and – as needed – to change'.

Stephen Foster (holder of SVP positions in Finance and Audit and Compliance) conveys a similar message about effective RCA:

'Sometimes you start an inquiry with certain expectations and the dreaded "preconceived ideas", but if it is done well you can find it's like a boomerang that can come back to hit you. Specifically, you can find the inquiry raises important questions and challenges for the very people who asked for explanations why something went wrong.

All parties need to be aware that this may happen and have a plan for how to manage it if it does. In mature, open environments, it can be managed well, and even constructively, "mea-culpa" can be a very powerful and rewarding signal.

However, though I have not experienced it, in the worst cases and environments, those sponsoring an inquiry, or RCA investigation, can constrain the boundary of what is looked at, such that important insights stay out of reach, especially if those insights will call into question some of the decisions they have made.'

Considering all that I have discussed up to now, it's time to introduce a hybrid approach to understanding root causes that combines RCA techniques and systems thinking.

Eight Ways to Understand Why, with Connections

The modified fishbone diagram that I shared at the end of Chapter 2 outlined 'eight ways to understand why', to arrive at the root causes of a problem. But systems thinking highlights the importance of recognising there may be connections between different causes.

To take a simple, hypothetical, example, building on the earlier discussion concerning electric vehicles: Suppose we set a goal to sell EVs and then find we missed our goal for the various reasons touched upon earlier.

Imagine we investigate what went wrong remembering prevention, detection and recovery and suppose we discover the following additional information:

In terms of prevention (P) – we missed our EV sales goals

(P1) because of faulty assumptions about sales of EVs to be used as a main car, because

(P2) we assumed EV sales would keep growing, as they had for years, and also because

(P3) we had assurances from EVSE providers about their plans to increase the number of charging points, but these were not completely in line with their earlier plans.

Regarding detection (D), we knew we needed to track EV car orders and customer satisfaction with EVs and EVSEs. However,

(D1) we didn't know enough about what was happening on the grapevine, where stories about 'nightmare journeys' were now reaching a tipping point and putting off prospective EV buyers, and

(D2) we didn't realise that this was going to cause such big problems for our EV sales until it was too late.

In terms of recovery (R) –

(R1) there was no plan B, for a serious shortfall in the sales of our EVs; as a result,

(R2) there was no plan in place with EVSE providers to build some additional dedicated charging points in crucial locations and – in any event,

(R3) this would have taken more time and effort, which was not a priority in the past.

Diagram 3.5 sets out the key points from this hypothetical example:

1. against the framework of 'eight ways to understand why', so we have an RCA perspective, and
2. with illustrative, high-level, causal loop connections, so we have a systems thinking perspective as well.

If we had more information about a specific, real-life case and a greater understanding of the way factors were causally linked, there might be more, or different, connections to draw out. But, in any event, we have – in one diagram – a way of seeing the range of reasons why things didn't go to plan.

What we find, as we shall see time and time again, is that a mindset that focuses on just one cause can miss the bigger picture. Thus thinking 'They should have made better forecast for their EV sales' (P1) misses the deeper issues about (i) *why the forecast may have been incorrect* (P3), (ii) the dependency of EV sales on charging points (EVSEs) (P2) and (iii) *weaknesses in the intelligence gathering about how important an issue this was becoming* (D1).

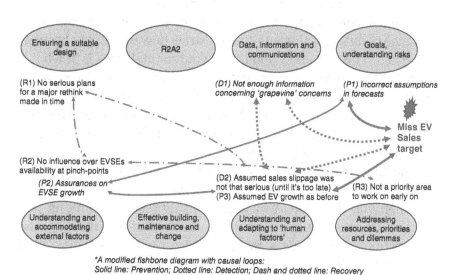

*A modified fishbone diagram with causal loops:
Solid line: Prevention; Dotted line: Detection; Dash and dotted line: Recovery*

Diagram 3.5   Eight ways to understand why, with connections (illustration)

It should be no surprise that Tesla has such an extensive network of fast charging EVSEs and that an increasing number of EV producers, (such as Ford and GM), and members of the public, are seeing the connections between an enjoyable EV experience and the availability of fast charging EVSEs.[28]

Thus, unless the two systems of EVs and EVSEs are designed to work better together, with a clear change programme to achieve this, maintain the network of EVSEs and overcome a range of constraints and dilemmas (e.g. charging for EVs without access to charging points at home), *problems are almost guaranteed for the future*. Already there are early warning signs that problems in this arena could impact the economy as well as our CO_2 reduction goals if 'the jigsaw is not joined up'.[29]

Summary

- Systems thinking has been developing throughout the twentieth century, first with concepts such as 'the ecosystem' (from the 1930s) and then in earnest after World War II.
- Systems thinking and systems analysis allow you to map out a range of different elements and illustrate how they might be interrelated. This can allow you to test your mental models of what is happening and see the unintended consequences of decisions.
- You can gain a good overview of the 2007–2008 financial crisis when you look at its causes from a systems analysis perspective.
- Systems thinking and causal loop analysis highlight how problematic it is to imagine one root cause.
- The dilemma with systems analysis is where to draw the boundary around any investigation or inquiry.
- When you do an RCA or inquiry using systems thinking perspective, you should expect that some lines of inquiry may raise questions about leaders' role in problems which they may think should be attributed to someone else.
- The book will use a hybrid RCA and systems analysis technique, a modified fishbone diagram with causal loops. In day-to-day

language, you can call it 'eight ways to understand why, with connections'.

- While this approach will be used as a framework to guide the subsequent discussions, it is fully recognised that this is just one tool to support RCA and systems thinking, which can complement other tools and techniques. There is no 'correct' or 'definitive' approach to use.
- Day-to-day problems we all know about, such as EVs and EV charging points, can be so much better understood when you approach the problems from a systemic perspective.

Section 2

Eight Ways to Understand Why, with Connections

'History does not repeat itself, but it does tend to rhyme'.
– Mark Twain[1]

Overview of This Section

Chapters 4–11 in this section of the book discuss the 'eight ways of understanding why', outlining root cause factors that can recur again and again in a myriad of situations.

Whilst I will be sharing real-life examples, it has been necessary to simplify and omit specific details about what happened for brevity and confidentiality. But I intend to highlight the following:

(i) *The gaps between the theory of how things should work compared to what happens in practice.*

(ii) *The significant shortcomings of having an overly simplistic analysis of why things go wrong.*[2]

(iii) *How taking a systemic perspective can help us head off problems in the first place.*

Note, however, that because this book is not a detailed 'how-to manual', it will not be possible to provide an in-depth analysis of all of the root causes for every example that follows. However, an analysis of the Titanic tragedy of April 1912 (in Chapter 12) illustrates how you might understand a major incident more holistically. It also makes some important links between what happened then and what we still see happening in the twenty-first century.

In the examples that follow, I hope readers begin to discern the fine details, the hairline cracks, that can separate success from failure and vice versa. So, if someone suffers a setback and you hear them exclaim, 'Why did we fail? We did so many great things!' it should become clear that 99% of the good things that were done counted for nothing if there were shortcomings in the wrong places at the wrong time. Moreover, it should become clear how often well-intentioned efforts to achieve objectives and manage risks can turn into a 'tick box' compliance exercise and result in a great deal of time and effort being expended in a way that may very well not make a substantial difference when it really matters. As Steve McConnell explains: '. . . the chain isn't as strong as its weakest link; it's as weak as all the weak links . . . together'.[3]

Chapter 4

Setting Appropriate Strategies, Goals, and Understanding Risks

'The best-laid schemes o' mice and men, gang aft a-gley'.
– Robert Burns[1]

The Successes and Failures of the Wright Brothers at Kittyhawk

Consider the flight of the first powered, controlled, heavier-than-air aircraft. The Wright brothers did this on 17 December 1903, in their motorised flyer at Kittyhawk, North Carolina. The first flight that day lasted 12 seconds and covered 37 metres, while the fourth and final flight lasted 59 seconds and covered 260 metres.[2]

Later that day, the flyer was damaged by a gust of wind and never flew again. However, the Wright brothers knew they had made a breakthrough. By 1905 they had designed and built a flyer that flew for 39 minutes, covering 24 miles. By 1909, they had signed a contract with the US Army, and 'the rest is history'.

In December 1903, the Wright brothers did not have a specific goal other than to keep testing their flyer. Although it was damaged beyond repair, the downside was accepted because the brothers knew that *they would make progress only by taking calculated risks and tolerating some setbacks*. Illustration 4.1 highlights the choice many face when setting a goal; if you aim for a very ambitious goal, you must be prepared for setbacks and disappointments.

To give their achievement more context, the Wright brothers started their journey towards powered flight by working on unpowered gliders in the late 1890s. Their efforts were inspired by the experiments and writings of Sir George Cayley, going as far back as the 1850s, and the inventor and glider pilot Otto Lilienthal during the 1880s until his death (during a glider flight that rose to some 50 metres) in 1896.[3]

So, when you consider the Wright brothers' achievements, it is essential to appreciate just how much this was a combination of

(i) recognising that the flyer was, in fact, a combination of different systems (flight surfaces, controls, power, etc.) that all needed to work together[4] and

Illustration 4.1   Goals, risks and acceptable losses

(ii) a step-by-step evolution of each piece of the jigsaw puzzle: designing, building and trialling different elements, and the flyer itself.

This was not a simple overnight success story.

The words of Wilbur Wright are still highly relevant today and applicable in many contexts:

'The [person] who wishes to keep at [a] problem long enough to really learn anything positively must not take dangerous risks. Carelessness and overconfidence are usually more dangerous than deliberately accepted risks'.[5]

Realism and Learning in Pharmaceuticals

Looking at the pharmaceuticals industry, with its setbacks but also a century of important innovations, the perspective of Dr Kevin Bilyard (former CEO and Board Director, Immodulon Therapeutics) gives us a window into goal setting, risk analysis, and having a clear tolerance for failure:

'The vast majority of board members and investors in biopharmaceutical companies have a deep understanding of how risk can vary between different stages of research and development.

Early in the discovery stage, a setback or failure will be a disappointment. Still, you won't necessarily conduct a full-blown investigation into why the candidate drug didn't meet your requirements unless there is cause. This is because you understand that in pharmaceutical research it's impossible to be sure that all research studies will succeed. After all, you are carrying out work at the frontiers of science where no one knows what the outcome is going to be. Most stakeholders accept losses, and setbacks are an intrinsic part of the business and will normally be concerned only if there is an excessive failure rate.

However, at the development phase, where a candidate drug has passed through the research phase, a different set of considerations are in play. It can be tempting to approach drug development in a very cautious, incremental way. But the problem is that you can find yourself having spent millions of dollars on one study after another. Then you carry out a major study that shows that you do not have a viable product, perhaps because of an insufficiently strong statistical signal on a key characteristic for the drug.

As a result, there has been a growing practice of using multidisciplinary teams of medics, scientists and clinical trial specialists to design and oversee drug development. These teams can design clinical trials to meet the key scientific, regulatory and statistical evidence requirements "head on" as well as understanding practical matters such as how you might recruit volunteers for the trial.

Nowadays, most clinical trial teams aim to approach the development phase with a clear, comprehensive and practical sense of what is a necessary and appropriate goal and what might be lost if the study fails, to which the answer is, sometimes, everything.

This approach can't guarantee success, but it can help to ensure trials are neither over-ambitious nor under-ambitious. Losses will arise, but they will typically be lower and sooner than if the development programme was poorly conceived. The phrase you hear now is "fail fast".'

Of course, you can extend the discussion on goals and setbacks towards a range of other contexts, such as trying a new medical procedure or developing a new IT system, etc. However, my key message is that *unless you are sufficiently clear about what you are aiming for and what you can accept that might go wrong, you are already going to have a problem with root cause analysis (RCA).*[6] After all, if you experience a setback and want to understand what went wrong, you need to be clear what 'wrong' means. As Yogi Berra said: 'You've got to be very careful if you don't know where you are going because you might not get there'.[7]

Of course, even when you do have specific plans and goals, things can still 'slip through your fingers' despite best efforts to the contrary.

Scaling-Up

Andrew Wright (Chairman of AW Hainsworth) offers a perspective concerning an industrial scale-up:

'I have worked in many different companies working on large programmes and projects. But sometimes, the delivery of what seems to be a sensible goal and well within your organisation's capabilities can catch you out. Take an example of a chemical plant that is working well at one scale and thinking it will not be that difficult to get a larger plant to deliver a larger volume.

The challenge is this. When you have experience from the past of scaling-up, you know there will be roadblocks and difficulties, and you learn how to overcome them. You recognise that overcoming challenges is a part of the scale-up process and understand each new project will have slightly different difficulties, and you prepare for this. But the trap you can fall into when you have a track record of success is to tell yourself that the obstacles in the next scale-up will be manageable.

I have now seen examples where a scale-up has proven to be much more difficult and a lot more expensive than planned. And the realisation that the scale-up is going to be much more challenging than you thought can creep up on you little by little, costing more and more. In the end, these difficulties can sometimes be big enough to undermine the commercial viability of what you were aiming for.

If you carry out an RCA into why things didn't go to plan, you realise that there was an assumption on something that seemed straightforward that was not correct. Therefore, it's very important to be clear about the assumptions you make at the planning stage. You need to recognise that just because you've made a similar thing work in the past, the similarity may only be on the surface. You need to be open to the possibility that there might be a "deal breaker" to contend with.

In one case I know of, if a more rigorous review of scientific papers from across the world had been carried out or if someone had talked to the world-leading experts in the field, you would have realised that what you were trying to do was going to be much more difficult than first thought. And an insight like this early on might lead you to approach a problem in a completely new, innovative way rather than end up with a failure on your hands. In another case, the design engineers involved were recognised as experts on the science underpinning the process being designed, but they missed an obvious step in creating the design, leading to a process failure that took a year to diagnose. A "peer review" of the design and design process might well have picked up the error and avoided a costly delay.

But it's so easy, when you have expertise in your company, to think that this expertise is "good enough." Of course, there would be an additional upfront investment in doing more rigorous due diligence on something that seems basic, which might take time and money and may only confirm everything is fine. But over the years, I have learned to pay close attention to critical risk areas that seem to be fine because sometimes they are not.'

If you take Andrew's account of what happened at a surface level, you might say the reason there was a problem was 'management was too optimistic about the scale-up'. But if you do this, (i) it could easily be interpreted as saying 'management got it wrong' (i.e. potentially suggesting they should be blamed) and (ii) it still does not explain *why management was too optimistic*. Further, it could lead you down a path that says, 'management should not be so optimistic next time', which can create a pendulum dynamic, i.e. a problem now risks an over-cautious approach in the future.

So, if you consider why things didn't go to plan and the details Andrew provided, you can see:

From a prevention perspective: (P1) The scale-up looked manageable because (P2) they knew there would be differences and challenges, but (P3) they had designs that had worked before when challenges arose in the past, and (P4) they had no sense there was a need for external advice or assurance, and (P5) anyway they were confident they could address unknown issues, and (P6) double-checking would just cost even more, and (P7) at a certain point, they couldn't afford to start all over again.

From a detective perspective: (D1) They got regular project updates (that had worked in the past), and (D2) they knew there would be differences and challenges, but (D3) they didn't know some of these would be show-stoppers, after all (D4) they have handled differences in the past, until (D5) eventually it became clear they had spent too much money and time and could not afford to start all over again.

(I'm omitting the 'Recovery' for the sake of brevity.)

So, you can map these explanations' why against the 'eight ways to understand why' framework and create Diagram 4.2.

Here, we can see that what happened wasn't just about management being too optimistic; there were other essential factors involved, such as pressures on cost and time, no 'early warning measures' capable of identifying a potential show-stopper issue and no clear basis for when to test things more rigorously before passing a 'point of no return'.

It's only when you start to see the systemic factors 'hiding in plain sight' (and going beyond five whys) that you gain a more holistic, rounded sense of what is going on and what issues need to be considered and, as appropriate, addressed. When you do, you are more likely to take a measured, balanced approach concerning what to do about problems rather than blaming someone or having a knee-jerk over-reaction. Rudyard Kipling's insight about taking a mature approach to events is worth remembering: 'If you can meet with Triumph and Disaster and treat those two impostors just the same'.[8]

An additional perspective we can get from Andrew's story is how big problems can arise from what appear to be relatively small 'cracks' or 'holes'. This perspective on RCA was first provided by Professor James Reason.[9] He introduced the 'Swiss cheese model' of risk failure, highlighting that setbacks and accidents can arise because of relatively minor shortcomings in control measures, creating 'holes' that allow harm to occur.[10] I often refer to 'hairline cracks' for those less familiar with Swiss cheese.

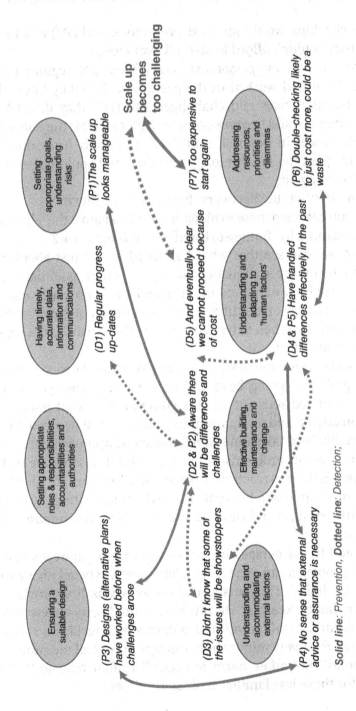

Diagram 4.2 Eight ways to understand why, with connections – scaling up surprises

*Solid line: Prevention, **Dotted line**: Detection;*

Setting appropriate goals, understanding risks

Having timely, accurate data, information and communications

Setting appropriate roles & responsibilities, accountabilities and authorities

Ensuring a suitable design

Effective building, maintenance and change

Understanding and adapting to 'human factors'

Addressing resources, priorities and dilemmas

Understanding and accommodating external factors

Scale up becomes too challenging

(P1)The scale up looks manageable

(P7) Too expensive to start again

(P6) Double-checking likely to just cost more, could be a waste

(D1) Regular progress up-dates

(D5) And eventually clear we cannot proceed because of cost

(D4 & P5) Have handled differences effectively in the past

(D2 & P2) Aware there will be differences and challenges

(P3) Designs (alternative plans) have worked before when challenges arose

(D3) Didn't know that some of the issues will be showstoppers

(P4) No sense that external advice or assurance is necessary

Business Case Transparency – Balancing Optimism and Realism with an Eye on Downside Risks

Even when we know that business ventures contain risks and downsides, you cannot be sure business plans will be presented transparently. Martin Ludemann (Corporate Psychologist) offers his experiences working with cross-functional teams:

'I have worked with senior executives and managers who are looking for new opportunities. Often they have some great ideas about how new business initiatives might be achieved through the delivery of new sales and marketing programmes supported by a project to build, for example, a new production facility. In their mind, the new initiative will deliver something valuable for their customers and provide work and success for the company, their colleagues and themselves. At this stage, commercial managers play an important role in getting the organisation prepared to move out of its comfort zone, which invariably involves engaging the emotions of others to get them enthusiastic about the new initiative. I like to think of this as the "rose-tinted glasses" phase.

There will also be discussions addressing the practical implications of what is proposed. As conversations take place, the commercial managers develop their thinking and arguments, and usually it will involve preparing a business case for a decision to proceed. The manager speaks to various colleagues and develops an estimate of the costs, at, say, €175 million over three years, and income of, say, €350 million within six years. And based on this, the initiative would be approved.

But in most organisations, such a high-level business case will not be sufficient to make a formal decision. For example, if a production facility is involved, the commercial manager must engage with production designers, engineers, surveyors, procurement specialists and finance staff. These professionals will prepare more detailed plans, consider risks and challenges to be overcome, and conclude that the costs will be at least €250 million, with €300–350 million of income, which may put the whole initiative in balance.

A big difference in forecasts can create tension and even conflict between commercial and other managers. Commercial managers may argue with the engineers and finance people. You will hear things like: "You are being too negative and cautious. We can find a way to overcome your concerns, so you should recalculate this."

Now the commercial manager may be correct in certain respects. Still, the problem is that they may also be taken up with their dreams and thoughts of being a success. So rather than a rational debate taking place, there is something of a fight, which may or may not take place out in the open. The finance and engineering professionals become an internal enemy to be "beaten down." You will hear arguments such as "You're not acting as part of the team," "You lack the 'can do' spirit we need" and "We'll never succeed as a company if we are not prepared to take any risks."

As a result, some technical and professional staff might feel under pressure to water down their concerns so that a more favourable business case can be presented to senior executives.

I want to emphasise that I am not saying that technical and professional staff will always be on the right side of these arguments. You need commercial managers, who have dreams for the future, who are passionate and emotional, and who see the glass as half full rather than half empty. There is a lot to admire here. But we need to recognise that these commercial colleagues may be pushing an optimistic case, with more chance of downsides than upsides.

You need an environment where commercial and technical staff can really listen to one another. And that is not always so easy. Commercial managers can sometimes resent what they see as a slow and cautious mindset from the technical staff. Conversely, the technical staff sometimes see the commercial managers failing to accept the reality of practical challenges.

So, even when there are many hard facts and technical details under discussion, there can be more psychology going on in business discussions than many people realise. If you don't get this balance right by facilitating high-quality discussions between different departments, you can have business difficulties, whether on the upside or the downside.

That is why I am happy I have clients here in Germany who are prepared to invest in trained facilitators, such as myself, so their businesses stand a better chance of getting the right balance between risk and reward.'

Here, we see the importance of making decisions 'with your eyes open' to the different perspectives of departments and functions in an organisation. Despite many saying that people in an organisation should be 'fully aligned', the reality is that views can differ. Engineers are paid to be thoughtful and measured, and commercial managers are paid to venture into the unknown without having all the facts. There is an inevitability to differences of opinion on occasions and the possibility of tensions and even rivalries. Thus, the oft-quoted mantras 'We're all on the same side' and 'We all want the same thing' are understandable, but they gloss over the checks and balances and the inevitable differences we sometimes need to save ourselves from groupthink.[11]

So, you need to design decision-making processes to ensure, as much as possible, there is constructive behaviour resolving differences, rather than win/lose dynamics between departments, or pretending these differences don't exist.

Alan Paterson (Global Accounts Director and Commercial VP at Santander) offers the following perspective on letting go of over-optimism:[12]

'When I look back over my career, I can see times when I needed the input of all stakeholders to drive the business forward but I can see how an "us" and "them" split can arise. Now, I've grown to appreciate the importance of quality discussions with all colleagues working in all the relevant areas, such as finance, risk, legal and compliance. I have also learned from the senior executives I work with. So, nowadays, if I propose something to a decision-making body, I will always be accompanied by colleagues from these other functions.

I might lead the business proposal presentation and answer commercial questions. However, when it comes to a question of risk or finance, I won't speak on behalf of my other colleagues. If it's a risk issue, the prime opinion that will count will be that of the risk manager. If they say you need to factor in a contingency in a business deal, then that's what will be included in the business case. If there is a finance or HR issue, those colleagues will be the ones whose voices will count the most. Of course, this requires working together as a cross-functional team, so you are all properly informed. And even if the cross-functional working is strong, there can still be judgement calls and even dilemmas. So, in the end, it will be the CEO or board who decides what we will do, considering all opinions.

But I learned that "ensuring all stakeholders have a voice and input" is the best policy from a business perspective. Have a culture where the business decision-making process is factual and respects all inputs. You must take ego out of the equation.

This takes a certain maturity because when I was younger and keen to get on, I sometimes regarded challenge and criticism as an obstacle to my career development. So, when I coach my staff, I try to stress that I will, of course, judge their work based on their ability to listen to the customer's needs and to create offers and solutions that will be attractive. But beyond that, I need them to have realistic plans, which will depend on their ability to work constructively with other colleagues. You want people who can be innovative and drive things forward but ensure they work collaboratively and listen to the experts in each field.

You want processes in your organisation which make projects succeed, and everyone feels a part of that success'.

Overarching Objectives (e.g. Compliance)

As well as setting business goals, organisations must comply with regulations, such as health and safety, data protection, etc. Following rules and regulations might seem 'basic'. Still, health, safety and environmental disasters and fines imposed on many organisations highlight it can be harder than many think.

You can explain this by recognising that a goal to be safe or compliant belongs in a category of what I call an 'overarching objective'. An overarching objective can seem straightforward, for example, 'Ensure no serious incidents or accidents'.

The argument that being safe and compliant should not be that hard tends to go as follows:

'Surely everyone knows that they need to be careful with safety? So, if we remind staff regularly, promote good practices and ask them to call out bad practices when they see them, it surely won't be that difficult to achieve! Likewise, suppose we find people who do the wrong thing. In that case, we will discipline or even dismiss them, sending an example to everyone else to take this seriously'.

Here, the argument is: 'What's the big deal about safety and compliance? It's mostly about staff doing what is common sense'.

However, Alan Dixon (former HR VP) highlights how such a mindset can miss the reality of what can happen in practice:

'I've seen things that have brought home just how hard it can be to keep health, safety and environmental risks under control.

For example, at a production facility, an articulated lorry was brought to the site containing chemical in a tanker. The driver of the truck, who worked for a haulage company, deposited the tanker in an allocated bay on site, with the ability to catch a small chemical spill, and left. It was the weekend, and he parked his cab at a nearby hotel but did not leave any contact details. All of this was done in accordance with procedures.

A few hours later, security guards on the site noticed that the tanker had started to "vent" chemical, suggesting the chemical inside was unstable, most likely too hot. Unfortunately, it wasn't possible to contact the lorry driver to clarify exactly what should be done, so it was decided that the sensible course of action was to cool down the tanker with water. This was practiced in drills in the past and should have been quite effective within a relatively short time.

So, a fire tender was brought close to the tanker, and it was drenched using a hose with water under pressure. However, instead of things calming down after half an hour, it took much longer for the venting to stop. And it transpired that this was because the chemical in the tanker was in a thermal blanket, so the cooling effect from the water was marginal. From a health and safety perspective, the steps taken were a success, no one was injured and the venting was eventually stopped. But from an environmental perspective, there was a problem. Because of the time it took to cool down the tanker, some of the leaking chemicals had mixed with the water poured onto the tanker. After a while, the chemical overwhelmed the containment area and then flowed into a nearby river. It resulted in the death of fish and other creatures.

What happened was all reported, and an investigation took place. It revealed that the chemical in the tanker got hot because the refrigerator on the tanker had stopped working. It also became clear that the standard drill to "cool down the tanker" did not work as planned because of the insulation around the tanker.

We also realised that not having the phone number to speak to the driver contributed to the incident because he could have suggested a better way to handle the problem. It seemed such an unimportant detail before the leak, made more complicated by the fact that the driver worked for the haulage company, but with the benefit of hindsight, you realise that small details can really matter.

The irony here was that despite all our efforts to manage health and safety, we ended up with an environmental problem that had not been thought through sufficiently. As a result of what happened, we carried out a series of "lessons learned" updates at the plant and with our contractors. We then commenced an initiative to improve our ability to identify health safety and environmental risks at a more granular 'on the ground' level and, in any event, to have a more robust chain of communication in the company and with contractors.

One of the most important lessons I learned from this episode is how easy it is for small details to catch you and for you to be held accountable, even when those involved are not under your direct control. Of course, the immediate cause of all of this was the haulage firm dropping off the tanker onto the site and not realising the chemical had become too warm, but one of the root causes for what happened was not realising that something routine could turn into a big problem quickly and become so hard to get on top of.'

Alan's example shows how a threat posed by an external factor (i.e. the tanker brought in by the contractor) can be underestimated and how, if you don't see the threat, you aren't going to be especially on the lookout for problems (until they happen). And not seeing all the threats you are facing might be explained by limitations in the experience and training of those who must make those assessments.

But the incident was caused by more than that; there were several good 'recovery' plans in place, but they were found to be wanting because of imperfect information, requiring a better exchange of information between the contractor and the company. It should be clear – again – that one root cause just doesn't cut it.

So, when an organisation sets itself an 'overarching objective', it is setting a series of mini goals along the lines of: 'No environmental or safety issues involving any of our staff, or contractors, at any time, across all of the activities we are involved in'. Such objectives have the character of saying: 'No one must spill a single drop, anywhere, or at any time, this year, or next year, etc.' Goals like this can be undermined by a range of things, including:

(i) an erosion of standards caused by other priorities, or cost pressures, or

(ii) an inability to keep the risk alive in the minds of busy staff[13] and

(iii) insufficient 'early warning' mechanisms to detect if standards are starting to slip.

Andrew Wright offers an additional insight in relation to what it takes to have an authentic safety culture:

'I was trained in BP about the importance of safety, particularly working in a high-risk environment. When I started my career, I remember thinking that what they were talking about to keep things safe was just common sense. I also remember hearing people who were rather fatalistic about health and safety. They thought it was unrealistic to aim for no accidents. They argued it's not possible; accidents happen.

But over time, as I saw how people behaved, reporting near-miss incidents at management meetings, doing root cause analysis, and sharing "safety moments," it became clear to me that aspiring towards zero accidents was something you could make a serious ambition.

Every now and again, I realise how outsiders might regard the level of attention towards health and safety as something rather bizarre. It can come across as somewhat obsessive, almost like belonging to a cult. But if you are serious about health and safety, you need to get to that level of focus and attention to stand a chance of not having any problems. This is because, in a high-risk environment, if you let down your guard for even a few seconds that can be enough to land you with big problems.

This means that the role of managers and senior executives to role model the right behaviours and to call out any problems they see is crucial. "Common sense' just isn't good enough".'

Many difficulties can arise in relation to goal setting, discussed in a range of helpful books, including:

- overconfidence following many past successes – see Danny Miller's book *'The Icarus Paradox'*,[14]
- too much subjectivity in risk assessments – see Douglas Hubbard's book *'The Failure of Risk Management'*[15] and
- a failure to consider the very worst things that might happen – see Nassim Nicholas Taleb's seminal book *'The Black Swan'*.[16]

And the fact that one can write a book on each of these topics highlights how big a theme we are looking at. But it's important to recognise that when you find weak spots in goal setting, the people involved at the time often didn't realise that the goals were unreachable or that there were show-stopping problems or risks, or the importance of being clear about their tolerance for failure.

And even if problems or risks are apparent to some people at the time, they would still need to voice these concerns, and managers would need to have the humility, and wisdom, etc., to take the right action as a result. This something we will return to again and again in what follows.

Summary

- Discussing failures and disappointments must start with what you were planning to achieve, how realistic the goal was, and what you were prepared to lose. Without this, you have no benchmark against which to judge a loss or setback that you want to understand the root causes of.

- I am not arguing that there should never be ambitious goals and that you should not take risks. Rather you need your eyes open when you are setting strategies goals and must not ignore the risks you are taking.
- A reluctance to analyse key parts of a significant goal and how it will be achieved, along with its principal risks and what downsides might be acceptable, may increase the chances of a problem.
- Making a change you have made many times before may not always be as easy as it was in the past.
- It's easy for business cases to underestimate costs and risks and to be over-optimistic on timelines and benefits realisation.
- Overarching objectives (such as compliance, cyber security and other environmental, social and governance [ESG] goals) are often much more challenging than you might think. They can be undermined by a single severe problem or a series of minor defects.
- There is more to compliance than common sense because staff in an organisation have other priorities simultaneously as well as constraints on time and resources.

Practical Suggestions

- When you are thinking about strategies, objectives and risks, the absolute size of the loss you might incur should always be clearly understood. A loss might be unlikely, but if you experience the loss, could you, or your organisation, cope?
- When it comes to forecasting, remember the advice of John Kenneth Galbraith 'There are two kinds of forecasters: those who don't know, and those who don't know they don't know'.[17] – so expect forecasts to be in ranges with confidence intervals.
- Be mindful of thinking trend analysis will be a magic bullet way of forecasting the future. Think how wrong trend-based

predictions were immediately before the 2007–2008 financial crisis, the COVID-19 pandemic, etc.

- Make sure you understand probability-adjusted calculations because these can easily 'mask' actual losses that might arise over a period.
- Feasibility studies, scenario analysis and getting an expert opinion on a business case (that is preferably not conflicted by those involved getting work if the decision goes one way or the other) are all good practices.
- If appropriate, get confidential feedback from commercial staff, technical, engineering, and finance staff, etc., in relation to how well they work with one another. If necessary, get some independent help to pave the way for more constructive dialogues rather than 'us' and 'them'.
- Approving plans on a provisional basis, subject to further independent review after a few months when key aspects are clearer, is a way of managing downside risks.
- The techniques of 'stress testing' and 'reverse stress testing' are worth understanding and adapting outside of financial services.
- If goals are being set in an uncertain, dynamic environment, establish what tools, such as VUCA and Cynefin, are being, and can be, used.

Chapter 5
Having Timely, Accurate Data, Information and Communications

'The most important thing in communication is hearing what isn't said'.

– Peter Drucker[1]

Lessons Learned in Cockpit Design

The Wright brothers' flyer had no seat, cockpit or control stick. Some years after, pilots flew in open-air cockpits where they could fly an aircraft with a control stick and a few levers. They could 'feel' how fast they travelled and how the plane responded to their course corrections. Aiming to fly in good weather as much as possible, they would navigate and land by eye. The relationship between the pilot and the aircraft was direct and visceral.

Sadly, unforeseen design weaknesses, poor construction, poor-quality materials, adverse weather conditions, etc., resulted in aircraft crashes. So, over the years, there were improvements in airframe design, cockpit design, construction techniques, available materials, etc., to allow pilots to fly aircraft in increasingly demanding situations (e.g. in poor weather and at night).

As time progressed, aviation electronics became a recognised specialist field (known as 'avionics'). With improved radio and navigation equipment, radar, and air traffic control centres, flying became increasingly safer, enabling long distance flights and allowing pilots to land safely in challenging situations. Cockpits were fitted with more instruments and controls. Inevitably, the crew of an aircraft was increasingly removed from the 'no filter' experience of the early days.

A turning point was reached during the 1960s and 1970s when it became clear that sometimes flight crews were becoming overwhelmed and confused with too much information in the cockpit. Wiener and Nagel, authors of '*Human Factors in Aviation*',[2] summed up the essential problem:

> 'Crew system designs and flight station layouts . . . frequently ignored the limitations and capabilities of the human operator'.

Henceforth, cockpits were built following Aerospace Recommended Practices (ARPs)[3] so that flight crew could:

- reach controls without effort,
- clearly see flight instruments and
- communicate easily with one another and air traffic control.

Insights concerning instrumentation and control design from the world of aviation have been distilled and adapted by organisations such as the Institute for Ergonomics and Human Factors,[4] which transmits its knowledge of appropriate instrumentation and control panel design to many High-Reliability Organisations (e.g. chemical plant and railway control rooms).

The critical learning about appropriate control panel design is captured in Illustration 5.1; not enough information is bad, but having lots of information is not always better. As I will explain shortly, the importance of this lesson may have yet to be appropriately recognised and applied in a range of other contexts.

Illustration 5.1 Communication and information

A former airline captain explains:

'For my flying career, I have been impressed by how cockpit design has evolved, with more augmented displays, touchscreen controls and a clear hierarchy of cockpit messages and warnings.

Regular flight simulator training also ensures that rarely seen messages are understood and – even more importantly – you can recognise when instruments are not working correctly and then "piece together" what is happening.

No matter how much you are used to relying on instruments, you must always be "on the lookout for trouble". You need to have situational awareness of where you are in relation to the topography of land and sea, etc.

Instrumentation is vitally important, but you must think about what it is and is not telling you, and above all, remember to fly the aircraft in the air.'

So, despite developments in instrumentation panels, there can still be shortcomings and difficulties in interpreting instruments and warnings, especially in high-stress environments.

Accounting and Business Performance Measurement

In the business world, 'keeping track of where you are' involved, among other things, the development of bookkeeping and accounting disciplines. First, accounting standards were developed to ensure businesses, investors and governments could understand what was happening in increasingly complex situations (e.g. foreign exchange, banking, insurance, etc.). Then, stock exchange rules required public companies to publish accounts audited by professional accounting firms. Audited accounts are intended to provide 'reasonable assurance' that the statements give a fair and true picture of a company's health at a given point in time for the benefit of current and potential future shareholders.

More recently, there have been growing requirements for greater transparency in corporate reporting, including disclosure requirements about the principal risks facing an organisation and the viability of the organisation as a going concern;[5] beyond this, disclosures regarding environmental, social and governance (ESG) matters are increasingly expected.[6]

In parallel with financial accounting and corporate governance developments, we have seen an evolution in management accounting.[7] This involves, among other things, analysing the viability of investment proposals and ensuring there is appropriate cash and credit available to fund business activities.[8]

But many board members and senior executives expect a more holistic picture of performance beyond the financial and management accounts. So, in the 1990s, 'balanced scorecards' were developed, combining financial and non-financial information.[9] Nowadays, managers often run their organisations using key performance indicators (KPIs), to show whether things are on track (e.g. with customer satisfaction), and key risk indicators (KRIs), to flag any impending problems (e.g. the level of outstanding debts).[10]

Executives and managers recognise they need to see clearly where they are and where they are going and to understand any difficulties ahead. However, it's still easy to lose track of things. Sébastien Allaire, (founding partner of Finaction & Associés) explains:

> 'I've seen many occasions when a lack of reliable data and information has caused issues to fester until they have blown up. In response, I have seen organisations embracing "digitalisation" and dashboards that are good in many ways. Here, you can "drill down" to interrogate information in detail. However, not all data in systems are high quality, so interrogation of what the data says can result in asking for data to be "cleaned" so it has the correct coding, for example.
>
> Even when the data is clean, it's easy to see managers becoming overwhelmed by the amount of data at their fingertips. Sometimes I liken it to a blizzard, and when you are in a blizzard, you can't see so clearly. In my opinion, it's easy to suffer from "too much of a good thing".'[11]

Here are some of the challenges that can arise when determining the right level of information that should be relayed to key decision-makers:

For the Board, the Right Kind of Filters

In my role, I have seen board members get frustrated when they get lengthy reports. And if something serious goes wrong, the board chairman might ask the CEO: 'Why didn't you tell us?', to which, a CEO might respond: 'Well, it was flagged on page 8 of the risk update last quarter'. After which, the chairman might say: 'We are going to need a better way of handling information being sent to the board; few of us appreciated that it was going to blow up in the way it did'.

Here, there is a dilemma to resolve: on the one hand, the board has been 'spooked', so there is an interest in receiving more information. But, on the other hand, the board is often overwhelmed with information. So, how might the quantity of information presented to the board be reduced while not losing the critical warning signs?

One large organisation I worked with had a finance and business reporting department that produced pages of information every month detailing financial and customer data, and progress reports on more than a dozen significant change projects.

This information and data were supplemented by a quarterly risk report covering the status of around 30 key organisational risks. But it was clear that board members were getting tired of what they were receiving. Also, the executive was finding they were getting questions from the board on details they genuinely didn't think were important. However, they felt obliged to deal with them, so they did not come across as defensive.

It was agreed to start using a new risk rating scale using the Failure Mode and Effects Analysis (FMEA) framework to strike the right balance.[12] This risk rating framework *challenges decision-makers to be more discerning in relation to what is really important.*[13]

When you apply the FMEA rating scale, you realise only a few things are critically important to the survival of an organisation. Consequently, we were able to halve the number of risks that deserved regular board attention. For the remaining risks, we clarified what early warning signs (e.g. KRIs) we should track to see if the risks might earn more executive, or board, attention in the future.

Thus, *it was agreed that if there was a risk with a dangerously high impact, then, even if it's very unlikely to go wrong, senior execu-tives and the board needed to know it was on someone's radar screen. They also need to understand what will trigger the next update regard-ing how it was being managed.* The aim was to avoid a common problem; a risk arises that management hope they can fix without 'making a big deal of it' to more senior executives. But sometimes, they find they can't resolve it the way they hoped. At which point, senior management and the board get a nasty surprise, often worse than if they had been involved earlier.[14]

Table 5.2 illustrates how issues were filtered upwards based on their impact and likelihood, so even a risk with a remote possibility (less than 5%) had to be reported to the executive team:[15]

Table 5.2 Disciplined filtering upwards including FMEA ratings

Probability					
>50%	Probable	Function	EXEC	Board	Board
10-50%	Possible	Function	Function	EXEC	Board
5-10%	Unlikely	Market/Entity	Function	EXEC	Board
<5%	Remote	Market/Entity	Function	Function	EXEC
	Financial loss* (£)	<1m	1m to YYm	YYm to XXm	>XXm
	Brand Image	Negative coverage barely noticeable	Negative local coverage & short-term disruption to local customer confidence	Extended negative national or industry wide coverage & some disruption to customer confidence	Extensive negative media coverage & enduring disruption of customer or industry confidence
	Consumers	Isolated cases of dissatisfied consumers	Loss of confidence leading to loss of some local consumers	Loss of confidence leading to loss of large number of consumers/major customers	Complete loss of confidence in key markets or material customer
	People	Small numbers of dissatisfied employees	Dissatisfied employees, some loss of key talent	Dissatisfied employees, significant loss of key talent	Loss of reputation as a good employer, unable to retain or hire effectively
	FMEA Score	Up to Moderate <6	High 7	Very High 8	Extremely High Dangerously high 9-10

All Is Going Well Until It Isn't. Metrics That Turn from Green to Red Overnight

Another problem you can see is when an organisation has identified a critical risk and has, in principle, measures in place to keep it 'under control', but then, suddenly, the risk turns into a crisis in the space of a few days. After which the board, senior management and other stakeholders ask: 'How did that happen?'

Hurricane Katrina, which devasted New Orleans and the surrounding area in August 2005 and resulted in thousands of deaths and costing billions of dollars, was an example of a risk that many thought was 'being worked on' (especially after Hurricane Isidore, Hurricane Ivan and the Hurricane Pam exercise). Hurricane preparedness was progressing, but some of the most crucial mitigating actions (building levees, etc.) were not improving as quickly as turned out to be necessary. The inquiry report provides a painful but powerful reminder of how easy it is to know about a risk, be in the middle of improving things, but be missing the fact that critical ingredients are still missing. The title of the inquiry report says it all, there was 'a failure of initiative'.[16]

I see similar problems quite frequently:

- A project is reporting positive progress, with a few minor setbacks, and then, suddenly, there is news that the project will be delayed.
- News that business continuity plans are mostly in place, with no serious 'red flags', but then things are shown not to be working (which happened a lot during the COVID-19 pandemic).
- Cyber security and ransomware risk is reported to be 'under control', and then it isn't.
- Work is underway to encourage staff retention; but then it transpires that some key staff (e.g. working on IT projects) have left for a consulting firm, resulting in project delays.

When a root cause analysis (RCA) is conducted, a common finding is that the relevant risk was on the radar screen, but it was either:

(I) not being reported upwards on a timely basis (as discussed) or

(II) not understood (and documented) in 'high definition', so that critical cracks might be more clearly seen[17] or

(III) reported from a 'glass half full' perspective rather than 'glass half empty;' again, masking the urgency of what may still need to be done. (Illustration 5.3 epitomises the problem, which can be encountered both in a business context and in daily life.)[18]

As a result, *it's not just the granularity of how key areas are reported upwards but the criteria by which we say whether we are 'on track' that increases or reduces the chances of getting a surprise.*

One perspective
'Look how much we have achieved'

Another perspective
'Look how much we still have to do'

Illustration 5.3   Perspectives on progress

Paying Attention to the Way Milestones Have Been Planned and Progress Is Tracked

Suppose we ask a team to ascend 6000 m up a mountain in three days, and we are asked to set goals and track progress. We have the following key choices:

- How we plan to climb the mountain?
  - In equal stages for three days (2000 m a day) or, say,
  - 1750 m/day for two days and then 2500 m on day three.[19]
- How we judge whether the team is 'on track'?
  - Only judge them as being on track (with a 'green light' rating) if they reach 100%+ of their daily target.
  - Or give them a 'green light' rating if they reach, say, 90% or 95% of their target.

Let's consider the consequences of what seem like innocent choices:

(I) If we agree to a 'slower start' of 1750 m ascent for the first two days, then the 2500 m required on day three is 43% more than the first two days – potentially more demanding to achieve. Here, all other things being equal, we are increasing our chances for a last-minute disappointment.

(II) If we set an equal ascent of 2000 m a day for three days, but allow a green traffic light for reaching 90% of the daily target, we could have a situation where the team climb 1800 m on days one and two (and still get a green rating), but then need to cover 2400 m on day three. This still means the team must go 33% quicker on the last day! So, again – all other things being equal – we are increasing the chances of a last-minute surprise, with no 'slack' as we approach a deadline.

As we can see from both examples, it's surprisingly easy to inadvertently 'set up' the chances of a last-minute disappointment by the way targets are set or the way progress is measured. So, whether it's climbing a mountain, flying over a mountain or reaching a project goal, if the 'mountain' we are trying to climb up or fly over is a certain height, *the way we plan to ascend can really matter to whether we are going to safely 'sail over', 'just make it' or crash.*

When I look at things that didn't go to plan, I quite frequently encounter organisations that missed the fact that risks were building up from the start. Reasons for this include: (i) 'It'll take time for the project to get started and for things to be set up' and (ii) 'Achieving 90% is good enough; we can't be too hard on the project team at the beginning'. This highlights there is often more to goal setting, the way plans are formulated, and how progress is tracked than meets the eye (see Illustration 5.4). A slower and lower 'hockey stick' approach is very popular but can push problems into the future and contribute to the last-minute surprises you might see.[20]

I am not advocating that targets and measures should be set in a specific way; instead, I am highlighting *that target setting, and the way progress is tracked, contain their own risks, which can increase the chances of a surprise unless you are careful.*

Further, the cause of targets and metrics being set in the way they are will often depend upon a range of other factors (e.g. pressure to meet a specific date from stakeholders, dependence on getting a contractor to start work quickly, the budget/headcount approval process, etc.) – highlighting the systemic nature of what might be happening.

Illustration 5.4   How will you reach your goal?

Project Oversight: Costs and Progress

A project management consultant I interviewed outlined a common problem with project reporting:

> 'Tracking the costs of a project, and understanding how these might evolve, is often more challenging than monitoring business-as-usual costs because it takes discipline and skill to "match" expenditure incurred to the relevant stages of the project. You cannot simply track project costs against a monthly budget. Many business reporting systems are set up to do this, but it's likely to be meaningless because the work you have done on a project, month by month, invariably won't exactly match what you first planned and budgeted.
>
> And even more challenging is anticipating the future cost outturn as well as the benefits that are forecast to be delivered from a project. In the latter case, it must be recognised that benefits forecasts often involve making estimates regarding how much money or time others might save in the future because of what the project delivers (e.g. because of what a new system should be able to do). Thus, benefits forecasts involve making inferences about the

functionality of any new system. So, these estimates can quickly get "out of sync" with what will be delivered. In the light of all of this, forecast cost and benefits for a project are often worth checking independently from time to time.'

Damian Finio, CFO Phibro Animal Healthcare Corporation, explains the need for direct data points as well:

'As a Finance Director, I have learned the importance of getting "direct assurance" from project and product leads and key team members. If something is potentially important or costly, you should get a formal update on progress, the current key challenges being worked on and the key risks that may arise in the future. If you do this, you can judge whether the team properly understands what is going on. After all, if someone doesn't flag a risk upfront and then three months later, it becomes an issue, it should raise some concerns.

It's not about expecting progress updates to be perfect; it's quite the reverse of that. So, if someone says they are "worrying" about key details, that puts me at ease. But, paradoxically, if they try to give me a picture that everything is fine or the only challenges they foresee are the ones that are being worked on, I get concerned. The aim should always be to avoid an environment where things are reported as fine until they aren't.

In this context, it's essential to hear from different team members beyond the team lead, with the chance to listen to what they think on critical points. Looking at their body language when questions are addressed can also be informative, and you can also start to get an impression, albeit a partial one, of how different risks, and even other teams, compare.

It's also useful because it can help "bring to life" what is happening with critical products and projects in a portfolio. Discussing the colour of traffic lights on a piece of paper or percentage completed statistics risks becoming detached from the real issues on the ground. As a Chief Financial Officer of a publicly traded company, I know this must be avoided at all costs.'

To summarise, it's understandable that organisations devote a lot of time and effort to collecting and reporting information.

The desire for timely news and good communication comes from the basic human need to know where you are and what's happening. Otherwise, it can generate anxiety to be 'flying blind'. However, as we know from the cockpit, it's easy to get overwhelmed, and find you are missing 'the wood for the trees', where it can be difficult to know whether you are hearing 'noise' or 'signal'.

As I hope I have illustrated, there are a range of design factors and human factors that impact the way information is presented, including the way we define the importance of risks and issues, how we set milestones to reach an objective and the way we report whether we have met these. Quite often, its subtle shortcomings can contribute to big problems coming to light too late.

There are numerous books and frameworks on good practices in setting targets, KPIs and KRIs which provide guidance on how you might avoid surprises coming out of the blue. The book 'It Should Never Happen Again', by Mike Lauder[21] provides a useful list of types of signals to consider, including routine, weak, messy, mixed, decoy, misinterpreted, etc. He also discusses other challenges associated with the way information flows, including 'loss of salience' (when a warning sign becomes normalised) and missing crucial early warning signals.[22]

The challenge, though, is to look afresh at the reporting of information and be open to the possibility that there might be subtle problems, or cracks, even when 'everyone is pleased' with what is being done. This is one of the reasons lacunae can exist for years, and their significance only coming to light when something comes at you from your 'blind side'.

Summary

- The aviation industry reminds us of the importance of giving decision-makers the right amount of timely data and information. However, it also highlights the importance of watching how much information is provided. Otherwise, managers can be overloaded.

- Businesses need to have a range of measures of where they are and where they are going. KPIs and KRIs can be helpful but they need to address the things that really matter.
- Filtering what information does and does not reliably make it to senior management, the board and external stakeholders is a fundamentally important question to keep in mind.
- Understand what arrangements are in place to 'fast track' potentially important issues to senior managers and the board so they don't get lost or delayed.
- How milestones are set and how achievement against milestones is measured is also a fundamental question to be understood at both a design and an operational level.
- 'Hockey stick' forecasts are a precursor to many surprises. So are metrics or traffic lights that allow for shortfalls to accumulate.
- Tracking the costs and benefits of a project is a highly specialist skill. Remember comparisons against a monthly budget may not warn you of problems. Good practice is to match costs against specific project deliverables and especially against the benefits that have been secured.
- Look for a range of sources of information so you can corroborate what you are seeing. Incidents and near misses are vitally important, as are meetings with those directly involved (sometimes called 'skip' meetings) or independent assurances.

Practical Suggestions

- The FMEA framework is an excellent tool to help 'push' thinking around critical risks. A helpful mindset to adopt is 'risk-based risk management', with a 'belt and braces' approach to understanding mission-critical goals and risks and analysing these in more detail than routine risks.
- Be mindful of 'motherhood and apple pie' risks that are generic (e.g. 'cyber security risk' and 'staff retention'); a good risk management process should be capable of revealing detailed data on critical sub-risks *relevant for a specific organisation*.

- Ensure you are clear what measures of progress are leading and lagging and don't let perfect data be an enemy of 'good enough' data, especially concerning things that matter, such as customer relationship management data (waiting times, turnaround times and understanding the causes of negative feedback).
- When a goal has been set, pay close attention to the phasing of how it will be achieved. The more that milestones and metrics are 'back-end loaded,' the greater the chance of a surprise with little time to put things right.
- Be very clear about how the organisation measures whether milestones have or have not been met; there are often many incentives for managers to give themselves the 'benefit of the doubt'.
- Appreciate that 'silence' can often be dangerous. Ideally you are looking for a culture where sharing and transparency of 'inconvenient truths' is encouraged.
- When you get survey results in support of a key point, clarify how many people did not respond. Likewise, try to unpick the extremes from the average and ask whether 'free text' responses were asked in any surveys and, if so, what they said.

Chapter 6

Setting Appropriate Roles, Responsibilities, Accountabilities and Authorities

'A body of people holding themselves accountable to nobody ought not to be trusted by anybody'.

– after Thomas Paine[1]

In Many Contexts, Clear Roles and Checks and Balances Are Essential

A commercial aircraft usually has two key roles in the cockpit. The pilot flying the plane and the pilot monitoring the flight. The pilot monitoring is there in case – among other things – (i) the pilot flying suddenly becomes ill, or (ii) it looks like the pilot flying might be about to do something inappropriate or dangerous.

You will find an insistence on clear roles and responsibilities in a maritime environment, in chemical plants, power stations, hospitals and in a military context, covering responsibilities for determining the organisation's strategy, operational decision making and more detailed day to day points, such as who can authorise salary payments.

In large organisations, at the most senior levels, you have key executive management roles such as the Chief Executive Officer (CEO) and Chief Financial Officer (CFO). Overseeing their work will usually be a board of directors, chaired by the chairman of the board, and then numerous sub-committees with specialist roles (such as an Audit Committee).[2] At the board and executive levels, roles, responsibilities, accountabilities and authorities (R2A2) are invariably considered in detail, cross-referenced against legal and regulatory requirements, and communicated to relevant senior managers.

There are three fundamental considerations:

1. It is essential to have clear enough roles, responsibilities, accountabilities and authorities[3] if you want an organisation to be effectively managed and governed.
2. No matter how competent or senior someone is, you don't normally leave them completely unchecked to do what they will. You can also see this with the US government, where the constitution enshrines a 'separation of powers' and 'checks and balances' between the President, the Executive, the Legislature and the Judiciary.[4]
3. R2A2 should adapt and change as things evolve, to cope with new goals, challenges, risks and unforeseen situations.

Yet, despite the fact it is well understood that R2A2 is critical to organisational success, you can still find problems with R2A2 in practice. For example, after the 2007–2008 financial crisis, where many banks and insurance companies lost money, investigations highlighted several instances where senior executives tried to blame others for what happened.[5]

As a result, in the United Kingdom, a new Financial Services Senior Management and Certification regime was implemented in 2016.[6] And in Australia, the Banking Executive Accountability Regime

(BEAR) was launched.[7] Both significantly sharpen competency and experience requirements before appointments to a senior role in financial institutions. They set out the responsibilities of key executives and the conduct expected of senior staff (e.g. to act with due care, skill and diligence, to pay attention to customers' interests, treat them fairly, etc.). Failure to comply with these regimes can have severe implications for the companies and key personnel involved (including sanctions and fines). Note, however, that the primary focus of these regulations is on senior leadership roles and responsibilities.

Despite a recognition that R2A2 should be appropriately managed, there remain many challenges in practice, for example:

Surely It Was Someone Else's Job?

Even though many organisations set out senior leadership roles and responsibilities, etc., unclear R2A2 is often one root cause of why things went wrong. Illustration 6.1 sums up the challenge.[8]

When it goes well:
Everyone claims the credit

When it goes badly:
It was someone else's fault

Illustration 6.1 Accountability

Here are some examples of problems that I have seen, where unclear R2A2 has featured:

(I) *A cyber security breach occurs because a business system owner and their local IT support did not execute the latest software update.*

The central IT department blames the system owner, but the system owner explains that the software upgrade had been scheduled for later in the month because they were in the process of making other changes to the system that customers had asked for and they didn't want to do anything to interfere with that upgrade. They felt they had the authority to make a pragmatic decision to delay the security upgrade for a few weeks, whereas the central IT department did not.

(II) *In a large business project for a new line of business, a considerable cost overspend arose that wiped out all the hoped-for profit of the venture.*

A review of what happened established that rather than insufficient finance oversight, three finance managers were involved. However, it transpired their efforts needed to be 'joined up'. Each finance lead assumed someone else was looking at expenditure commitments being made by various business managers. They said they had got an incomplete understanding of everything that was happening in the business while they were often busy with other matters.

On the other hand, the business managers explained that they were working 'flat out' to deliver the project to a timeline, and they didn't have the time to keep track of everything they had discussed and check all the paperwork they had received. They assumed colleagues in legal and finance were keeping track of things.

(III) *A warehouse has a fire, and stock is damaged because of a lack of sprinklers in a new section of the warehouse.*

A health and safety audit before the fire recommended sprinklers should be installed in a new section of the warehouse. However, the warehouse manager said the installation of sprinklers would need to wait until funds were available in the next year.

The head of health and safety explained, 'I did my best to raise the issue, but I have no authority to make the logistics director and warehouse manager install fire sprinklers since that was a business decision'.

The logistics director and warehouse managers said, 'If health and safety were not happy with our plan to do it in a year, they should have told us and escalated their concerns upwards so that we could get funding sooner, with their help'.

(IV) *As part of a regional expansion project, a new production plant is built but cannot be used for exports until a crucial approval is obtained (which comes many months later than planned).*

The project takes several years; land is acquired, a building contractor is engaged, various permissions are granted to build the facility and get authorisations to produce products (involving an overseas lawyer), etc.

Millions of pounds were spent, and the plant started the commissioning phase to go 'online' in the region. As detailed logistics planning begins, it becomes clear that no export licence has yet been issued from the authorities, which is essential if it is going to be used as a regional supply centre.

So, fingers start pointing: Can we get a licence to export in time? Who chose the external lawyer? Who should have supervised what they were doing? How long should we have waited for the 'pending' approval before escalating the matter?

There were arguments between various business managers and within the legal function (in the headquarters, regionally and locally).

(V) *An Internal audit team examines an area and only finds a few minor problems. But six months later, there was a serious fraud.*

Senior management and the Audit Committee ask the Chief Audit Executive (CAE): 'Where were you? You said that area was mostly fine, and now we have a fraud!' The CAE replies: 'We did a high-level review of the area and found some problems, but it would have taken a lot more time and effort to dig into details to find the fraud'. As the discussion ensued, the CAE explained: 'Anyway, it's not the role of internal audit to 'provide absolute assurance on everything, we only provide "reasonable assurance". The procurement and finance departments should have stopped the fraud, not internal audit'.[9]

I trust the pattern is clear; on the ground, it's easy to encounter situations where roles and responsibilities, etc., are unclear. And for months or years, this may not matter. But *R2A2 gaps and overlaps can lie around like landmines, creating the conditions for significant setbacks and problems later when the question of exactly who does what will matter.*[10]

Who Is Accountable for Pinning Down Unclear Accountabilities?

Of course, whether an organisation has problems with operational R2A2 often depends on how much effort relevant senior leaders have put into pinning things down in detail. In some areas where there is a significant operational or regulatory requirement for clear operational roles, or there was a problem in the past, you can find roles have been clarified proactively and things work well.

Where this is not the case, internal audit departments are often the 'canary in the coalmine' identifying R2A2 problems. For example, an auditor will start an assignment, and a manager will say, 'That's not entirely our responsibility; you need to speak to the finance/procurement/IT manager'. And there can then be a wild goose chase to establish who does what. Sometimes these uncertainties, confusions or disagreements in R2A2 won't matter enormously, but at other times, they do.

Of course, internal audit departments can't visit all parts of an organisation every year, which raises the question: '*What is the management process to flush out unclear roles and responsibilities on a proactive basis?*' and '*Where do managers or staff go to flag up concerns in R2A2, and what's the process to resolve gaps or uncertainties?*'

Accountability Mapping Tools

This is why 'accountability mapping' tools, such as the McKinsey RACI model,[11] the Bain RAPID model[12] or swim lane diagrams,[13] are so important. They can set out on just a few pages who does what, but *they can also be used to capture different views concerning R2A2, enabling relevant managers to see, sometimes for the first time, the confusion around who does what.* Table 6.2 sets out a series of activities (e.g. tasks) and roles and then sets out which tasks stakeholder thinks they are accountable or responsible for and which are the accountability and responsibility of someone else, etc. This will often make visible where there are differences of opinion.

Based on such a mapping exercise, you can then work to 'join up the jigsaw' with an updated accountability map, where it is agreed – for example – which manager is accountable for each activity, overseeing what is done, and who is responsible for doing what must be done, etc. After which, you can then adjust job descriptions, authority levels, experience levels, training needs, and appropriate

Table 6.2   Accountability mapping as a tool to clarify role clarity or role confusion

	Role 1	Role 2	Role 3	Role 4
Activity 1	A	C A	R R R	
Activity 2	A A A	C	I R	R
Activity 3	C	A A A A		R
Activity 4	C	C A	A A	R R R
Activity 5	A A A	C	A	R

Key
Accountable (A)
Responsible (R)
Consulted (C)
Informed (I)

Ideally
One A and one R
for each key task

Different fonts signify different views concerning who does what. Reading across:
✓ *The same letter in a different column highlights a need to gain further agreement, e.g., Activity 1, A is unclear between Roles 1 and 2.*
✓ *Various letters in the same column indicates consensus who is either R, A, C or I; e.g., R consensus - Activity 1, Role 3; A consensus - Activity 3, Role 2*
✓ *Sometimes stakeholders may not have an opinion (hence no comment recorded)*
✓ *In practice you need the requisite authority to determine R2A2 - it's not simply a matter of consensus.*

resources and targets to bring to life, in practical terms, what is required of each role.

In my experience, these tools are not used as often and systematically as they should be. Likewise, not all internal audit teams flag up the accountability issues they are finding, which is a missed opportunity.[14]

The Role of Policy Owners and Accountabilities for Third-Party Interactions

Paradoxically, even when some roles have a formal legal or regulatory responsibility, such as a head of health and safety, head of data privacy, head of compliance, etc., you can find unclear R2A2s. Here is what I have heard from policy owners on a number of occasions, 'I am accountable for the policy development and communication, for delivering training, offering advice and reporting to the regulator. But that does not mean I can make sure the whole organisation is compliant with the policy. I rely on others to do what is needed and ask me for advice if they are unsure. In practice, *I have no direct authority to instruct them what to do or to allocate resources in their direction; that is the job of operational management*'.

Alongside this, I have also heard line managers say, 'Everyone is accountable for compliance', which may be true in broad terms, but can lead to a diffusion of responsibility, where managers and staff say, 'It's surely [someone else's] job to do something! Why would it be down to me to act when others have equally been involved, and nothing terrible has happened?!'[15]

Other areas where R2A2 can be challenging include the following:

- When a steering group or committee is involved (After all, if a committee decides something, which individuals are accountable and responsible?).
- When a third-party contractor or agent is involved.

- When – more broadly – different organisations need to work together on specific issues (e.g. border control, fire, police, ambulance, local government, intelligence services, etc.).

It's outside the scope of this book to embark on a detailed discussion of how to address the many R2A2 issues that can arise[16] because it's such a big topic. However, if you encounter, or suspect, unclear R2A2 in a critical area, it is invariably worthwhile asking for roles and responsibilities to be pinned down because so long as this is not the case the risk of a problem occurring will just grow.

The Causes of Unclear R2A2

While unclear R2A2 is often an important reason why things don't go to plan, it shouldn't be a surprise to recognise that R2A2 issues are invariably not a 'free-standing' root cause.

So, assume we have a risk that is not being effectively managed (P1) because of unclear roles and responsibilities at an operational level. It's possible to see the following 'chain' of reasons explaining this. For example:

Considering Prevention:

(P2) While there are senior level R2A2, there are no enforced operational roles and responsibilities, because

(P3) there is a mistaken assumption all people will take up responsibilities voluntarily (or flag this up if it is unclear), but

(P4) most people are busy and don't have time to resolve these unclarities (after all, not everything can be totally clear), and

(P1) it's not clear that it's their role to do this (note the circularity of unclear roles here).

Considering Detection:

(D1) There is no precise, systematic measure to say that R2A2 is unclear, and

(D2) there is no one in place to proactively take an interest in whether R2A2 is clear (again, a repeating causal factor), because

(D3) few staff have been trained to do this, or have the tools to understand how to map accountabilities, because

(D4) it's not clear why you would prioritise training managers on such an esoteric topic. Afterall, it might be argued there is no evidence this is causing a big problem. (And, again, there is a circularity here, because without any information about unclear roles, how could it become a priority for anyone?)

Considering Recovery:

What typically happens is that when an incident arises and a root cause analysis (RCA) is carried out, the lack of clarity of R2A2 can emerge as a causal factor, *which is then fixed for that area by pinning down roles and responsibilities at the level of job descriptions and targets for the relevant staff.*

The precise reasons for unclear R2A2 will depend on the specific facts of each situation, but the 'fact pattern' detailed is not unusual and can be set out in Diagram 6.3.

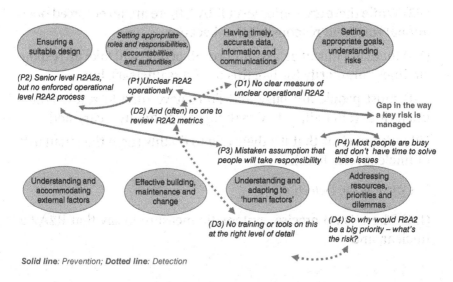

Solid line: Prevention; **Dotted line**: Detection

Diagram 6.3   The systemic nature of unclear roles, responsibilities etc. (illustration)

Whatever the analysis for unclear R2A2, simply saying that you need to agree on clear roles and responsibilities for a specific problem area for the future *does not address why R2A2 were unclear in the first place*, nor does it proactively prevent similar issues from repeating.

Organisations need to be able to detect critical R2A2 gaps and have a clear process for clarifying and resolving role ambiguities proactively as they arise. Pinning down accountabilities at a senior level may not be enough; senior accountable persons would need to ensure a robust accountability framework at an operational level and may even require the authority of the CEO to resolve differences of opinion across departments.[17]

So, if you hear someone say, 'we have a culture of unclear roles and responsibilities', *'culture' may be referring to a range of factors that are causing the problem* (e.g. as shown in Diagram 6.3). Thus, the 'eight ways to understand why' framework, with connections, can provide insights into the factors that might be creating 'cultural' or 'systemic' problems.[18]

I am sure the importance of R2A2 at the right level is going to be picked up by more organisations, regulators and others as we look to the future.[19] For example, what would an accountability map look like for a zero-carbon goal for an organisation and its suppliers? And as Artificial Intelligence (AI) capabilities are developed, how should we understand R2A2 between the organisations involved and different regulators across the world? How do we manage gaps and overlaps between regulators when AI may have implications for data privacy, consumer protection, etc., as well?

Unless we 'turbo charge' our ability to untangle the spaghetti of unclear R2A2, and develop more tools and techniques to address concerns, there is every chance the complexity of contemporary global challenges will run far ahead of our ability to keep track of who is doing what. And this is more than just about the 'hardware' of who does what; it's about the softer 'human factors' that help people to take up and carry out their roles to the full. And without clear R2A2 that people want to uphold when no one is looking, how can we even start to protect ourselves from the worst that can happen?[20]

Summary

- R2A2 should be sufficiently clear for important matters.
- Even the most senior people need reasonable clarity about who is doing what, including the need for a 'separation of duties' (e.g. between CFO and CEO, and CEO and board of directors).
- The UK Senior Managers and Certification Regime and Australian BEAR provisions provide valuable insights into pinning down R2A2.
- Of course, not every role and responsibility, etc. needs to be pinned down; the idea is *to pin things down in relation to the objectives and risks that matter the most.*
- Equally, roles need a degree of flexibility in some situations and over time, which adds to the complexity of how to get this right. This is where 'adaptive accountability' thinking can be helpful.
- Accountability mapping tools are essential to help you 'get your arms around' these questions. They can be used not just to set out the ideal position, but to map out the 'as is' so stakeholders can visibly see any differences of opinion about R2A2.
- The role of a policy owner is more complicated than many realise. Policy owners may carry legal accountability, but, in practical terms, they may not have the authority they need to enforce and resource the management of specific risks at an operational level.
- Understanding accountabilities can also be challenging when third parties are involved (including those working under contract and external consultants), and when management teams, committees and steering groups are involved.
- Be mindful of any discussions that suggest managers rely on a regulator for assurance, for example, 'The regulator didn't find anything when they looked at [an area], so it should be OK'.
- Unclear R2A2 is a commonly found explanation of why things can go wrong. Still, it does not stand independent of other root causes.
- Accountability mapping tools currently in use need to be evolved to address the challenges we see in the twenty-first century.

Practical Suggestions

- Take great care with the assumption that because top-level R2A2 are clear, it will be equally true elsewhere in the organisation.
- Clarify what tools the organisation has in place to clarify R2A2 – RACI? RAPID? Swim lane? And what training do relevant staff get to use these tools?
- Clarify how well the segregation of duties works for the most high-risk activities. What training do those involved get?
- Is there an ongoing process to update policies and procedures at intervals and to reconfirm that R2A2 is agreed upon and operating in practice? What management information, if any, is available to detect if R2A2 is unclear proactively?
- Leverage what the Internal Audit department and other cross-functional bodies see. However, recognise that the clarity of R2A2 needs to be an area to check proactively in the management system, especially for the most critical risks and sub-risks.
- Is there any mechanism for staff to flag up a concern or question about who is accountable for what?
- Clarify how R2A2 is kept working if someone is ill or moves on (i.e. emergency cover and succession arrangements).
- Clarify with any policy owners how they see their role vs. that of the business. For example, if there is a resource stand-off, what is the mechanism to escalate and resolve the risk or to have the business accept the risk?
- Look into Organisational Role Analysis (ORA).
- Commonplace areas to check:
  - What is the role of a policy owner vs. a business area manager in maintaining compliance?
  - Do managers recognise Internal Audit operates in the 'third line', i.e. it is not accountable for checking things are working on behalf of local management?
  - Do managers understand their role in monitoring the work of their staff and the fact that they can't just say, 'No news from my staff is good news?'
  - How do accountabilities work with third parties and committees?

Chapter 7
Ensuring
a Suitable Design

'Design is not just what it looks like and feels like. Design is how it works'.

– Steve Jobs[1]

Ahead of Its Time and Still Standing Today: The Eiffel Tower

If you talk about Paris, France, it doesn't take long for most people to mention the Eiffel Tower. The Tower was constructed for the Exposition Universelle of 1889 in Paris, with a projected life of a few decades. But instead, it was the highest building in the world for over 40 years, and it still stands after 130 years.

A crucial part of its appeal is its curved 'A' design. The original design concept came from Emile Nouguier and Maurice Koechlin. But it was Gustave Eiffel who was able to see both the potential and the challenges in the first design and to develop and build what we see today. The design looks simple, but was perfected after years of experience designing and building a range of important bridges (e.g. the Garabit viaduct and the Maria Pia bridge) as well as other structures, including the frame for the Statue of Liberty in New York, USA.[2]

Eiffel developed expertise across a range of important, progressive engineering specialisms, including stress and load calculations, understanding the effect of wind on structures and how to build solid foundations using compressed air caissons. He was also a 'hands-on' designer and engineer and understood the need to design structures from a practical perspective. This included calculating loads on each of the four pillars at the bottom of the Tower as they were built higher and leaning inwards. He created scale models of the Tower to understand better the practical challenges that would arise and thought through how the four foundation pillars could be joined together to create the first floor of the Tower, with a precision of millimetres, some 57 m high.[3] Illustration 7.1 highlights Eiffel's ability to think through practical details when designing the Tower.

Illustration 7.1   Design

Eiffel's genius was to recognise that the Tower could not be built so high as a closed, solid structure. Instead, the structure was able to hold its own weight because it is comprised of a lattice of relatively thin wrought iron girders.[4] Thus, we have an engineer with tremendous passion and ambition who paid great attention to practical details. He did not live in an ivory tower, and as a result, the Tower, bearing his name, is still standing today. As he explained:

> '[Do you] think that because we are engineers, beauty does not preoccupy us or that we do not try to build beautiful, as well as solid and long-lasting structures? Aren't the genuine functions of strength always in keeping with unwritten conditions of harmony?'[5]

Good Design Applies to More Than Just Buildings and Structures

The need for good design has already shown its importance in the earlier chapters, for example:

- The design of a clinical trial to maximise its chances of success.[6]
- Cockpit design, so the crew in a cockpit have critical information without being overloaded.
- The design of appropriate roles, responsibilities, accountabilities and authorities (R2A2), so key people working on a goal, or managing risk, know who does what, with proper checks and balances.

However, getting the right design can be a challenge since it can involve achieving a range of different goals, such as (i) serving the purpose needed, (ii) being easy to use, (iii) being clear and uncluttered and, in today's world, (iv) being sustainable, and all within an agreed budget.[7]

Thus, it should be no surprise that designing skyscrapers, production plants, offices, computer systems, etc., can be very demanding and requires a great deal of skill and specialist knowledge. For this reason, I do not propose to get into a detailed discussion about structural designs, which are addressed thoroughly in technical literature. Instead, I want to examine 'design' from a more general perspective to highlight some 'day-to-day' issues and concerns I have seen in several contexts.

The Pendulum Effect on Design: Security Overkill

In the years before 2001, it was possible to ask if the captain of an airplane would permit you to go 'upfront' to the cockpit. But after 9/11, that changed. As a result, airport and aircraft security protocols changed: all bags were to be passed through an X-ray, no liquids to be taken on board above 100 ml, closed cockpits with no passengers allowed and countless other measures 'behind the scenes'. I am sure many changes in the design of airport security measures have helped reduce the likelihood of passengers planting a bomb or hijacking an aircraft. That said, this has been at the expense of a huge amount of time, cost and disruption, often borne by the mostly innocent travelling public.

If we turn our attention to online security, we regularly see software upgrades that contain 'critical security' updates for the computers and systems we use.[8] We must also type in passwords to access our online data and information, with instructions and guidance about secure passwords.

However, the more safeguards you put in place to secure buildings and IT systems, etc., the harder it can be for legitimate users to gain access. A rigorous design for security can therefore create a spin-off problem where we need to have password recovery protocols and 'workarounds' (e.g. if we forget our password, we might have it written down somewhere).[9]

It's the same with security passes for office buildings. In theory, staff are supposed to show their access pass each time they go in and out of a building; but suppose they forget their pass on some occasions. In that case, they might be 'waved through' by security staff because they know the person (but strictly, they shouldn't do this because the person concerned may have just left 'under a cloud').

Bruce Schneier highlighted the challenge of getting the right mindset towards security measures in his book '*Beyond Fear: Thinking Sensibly About Security in an Uncertain World*'. He argues that the design of security measures after terrible events such as 9/11 can easily turn into overkill and, paradoxically, create gaps elsewhere.[10]

Sandeep Das (Head of Internal Audit, St John Ambulance) offers his perspective on being on the receiving end of a significant regulatory and compliance burden:

'For some organisations I have come across in the past, where resources are plentiful, it is easy for them to over-engineer new processes and procedures, especially when a new regulation is launched. And then, after a few years, it becomes clear that the new measures are so burdensome that they are either a tick box, where no one really knows what the checks and signoffs are for, or they become subject to workarounds or exceptions.

Over time, attitudes towards compliance shift, and a new "status quo" may evolve. However, if this is done as part of a managed process, then a new "real-world" process design can be established where there is still discipline and a sense of minimum standards but where "theatre" and overload are avoided.

But if shortcuts occur, without any "stock-take", there can be inconsistency in what an organisation does and – worst of all – an absence of control in some areas because "nothing bad has happened". Of course, when an issue does "blow up", everyone asks, "How did that happen?" when it was an open secret that standards had declined over time.'

While there will inevitably be new regulations, processes, etc., after a crisis, it is essential to recognise they can act as a heavy weight on day-to-day operations. Amilcar Zambrano (Global Practice Lead of Inspections and Root Cause Analysis, DNV Energy Systems) explains:

'Regulators have a difficult job. Something terrible happens, and they want to create a solid framework that will guarantee the same or similar problems won't occur again. But if they are not careful, it's easy for regulators, or policy owners, to underestimate or misunderstand the practical human dimension.

If you over-design things, the operators who must implement these requirements pick up that what is being asked
of them is unrealistic. This may create scepticism and either
a degree of resistance or a sense of needing to "go through
the motions".

This matters because regulations and procedures are often
written for a point in time, but this can fall behind good practice
as it evolves. This is a dangerous combination because if things
are designed so that operators go on "auto pilot" and stop thinking about risks, you have a greater chance of problems.'

A Human Factors expert (who wishes to remain anonymous),
working with High-Reliability Organisations, offers their perspective on how to design things appropriately:

'When I work with clients who want to implement a new process
or way of working, I will often ask that we ground any discussion
about what is wanted in the future upon two key pillars. First, what,
in practice, are staff at the operational level currently doing? What
can we learn from their experiences? It requires us to watch what's
happening in detail and engage with users on what they think
about what they are doing. Second, if new ways of working are
envisaged, what exactly does it mean practically? This is the "task
analysis" phase. It's crucial because it's where "the rubber hits the
road", and it is where errors and mistakes can happen at the design
stage, detached from the reality of those who do the work, day in
and day out.

This is where user groups and operator groups are so important. My goal with clients is to understand and then help to engineer out any potential practical problem areas from the beginning
and provide the functionality that users need and expect.

A policy, procedure, new system or new building, or piece of
equipment may look good on the surface, but the most critical
question to ask is, "Will it work? Is it practical? Will operators see
an improvement?"'

I cannot stress enough how often what appear to be good designs
on paper can turn out to be a root cause of problems because they
underestimate the human side of what is needed to make them

work in practice. Again, this is where we can learn from aviation; pilots don't follow 40-page policies; they use checklists that cover key points to work through in certain situations.[11] Likewise, in the healthcare sector, protocols and checklists are regularly used for life-and-death situations.[12]

Thinking about the Overall Burden of Control and Compliance Measures

Beyond the appropriate design of individual systems, policies, procedures, etc., it is also essential to think about an organisation's overall burden of control and compliance measures. I saw this working in AstraZeneca, moving from Finance to Human Resources and becoming Chief Audit Executive. It was judged that I would appreciate the importance of not thinking yet another policy or procedure would solve every problem the Internal Audit team found. The 'Lean Auditing' approach that we implemented sought to improve governance, risk, and compliance (GRC) in the organisation in a 'fit for purpose', non-bureaucratic manner wherever possible.[13]

Subsequently, my consulting work has entailed helping organisations overhaul their policies and procedures. The problem can be summed up by one of my clients telling me they had more than a hundred policies, hundreds of procedures and, in total, several thousand control activities to maintain and monitor.[14]

Others have identified similar challenges. John Bendermacher (Chief Audit Executive, Euroclear) observes:[15]

> 'It's important to recognise the amount of regulation that might impact an organisation. This can be at national laws, international regulations and sector-specific requirements. Think of these as a pile of "blankets" covering what you want to do. They all have a reason for being in existence. Still, collectively, they amount to a lot and can smother attempts to be more agile and adaptive to customer needs.
>
> It's why those working in GRC, and audit have a responsibility to coordinate and, where possible, combine the key things that

need to be done. But most of all, you need to work with business colleagues to link requirements to practical day-to-day tasks and not make them a "bolt-on".'

I think it can be helpful to consider how structures, systems, policies, procedures and other internal control (or GRC) requirements make up the 'skeleton' of an organisation:

(A) If you have too many rules, procedures, and checks and balances, or they are too 'burdensome', you end up being weighed down by these requirements, often created by managers with no 'skin in the game'. Nassim Nicholas Taleb observed: 'People who are bred, selected and compensated to find complicated solutions do not have an incentive to implement simplified ones'.[16]

(B) But suppose you have areas without appropriate rules, processes, procedures, checklists or protocols. In that case, you may get innovation and creativity, but you may also get weaknesses and problems (e.g. exposure to a cyberattack, fraud or manual activities where staff might forget what needs to be done).

It is outside the scope of this chapter to go into more detail about how to design an overall framework of policies, procedures or other control measures, but it's a hot topic for many organisations.[17] As one manager explained, 'We want to Simplify, Clarify and Strengthen management control requirements, so we don't have surprises on the 'basics', but beyond this, we want to allow for flexibility and innovation'.

Thus, a good design can't be created in a vacuum. There are many considerations to bear in mind, including how well it considers human factors and the workload burden involved. Brian Reed sums it up perfectly: 'Everything is designed. Few things are designed well'.[18]

So, it's worth considering:

- If we look at structures, systems, policies, processes, infrastructure, etc., what designs have we become so accustomed to that we might have underestimated how they might cause problems?

- As things evolve in the future (e.g. ESG requirements, AI, etc.), do we have the tools and the language to articulate what it would mean for things to be 'well designed'? Especially given the fact that things will evolve in ways we cannot yet imagine.
- To what extent do we need to reappraise the design of some of the RCA tools in use (especially those without a systems perspective) to see whether they are suitable for the problems of today?

Summary

- Good design is something we expect in day-to-day life, a nice-looking computer or smartphone or a kitchen gadget. We also know that buildings designed by an architect can create a lovely space to work and live.
- Good design involves considering the context and application of what must be done. Over-engineering and too many controls can create a burden on the organisation. But if there are not enough controls, the organisation's skeleton will have gaps.
- Beware of the tendency to over-engineer policies and procedures (especially after a significant setback or in response to a regulatory change). Be mindful of policy owners and regulators who write policies and procedures without 'skin in the game'. Sometimes idealised policies can cause problems because they do not sufficiently consider human factors or resources, priorities and dilemmas.
- Coordinating different policies and procedures across an organisation (and automating them where appropriate) is often an essential task to 'reduce the burden' on day-to-day activities.
- Where the stakes are very high, high-reliability design principles are worth exploring and adapting as appropriate.
- Sometimes checklists can be of value, but equally, on other occasions, you need a 'belt-and-braces' design; this can depend on the objective or risks involved.

Practical Suggestions

- Recognise the design question when considering a range of activities:
  - Projects and their metrics;
  - R2A2;
  - Policies, processes, procedures, systems, buildings or other structures;
  - Clarify who has the expertise/authority to sign off designs are fit for purpose;
  - Staff engagement in the development of policies, procedures, processes, systems, machines, structures, etc.;
- Remember that over-engineering things can be problematic in certain situations.
- Consider engaging 'Ergonomics and Human Factors' engineers on occasion to identify problems at a task level to see if it makes a difference to design proposals.
- Consider checklists and protocols to communicate what is essential to be done.
- Before implementing a new system (e.g. a GRC system), consider undergoing a Lean review (using tools such as Kano, SIPOC and Kaizen) to analyse what is essential at an operational and senior level and what is of secondary priority.
- Get ongoing feedback from staff on how 'user-friendly' are systems, policies and processes. Refrain from regarding their concerns as a sign of poor commitment; it maybe that they see shortcomings that those who promoted systems and policies don't want to be brought to light.

Chapter 8

Understanding and Accommodating External Factors

'[People] will not look at things as they really are, but as they wish them to be – and are ruined'.

– after Niccolò Machiavelli[1]

External Factors Are Not the Root Cause of Problems

Despite the understandable desire to blame external factors for some of the problems we experience, they are not the root causes of why bad things happen, though they may be immediate and contributing causes.[2] This casts a fresh light on daily conversations, such as:

- Q: Why are you behind on your budget? A: The economic environment deteriorated; it's not our fault.
- Q: Why is the project not delivering as planned? A: The consultants have let us down.
- Q: Why are you late? A: My alarm didn't work, my train was delayed, etc.

Of course, external factors are often a source of problems but the underlying root causes to focus on relate to our ability to recognise their inherent uncertainty and adjust our goals and risk management strategies accordingly. So, if you don't want to be late for work, you set a backup alarm and aim for an earlier train.

In aviation, bad weather is a risk factor. So, pilots obtain up-to-date weather forecasts and choose a flight path and time that should avoid storms if they can. However, suppose they foresee a severe storm en route, potentially outside the safety parameters of the aircraft. In that case, they will ask for an adjustment to the flight plan. And if the weather is very bad or forecast to be a grave concern, the flight might be cancelled or delayed.

Thinking this through with the aid of the Bowtie diagram:

  (i) you detect a possible threat;

 (ii) you consider measures that you think will protect you;

(iii) you hope that if there is a problem, you will be able to deal with it, but

(iv) *how well do you know and understand the scale of risk the external threat poses? And*

 (v) *how certain are you that you can handle what happens? And, if you are not, can you take another course of action?*

After all, how many of us have seen a horror film or a film about aliens and thought, 'For goodness' sake, don't open that door!' (see Illustration 8.1).

As Carl Sagan explains, '. . . it is far better to grasp the Universe as it really is than to persist in delusion, however satisfying and reassuring'.[3]

Here are some more examples where external factors entail risk or uncertainty, alongside some steps that might be taken to understand the situation better or mitigate the threats posed:

- *When moving into a new market,* managers often engage a consultant to do market research and competitor analysis. The consultants will help them make sales and marketing decisions 'with their eyes open'.

Illustration 8.1   External factors

- *If concerned about the cost of supplies for key materials, or utilities*, managers may consider (i) entering long-term contracts at fixed prices, (ii) using a new supplier or even (iii) acquiring a supplier if the price is right. However, before proceeding, the manager will likely commission 'market analysis', 'due diligence' or a 'supplier evaluation'. The due diligence helps managers decide whether the price they are paying is appropriate and understand the risks that need to be managed (e.g. through proper warranties or contract terms).[4]
- *If concerned about possible changes in laws and regulations* that might impact what the organisation does, managers might speak to experts in the field and – if the stakes are high enough – consider lobbying activities directly or indirectly through an

industry group or other professional association (recognising what is permitted by law).

- *In a medical context, before treatment,* a doctor will endeavour to review the patient's medical history and the medication they are taking, check their blood type, etc.; they won't just assume every patient is the same.
- *From a financial perspective, various points arise, from potential exposures to interest rate and currency movements, to cost and market movements.* Here, a manager might need to take specialist advice on the options for 'hedging' and contemplating different out-turns and how these will be managed (e.g. by a freeze on non-discretionary spending).

Know Your Customer

Considering external factors includes understanding what customers need and adapting to this as required. Alan Paterson explains:

'I've always enjoyed working in sales and marketing because it's a role where I am "on the front line" of the business. I enjoy meeting existing and potential new customers to find out what they want. I get a great deal of pride and satisfaction if I can match people up with an offer that will create a win/win. On this point, I learned very early on to be mindful of going for a quick sale because if you sell something that a customer later thinks is not right, it can backfire on you in the long run.

A role I have learned to take up when necessary has been to work with colleagues internally to be a "voice of the customer" back to them. This has meant working to adjust or change plans when I was certain it could adversely affect our relationship with the customer. Often my role has been to "fight their corner" when some might have been tempted to downplay these external factors. Here I believe a key ingredient of being successful in business is to see what things look like from the other side of the table. This is important so you can consider concerns seriously and gauge when you might be pushing things too far.

Running a business for the long term is about seeing customers as real, equal people whose interests must be kept front and centre. Of course, we won't always get that right, but the critical bit is not to go into a defensive mode automatically or "what does the contract say," but rather to try to see it from their side and create a mutually beneficial way forward even in the tough times. When you accept that other customers and companies are free to move their business and cannot be controlled, you realise it's all about getting an atmosphere of mutual respect and understanding.

This approach has served us well in the recent COVID-19 pandemic, which significantly impacted some of our customers and business partners and their customers in turn. We saw the sorts of pressures that people would be put under because of lockdowns, and rather than waiting to be asked, we started to work on a series of "no need to ask" offers that were likely to be helpful to our customers. These initiatives recognised the pressures on others and created an opportunity for staying in contact with our customers and offering tailored support to meet specific needs or concerns.'

Given that many organisations understand external factors are an area to be understood and managed proactively, let's examine how efforts can, nonetheless, be severely tested or undermined:

Recognising Different Perspectives Concerning Ethics

To address external threats, some managers seek to rig the table in their favour rather than being subject to adverse headwinds. So, beyond gathering market intelligence or engaging in legitimate, legal lobbying activities, you can find some engaging in industrial espionage to understand the strategies and plans of their competitors or to obtain their know-how and intellectual property. This may be done via third parties or by hiring employees with know-how from, or intelligence about, other companies.

Sometimes managers will participate in cartels, where competitors share information and try to work 'in step' to protect prices and market shares. Of course, such activity is illegal, but that doesn't mean it doesn't take place.[5] We also have bribery and corruption, where payments are made to secure lucrative contracts or block adverse regulatory changes.[6] Payments can be organised through third parties to maintain a shield of respectability. And since this can sometimes involve senior managers or be made via intermediaries, it can be (i) challenging to spot and (ii) even harder to prove.

The paradox is that whilst questionable or illegal behaviour creates exposure for an organisation, it can translate into a business that seems – on the surface – to be 'in control'.[7] Alan Dixon explains:

> 'I have seen the best and the worst of what can happen with overseas organisations. When it goes well, you have an experienced, respected company president who understands business and does this all above board. They are supported by a solid team of local managers and by some secondees from headquarters. With this combination, you hope to get the best of both worlds: commercial savvy in the market and people who understand how the organisation "back home" works. This is what happens most of the time.
>
> But some of the senior people you recruit or work with through agents and distributors may not be everything they seem. The very things that have brought them success and status are things that can create a significant risk for your organisation. According to our standards, excessively close connections can cross a line. However, in the context of the culture of the other country and its culture, it may not be regarded as anything particularly out of the ordinary.
>
> Consider business activities with connected parties, such as family members or friends we go on holiday with. Of course, most companies want connections to be declared because of a potential or actual conflict of interest. But in that country, suggesting that work be done by an uncle's company, or the company of a trusted friend is, for them, about choosing someone they know that they trust and – from their perspective – not at all corrupt.
>
> Another point to remember when working in some cultures is that sometimes regulators and law enforcement agencies may operate in a questionable or corrupt way. So, following the law or reporting something to a regulator has a different meaning overseas.

I'm a great believer in companies trying to do their very best to emphasise their values and to offer ways for people to escalate concerns or blow the whistle, but you must understand that these efforts are often up against the whole way a local system is set up. Indeed, they can be up against the entire way a country or business sector operates. It's why efforts to tackle these issues must be savvy because, over the years, I have learned never to be surprised by what some people will do to get on.'

Andrew Wright offers his perspective when considering overseas investments:

'I have worked for many years in Asia and South America. I have learned to love these cultures and the people there. However, sometimes you must be very level-headed about what you can and can't do overseas.

As a board member and consultant, I've worked with colleagues with plans to expand overseas. I will learn, for example, that there is an opportunity to acquire some land through a local consultant who has said that they know a reputable builder who can help with construction. And their references may seem to be great. I also see the organisation's planning to send trusted managers to the country to represent its interests as the new overseas entity develops.

And I will say, "There is a significant risk that the person you plan to send over to the country, at great expense, will not be the de facto leader of the local organisation." I can offer this warning without ever having met that person. Because time and time again, this is not how things work in some countries. There are networks and unofficial alliances that are hard to see from the outside. As a result, it's easy for overseas secondees to become isolated, even if they are nationals and speak the language.

The best you might get from them is an information channel. And even then, unless they are very good, they will sometimes be excluded from some of the things that are going on in the detail. Or it may be as simple as not having the bandwidth to monitor everything that's happening in the depot or when procuring products and services.

So, I tend to say, "You can arrange for a new factory to be built but be careful how you structure your ownership. Because if you are not very careful, you can put a lot of money at risk and find that, if there is an upside, it's not as big as you thought. Even worse, you might find that if something goes wrong, such as a legal or environmental difficulty, the allies that you thought you had cannot or will not help you, so you will be the one left carrying the can."

No matter how big you are, no matter how much due diligence you do and no matter how good your processes are in some countries, sometimes you simply won't have the understanding, the horsepower, the networks or the place in the culture to guarantee no surprises. I say this not only because I've got the T-shirt from working in countries such as China or Brazil, etc., but I also say this because I have now learned that no matter how long you have worked overseas and no matter how well you think you know another culture, you can never know all the underlying motivations of people and other players.

After all, even with someone you know and trust, if a family member of theirs gets into trouble and gets involved with the wrong people, it might impact the behaviour of your trusted person and your business despite decades of reliable behaviour before that.'

So, when it comes to overseas countries, third-party suppliers, agents, distributors, etc., managers need to keep their wits about them and prepare for the unexpected.[8] If they hear rumblings of trouble, they need to switch from a mindset that says: 'They have worked for us for years, that can't be true', to one that is a bit more open to the possibilities of either bad or 'grey zone', behaviour and therefore tackle emerging issues robustly and without undue delay.

Learning to see what is 'behind the mask' is a crucial skill to develop, and it's worth remembering that it can happen in your own country, not just elsewhere.

Third-Party Relationships and Warning Signs

In addition to ethical questions, I want to discuss the competence, ability and will of a third party to do a job it has been contracted to do. Many organisations use a supplier selection process and due diligence to ensure they are working with someone qualified to provide a product or service and do this reliably. Further, organisations will usually negotiate a service level agreement (SLA) that will specify what needs to be done (e.g. the supply of IT services) and the information to be provided (e.g. performance statistics on relevant systems and networks) so that everything should work smoothly.[9]

Over and above this, you might see regular catch-up discussions with third parties to discuss how things are going and to address any issues, concerns or questions.

Most of the time, things will go well, but despite the desire to keep things 'on track', here are some of the things that can go wrong with third parties that I have seen result in unpleasant surprises:

• *People stop paying attention.* If you engage a third party, there is often a flurry of activity to get things up and running: project meetings, transition teams, etc. Then, hopefully, things run smoothly, and the excitement that was there at first starts to dissipate. Managers may have reasonable grounds to believe that the third party is doing as good a job, perhaps an even better job than was being done before.

Then someone takes over the lead role for managing the contract, has a busy diary and asks, 'Why am I meeting them again?' and at some point, unless something terrible is happening, attention can turn in another direction. Then sometime later, things may go wrong, and the organisation realises, 'No one was managing the contract properly from our side'. In other words, just because there is a contract in place and potential penalties may arise if things go wrong, that does not mean that everything will run smoothly with a third party.

Ian Brimicombe (SVP, Specialist Finance, and Projects, Burberry) stresses the importance of properly attending to third-party relationships:

'We work with a wide range of third parties and regard it as central to our business model to have a laser-like focus on not only what they do for us but also how they operate. As a result, we demand high standards from our suppliers across a range of dimensions and recognise the need to monitor product quality, environmental impact and employment standards frequently.

Equally, we are always open to feedback from suppliers and contractors regarding process improvements to meet or exceed required standards. If you see regular improvements in operations, that's a good sign the supplier is treating the standards seriously. If things stagnate, this can be a warning sign that suppliers are not paying sufficient attention to the detailed requirements.'

- *Third-party responses may depend on who they are dealing with.*
  You might see some or all of the following 'influencing strategies' from third parties:
  - Those who put a 'positive spin' when it comes to presentations for senior executives (highlighting good news stories that happened and proposing new things they can do next year).
  - Organising client 'networking sessions' and conferences, where their customers meet one another and hear about recent achievements and potential future developments, which can provide new ideas but may also have an element of 'feeding egos'.
  - Corporate entertainment.

  None of these third-party influencing strategies necessarily cause problems. But these 'best foot forward' activities by third parties can sometimes buy them the benefit of the doubt if there are problems. Damian Finio observes:

'You need to recognise, when you are dealing with senior people, that part of the skill they have is their charisma and ability to impress. They can explain things in a credible way. They can answer questions truthfully, but without necessarily telling you everything you might want to know.

It's something you need to look out for as you gain more experience, the little details that get masked. And this isn't always about them deliberately hiding things; it's about them knowing how to highlight the best of what they have done and have explanations for things that have gone wrong.

For that reason, showcase events are not always the best way to understand what's happening "on the coal face". This is where digging into data, not just the averages, but specifics, can be so valuable. Likewise, pay attention to whether explanations for problems seem to explain symptoms or root causes.'

- *Exercising audit rights and paying attention to 'weak signals'.*

  If a third party is performing a critical role (e.g. IT services, call handling, payroll, etc.), managers might put arrangements to audit aspects of what they are doing. For example, how the third party handles data and information (e.g. so it stays secure) and accounts for revenue or costs (e.g. so any fees paid are correct). The results from these audits can give managers assurance they wouldn't get from a standard performance report, a catch-up meeting or even visiting their facilities. However, it's essential to be clear about the scope and depth of any audit work done to understand the level of assurance given and in which areas. Good practice I have seen to 'head off' issues can include:

  1. Expecting to see in-depth updates on the progress being made to address any previous areas of concern.
  2. Getting copies of other audit reports concerning the activities of the third party, to get more confidence in what is being done.
  3. Commissioning audits on specific topics of particular importance to probe, for example, information security, the integrity of non-financial information and other important information that might reveal important business or reputational risks (e.g. the quality of call handling and complaint resolution, beyond numerical metrics).

  And a simple, low-cost way of getting 'signals' that things may not be going as you would like is to ask operational staff how easy they find the third party to deal with on day-to-day matters. You'd be surprised how often delays on little issues at an operational level can be an early warning signal that your organisation is no longer its highest priority.

The Effective Use of Consultants

If managers do something new or something that requires specialist capabilities, using a consultant might be invaluable to help them identify 'what they didn't know they didn't know'.[10]

However, the inappropriate use of consultants can sometimes be a contributing factor when things go wrong.[11] Here are examples of problems some have encountered:

- *There is a contentious issue, so a manager proposes to engage a consultant to look at the problem.* Work is done, and a report is issued, but the scope and results arising have been influenced by the manager commissioning and paying for the work. Indeed, some managers speak of consulting assignments being weaponised. As a result, specific issues may not come to light early enough for appropriate action.
- *To move a business in a new direction, an organisation might need consulting support, but it may take existing staff well out of their comfort zone.* Andrew Wright explains:

'I firmly believe that there are situations where you need to engage a consultant. For example, if you want insights into a new market or want to know whether you have the best cyber security arrangements, it's hard to have the latest knowledge and expertise in-house.

In other situations, if someone wants to engage a consultant for a strategic priority, you need to (i) get real validation who knows what in the consulting firm, so the right people are working for you, and (ii) think about the state of your internal capability. After all, if no one in your organisation has a good understanding of a new topic, how are you going to be able to judge what the consultant is telling you?

Consultants will inevitably be interested in continuing to work for you as long as possible, so you must be conscious of building your capability quickly and avoiding a culture of dependency.'

This theme is also touched upon in the book '*The Blunders of Our Governments*', by Anthony King & Ivor Crewe[12]: 'You do not need to be a leftist conspiracy theorist to see that consultants tend to come up with schemes that require more consultants, and which err on the side of complexity'.

- There will be some situations where the use of a consultant must be weighed up very carefully because of potential dilemmas. Andrew Wright explains:

> 'I have had board-level conversations where we have asked ourselves: If we give this consultant this experience working with us, what are they going to do with it? I'm sure most of the time, confidentiality arrangements work. Still, suppose an industry-level challenge arises, and a consultant helps you work through a solution. In that case, they will have this story in their kit bag when talking to other clients facing similar issues.
>
> The dilemma is that, on the one hand, there are many benefits to treating consultants as part of the team. But on the other hand, you need to recognise they are working for a separate, external organisation and will therefore have motives that are not identical to those of your organisation.'

The themes of financial and ethical risk, third-party risks, the use of consultants and the need for effective oversight are by no means an exhaustive list of all topics that could have been chosen in relation to external factors.[13] But my overarching message is to highlight that whilst the appropriate use of third parties has an essential place in twenty-first-century organisations, contracting with others comes with a range of risks that must be thought about carefully and managed diligently and creatively.[14] As readers will appreciate, third parties will have other clients, some of whom may be significantly more important than your organisation. So, even though they may risk letting you down, they are often bound to favour (i) their most significant clients and (ii) the clients that monitor their work most closely. In many ways, organisations get the third-party service that they expect and pay for.[15]

Likewise, unless an organisation can accept the inevitable uncertainty around external factors and create lines of defence to protect itself from the worst, it cannot be surprised when this is a regular source of surprises and setbacks.

However, as outlined in other chapters, 'understanding and accommodating external factors' as a root cause explanation for problems will often be caused by other factors:

- Poor supplier management policies and monitoring – perhaps due to contract design limitations or unclear roles of who should monitor what (especially during a period of change).
- Weaknesses in third-party due diligence – perhaps due to resource constraints.
- Projects and programmes are let down by third parties or external factors – perhaps due to weaknesses in the target setting process that did not sufficiently consider these uncertainties (e.g. when appropriately skilled consultants would be available to start work).

Summary

- An external factor is not the root cause of problems. Instead, it's the inability to properly understand, and adapt to, external factors that may be a root cause.
- It's important to recognise the different types of external factors that may impact an organisation: e.g. weather, other natural phenomena, suppliers, consultants, distributors, agents, regulators, competitors, customers, patients or other stakeholders.
- When dealing with different countries and cultures, remember that something you might think is unlikely in an environment you are familiar with may be quite possible in another context. No matter what you say in terms of organisational values and ethics, and codes of conduct, every culture has its own interpretation of what is ethical and unethical.
- Recognise that there will always be a temptation to cross a line regarding competitors and dealing with regulators or government officials. This may involve senior staff, or take place through intermediaries, so expect it to be hard to detect.
- A third party or an employee can pass due diligence or a selection process with flying colours at one point in time. They may

work for you diligently for years, but that does not mean things might not change over time.[16]

- Even though a third-party supplier may be legally required to do things for you according to an SLA and may pay the penalty if they do not do what is needed, your organisation remains accountable for the work they do on your behalf. So, do not get lulled into a false sense of security by dropping your interest in monitoring their work, even when things are going to plan.
- Recognise that some third-party activities (not just customer entertainment, but participation in forums, etc.) can influence management's opinion favourably towards them.
- Recognise the dilemmas that can arise when using consultants. On the one hand, consultants may be 'head and shoulders' above you regarding knowledge and capability, and their input may be invaluable. But, on the other hand, consultants will invariably put a 'best foot forward' when it comes to presenting their capabilities, so you need the ability to test what they really know and can do.
- Likewise, beware of developing a dependency on consulting support and be mindful of the ways in which consulting assignments can be weaponised.

Practical Suggestions

- Never accept 'external factors' as a root cause, it will be an immediate or contributing cause.
- If you plan to do business in a new country, get expert input on the risks you will face from a legal, compliance and competition law perspective, best of all from an organisation with hands-on experience in 'cleaning up' after problems.[17]
- Be mindful of the ability for things you thought you knew to change, so always pay attention to the last time you double-checked things directly, in detail (e.g. via an internal audit or independent consultant review).

- Recognise that accountability and responsibility for managing a third party must remain in your organisation at a level commensurate for what is being done. Specifically, are you clear who monitors service level agreements (especially for your top suppliers and agents) and what the frequency and the rigour of supplier reviews should be and is?
- If a problem arises in the middle of the night, or during a public holiday, will managers in your organisation be able to contact the right people working for any relevant third-party supplier, so they can help you?
- When was the last time key suppliers provided certificates of assurance over critical matters or when were they last audited? If audited, what was the breadth and depth of the review and were there any gaps or issues to be addressed?
- If your organisation engages in conferences and third-party forums, clarify what information was shared, what valuable insights were obtained and what practical purpose these were put to? Discipline around the outcomes from such events will help concentrate the minds of those involved regarding the cost/benefit of these forums beyond general networking.
- Are there any areas where you are too dependent on consulting support? And are there areas you need to get a second opinion or build internal capability much more quickly?

Chapter 9
Effective Building, Maintenance and Change

'If your project doesn't work, look for the part that you didn't think was important'.

– Arthur Bloch[1]

You don't have to look very far to see projects and programmes identified as a cause of problems. But on the other hand, it's important to remember problems can arise because you can't maintain the status quo (e.g. maintain a consistent level of service or maintain product quality). In other words, *in a world with entropy, it takes effort to build things, to cope with change and to keep things the same.*

One Side of the Coin: Building, Change Management and Project Management

If we consider the construction of the Eiffel Tower, the Titanic or an aircraft, there would have been a good understanding of the problems that might arise during the building and construction phases and how to head them off. Indeed, this will have involved creating a written plan of what would be built and the intention to follow this through, making adjustments where things were not going to plan. It may not have been called 'project management' then, but that was what was happening.

The necessary skills and capabilities to manage programmes and projects broadened and deepened during World War II, where, for example, the Manhattan Project utilised the discipline of Gantt charts[2] and dedicated programme management roles.[3] And after World War II, it became increasingly clear that the construction of a building, a machine or a production plant required similar skills.[4] As a result, project and programme management has become a recognised profession, supported by institutes that disseminate relevant know-how, tools and techniques.[5]

Prince II

One well-respected framework for delivering change projects is the Prince II framework, which incorporates the following principles:[6]

- Ensure the project justification is refreshed and don't be afraid to stop;
- Have clear roles and responsibilities both within the project and around it;
- Work in stages;
- Escalate things following clearly defined tolerances;
- Adapt what you are doing to suit the context;
- Learn as you go.

Other project and programme management can be found (e.g. the PMI PMBOK), with variations in what is regarded as important, depending on their history and focus.[7]

Over a period, it was recognised that Prince II and other so-called 'waterfall' project management frameworks were sometimes constrained because of their emphasis on making relatively firm plans upfront. Of course, upfront planning is fine if what you are aiming for is not going to change (e.g. when designing a nuclear power plant) or cannot be changed as it is being built (e.g. a TV). But in some situations, you may not be entirely clear about precisely what you are aiming for. This can happen when requirements may not be fully clear at first or they change because of, for example, changing customer needs or regulatory requirements.

Agile

Agile is a way of working that allows for a more flexible, iterative approach to change. It emerged out of adaptive IT software development and involves ensuring applications are developed in line with the following principles:[8]

- Interact with customers regularly and hear what they have to say;
- Create a minimum-viable product quickly and get feedback; [9]
- Be prepared to iterate what you have done, with a mindset that is happy to adapt and change focus based on a prioritised 'backlog'.

To maintain some control over what is done, agile stresses the importance of several of the causal factors covered in this book, for example:

(I) R2A2 – via roles such as the Scrum Master, Product Owner and Development Team;[10]

(II) The design of critical checkpoints – called ceremonies, such as sprint plans, daily standup meetings, sprint reviews and sprint retrospectives.

Where organisations have effectively deployed agile ways of working in IT you can sometimes see them applying this approach in other areas. This is often because of the way agile challenges the tendency to set over-ambitious goals or to design things detached from their use. It also utilises other ways to minimise the chances of something going off track, for example:

(I) being clear about which tasks are a priority and keeping issue logs up to date,

(II) identifying key risks and difficulties on a timely basis, and

(III) focusing on action within a short timescale to resolve concerns.[11]

However, despite these strengths, *agile ways of working don't work in all situations.* For example, you can't build a machine, an aircraft or a production facility by deploying a pure agile approach. This is because the fundamental premises upon which agile is based include (i) that a minimum-viable prototype can be achieved quickly and (ii) that it won't be too costly, or time-consuming, to make changes to your prototype.

Already I have seen several organisations 'stung' by using agile inappropriately. For example, the agile mindset of pragmatism, and minimal documentation, can clash with (i) requirements to maintain high levels of security, (ii) the need to maintain evidence of control or compliance that a regulator might want to see, or (iii) incorrectly assume operational details after 'going live' can be resolved later (i.e. a 'let's not worry about that now, we'll sort that out in due course', approach). In each case, the inappropriate use of agile was identified as a causal factor in problems because it was an 'inappropriate design' for the task in hand, in part, because of the human tendency to 'latch on' to something popular and 'on message'.[12]

The Other Side of the Coin: Keeping Things the Same

Keeping service and product quality at a high level is often underpinned by having facilities and equipment that is well maintained and in good working order. This is essential whether we are talking about the engine room of a ship, a hospital, school or a production plant. Some of the essential disciplines needed to achieve this include:

- Inspection and testing of machines or equipment;
- Planned maintenance, such as routinely replacing the oil and filters on a truck, changing the tires, etc.;

- Condition-based maintenance, where information is collected and if there are warning signs about equipment, repairs are made before things go wrong. Noticing excess wear on a bearing and then repairing it at that point would be an example. The same would apply when checking medical equipment before a procedure.

In day-to-day life, going to the garage if you see certain warning lights on your car dashboard or 'cleaning' your computer if it is starting to run more slowly, often reminds us of the wisdom in the old proverb 'a stitch in time saves nine'.

In the context of High-Reliability Organisations, these principles have been taken to another level, and you will find Reliability-Centred Maintenance (RCM).[13] RCM strategies can include:

- Preventative maintenance;
- Detective maintenance;
- Predictive maintenance (which can incorporate active detection activities, such as vibration and temperature monitoring);
- Explicit 'Run to failure' decisions, where there are core, hard-to-change components.

Illustration 9.1 tries to encapsulate the essential ingredients when thinking about effective building, change and maintenance.

Richard Brilliant (VP of Risk and Assurance, Carnival Corporation) offers the following perspective regarding maintenance in a maritime context but broadens the number of factors to bear in mind:

'It's easy to look at a company that organises cruises and runs a fleet of ships and think of repairs and maintenance activities to keep the ship's physical plant in good condition and in compliance with laws and regulations. Make no mistake – there is a lot of equipment to maintain on a modern cruise ship. Effectively, a cruise ship is a large resort hotel that sits above a power plant, waste treatment facilities and freshwater production facility that must also provide propulsion and navigation capabilities to move the ship safely and efficiently around the world – all the while

Illustration 9.1 Building and maintenance

being mindful of safety, the environment, and the health and security of all souls aboard.

Clearly, the stakes are high if we don't pay close attention to all these elements, so we have certified high-quality safety and environmental management systems. These act as the backbone for all policies, procedures and accountabilities that are required by law and regulations[xi] and, in many cases, in accordance with higher standards and expectations set by either the industry or the company.

When you think of all of these "hardware" and process factors, it is critically important, and not mentioned enough in my view, to recognise the importance of managing human factors within the management system. Carnival understands there are risks here that must be proactively managed and have invested heavily to mitigate risks such as "skills fade".

Examples of steps we have taken to address this intangible but vitally important area include the development of a state-of-the-art training centre in the Netherlands which provides full mission and virtual-reality-based simulators as well as "Bridge Resource Management" and "Engine Room Resource Management" that seek to instil a wide range of skills, attitudes, communications, situational awareness, problem-solving and teamwork that support error-free decision-making. This is further supported by various types of supplemental training, including computer-based training, to keep their skills fresh. Furthermore, we have a fleet support and mentoring programme where experienced crew members offer their insights and perspectives to other colleagues so that we try, as much as possible, to keep our "ears to the ground" in relation to new and evolving training and development requirements.'

Much of what Richard is discussing can be used as a reference point for other areas where keeping things 'up to scratch' is important.

It is also important to recognise how easy it is to 'take your eye off the ball' from 'business as usual' if change programmes are absorbing everyone's time and attention. Richard Taylor (Audit Support Director, Aegon Asset Management) explains:

'It's understandable that people think and talk about implementing new systems and processes. This can be exciting and motivating because you can start to sense a world in which current difficulties will become a distant memory.

But when you focus on one thing, you can easily forget other risks. The most obvious area is keeping the business-as-usual IT system going while a new IT system is being developed. And sometimes you can reach something of a "no man's land" period when people start saying, "There is no point in making changes to the old system now because the new system is only six months away". But then there is a delay in implementing the new system, and before you know it, you are running with an old system that is creaking.

Even more subtle than this risk is the fact that, as you implement something new, there is an old system that has a lot of data in it that will need to be decommissioned, so first you have a data security risk to manage. Second, not everyone working on the old system will get a job working on the new system. So, here you have a potential fraud or conduct risk to manage.

It pays to watch these softer aspects in particular parts of your business. Managing and motivating staff who may be leaving your company is a skill not to be ignored or underestimated.'

For the rest of this chapter, I will focus on the ways in which 'hairline cracks' can arise in a project management context despite efforts to ensure significant setbacks will not happen.

A Big Project: 'Fire Control'

In 2004, a major project was commissioned in England to reduce the number of control rooms used to handle fire service emergency calls from 46 to 9 Regional Control Centres (RCCs). The benefits planned included greater resilience as well as efficiency gains. It was intended to implement the new RCCs between 2011 and 2012, but during 2010 it became clear there were serious flaws with the project, which was scrapped by the end of that year.

There were two inquiries into what happened, one for the UK Parliament Public Accounts Committee (PAC)[14] and another by the UK National Audit Office (NAO).[15] Not surprisingly, the two reviews found similar issues. I have mapped many of the key causes identified by each inquiry against the 'eight ways to understand why' and set these out in Table 9.2.

To deepen our understanding concerning what caused things to go off track, I spoke to Charlie Hendry (former Fire Chief of the Kent Fire Service), who was involved in the project:

'I was involved in the later stages of the Fire Control project. It was a much more complicated project than many realised. First, it involved new technology; second, this sort of thing had never been done before in the Fire Service; third, and most important of all, the local Fire Services hadn't really bought into it.

The lack of buy-in was partly because of factors such as changes in roles, potential job losses and who was going to be in control of the RCCs. But it was also because of genuine concerns

Table 9.2   Overview of Key Findings Concerning the Fire Control project

Report	National Audit Office (July 2011)	Public Accounts Committee (September 2011)
Ways to understand why		
Appropriate goals	1. Underestimate of the complexity of the project 2. Unrealistic costs and savings	(A) Failure to understand the complexity of the IT system
Communication and information		(B) Weak project oversight
R2A2	3. Governance arrangements were complex, which led to unclear lines of responsibility	(C) Despite the scale of failure and waste, no one has been held accountable
Design	4. Poor contract design impeded the resolution of issues	(D) Insufficient early milestones
External factors	5. Insufficient grip to sort out early problems with delivery by the contractor	(E) Weak mechanisms to manage sub-contractor performance
Change/maintain	6. Changing direction	(F) Failure to apply checks and balances from the start
Human Factors	7. Levels of support incentives	(G) Failure to secure the cooperation and support of others (H) Including over-reliance on consultants
Resources and priorities	8. High staff turnover and poorly managed consultants	(I) The focus was on building the new RCCs

and questions, such as the likely loss of local knowledge when using a regional model. Remember, in the context of a fire, if you misunderstand where a fire is taking place, you are putting property and lives at risk.

I attended project board meetings that were centred around following the Prince II project methodology. Sadly, the mention of Prince II tends to bring me out in a rash nowadays because I saw an excessive focus on what was going on at a micro level, which got in the way of bigger, less tangible factors.

I felt we were losing the wood for the trees. Numerous problems were encountered years before the final decision to stop the project. But it seemed to me that that if you reported problems, said you were working on them, and provided new deadlines, then that was fine. It seemed fine to defer things into the future, where there appeared to be time and capacity, without seeing the cumulative effect of doing this. Furthermore, I think what got missed were the cultural and behavioural challenges that hadn't been scheduled to be addressed until much later in the project.

My sense is that not enough was done early on to challenge what was being planned against the "on the ground" hopes and fears of people who used existing systems on a day-to-day basis. If there had been the right kind of engagement at the early stages, it would probably have been realised that there was the kernel of a good idea to progress but not through a top-down, technology-based, one-size-fits-all solution.[16]

As a result of not getting the buy-in right at the right level, in detail, during the early stages, you end up with a flawed design concept, assuming the wrong processes will work in the future and following a flawed implementation path.

I made myself unpopular on occasions because I could sense that practical problems were building up. And it was tricky because the project had been going on for years. So, much money had been spent already. I could sense how invested many players were in the project and how much they would lose if they admitted defeat. I feel I did my best to raise concerns, as did others, but the reality was that it probably needed someone independent to dig into the various problem areas, as well as the hidden cultural buy-in problems at an operational level, to then call out "the emperor has no clothes".'

Charlie points to a common problem: how easily we can underestimate the behavioural and cultural aspects of what seems to be primarily a project concerning systems and infrastructure.

He offers a few additional reflections about target setting and accountabilities:

'There is an interesting question about how we think of targets. On the one hand, you can have a target, as in Fire Control, where it's a specific new, big, national system, costing millions and taking years. Alternatively, you can set more modest aspirations that are more a "direction of travel", such as "We need more resilience in our control centres, and it will be useful if we try to save some money as well". From this sort of target, alongside pressure on budgets, you can get more of an organic, emergent approach that tries new ways of working in a "bottom-up" manner. On the downside, no fanfare and no swanky new system, but on the upside, no hundreds of millions spent on consultants, no distractions from business as usual and no newspaper stories about wasted taxpayer money.

There is also a fundamental problem with the way responsibility and accountability work at a senior level, especially in relation to projects and programmes in the UK public sector. In theory, people at senior levels are given specific accountabilities to run organisations effectively and efficiently. This can work when the organisations' boundaries are clear, and measures of success are realistic, specific enough and not subject to "finessing". But when you turn to projects and programmes, with steering groups and governance boards, you automatically get a blurring of roles and responsibilities because decisions are often made on a collective basis. Worse, big projects are often multi-year and people move on, so by the time a project gets into difficulty, a good proportion of the key personnel will have changed.'

Charlie is echoing a point discussed in the chapter on R2A2. In our modern, complex, matrix world, our ability to keep track of what people have and have not done is not always easy. This includes what goes on at the level of steering groups and other committees. So long as we are unable to properly create an 'adaptive accountability' that retains an audit trail of who made what decisions and with what information, we will have a rather important fault line that may be exploited in some situations.[17] As the saying goes: 'The secret of success is having someone to blame for your failures'.

The points Charlie raises can be found in other projects that have ended up disappointing stakeholders. Here is a 'fact pattern' that you might see:[18]

Concerning Prevention:

(P1) The project goals may not recognise the full complexity and risks of what is being planned because

(P2) those with insights about what the real issues might be were engaged in 'sell mode', so their concerns were not taken on board, and

(P3) while there were checks and balances (i.e. board and steering group meetings) regarding the project plan, these were not always effective given the constraints of time and the data available, and

(P4) consultants cannot always be guaranteed to challenge what is proposed unless they are independent and specifically commissioned to pressure test the project ambition level (which is a matter of judgment in any event, especially at the early stages) and

(P5) group dynamic pressures can make it challenging to call out concerns in key meetings, especially early on, without appearing overly negative, and anyway

(P6) it would take time and effort to 'dig' into the facts, issues and risks to identify any 'showstoppers' or definitive implications for the project budget and timeline.

Concerning Detection:

(D1) Project data and information was supposed to be able to highlight critical issues (often red/amber/green ratings alongside criticality);

(D2) however, there are multiple reasons (psychological and structural) why metrics may be not designed as required or not accurately reported (especially at the early stages of the project), and

(D3) there are limits around what information and data can be pressure tested before it reaches the board or a steering group, and

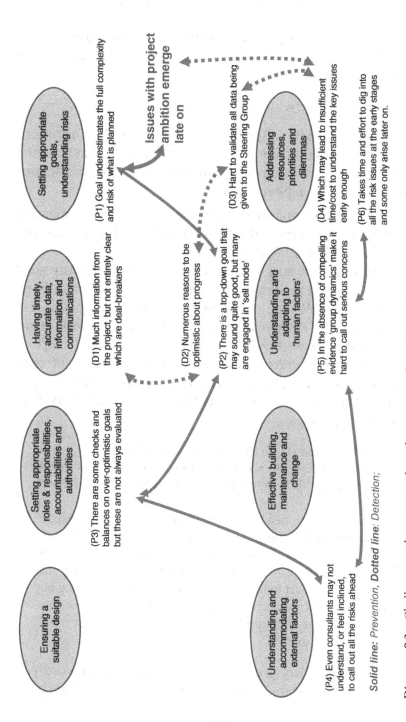

Diagram 9.3 Challenges with a project where there are stretch goals, top down (illustration)

The diagram contains the following labelled elements:

Setting appropriate goals, understanding risks

(P1) Goal underestimates the full complexity and risk of what is planned

Issues with project ambition emerge late on

(D3) Hard to validate all data being given to the Steering Group

Addressing resources, priorities and dilemmas

(D4) Which may lead to insufficient time/cost to understand the key issues early enough

(P6) Takes time and effort to dig into all the risk issues at the early stages and some only arise later on.

Having timely, accurate data, information and communications

(D1) Much information from the project, but not entirely clear which are deal-breakers

(D2) Numerous reasons to be optimistic about progress

(P2) There is a top-down goal that may sound quite good, but many are engaged in 'sell mode'

Understanding and adapting to 'human factors'

(P5) In the absence of compelling evidence 'group dynamics' make it hard to call out serious concerns

Setting appropriate roles & responsibilities, accountabilities and authorities

(P3) There are some checks and balances on over-optimistic goals but these are not always evaluated

Effective building, maintenance and change

Ensuring a suitable design

Understanding and accommodating external factors

(P4) Even consultants may not understand, or feel inclined, to call out all the risks ahead

*Solid line: Prevention, **Dotted line**: Detection;*

131

(D4) some key information may only come to light towards the end of the project at which point delivery to time, cost and quality may be challenging.

Concerning Recovery:

My experience is that it often takes a visible setback or a concern from an influential senior executive to trigger a fundamental rethink and reset of a project or programme and before serious 'Plan B' options are explored in detail.

Based on such a scenario, you can create a causal loop diagram at a high level,[19] using the eight ways to understand why, with connections, as set out in Diagram 9.3.

The diagram shows us that it is easy to see how many good project management processes can be wasted if subtle 'fault lines' are not understood. Worse, as Charlie explains, *the very presence of project management dashboards, consultants, etc., can mask subtle, hard-to-measure issues, such as the absence of real buy-in to operational matters, a clear understanding of how these would be addressed and whether there was sufficient time and budget left to address them.*

Andrew Wright stresses the importance of having safety margins and clear priorities:

'It's not just an urban myth that projects tend to be over-optimistic on benefits and light on risks and extra costs. More and more research tells us this is an endemic problem in both public and private sectors.

The mindset you need to develop is one in which you expect to see scenarios for the project and critical dependencies and force yourself to imagine how you would feel if things were wrong by a factor of one and a half or even two times. When you think this way, you can start to be more thoughtful about balancing big spending on major projects versus more modest upgrades. You can also be stricter about project priorities, what is "must have" and what is "nice to have".'

Gary Kline's Project pre-mortem technique is also worthy of note. Here, a project team are asked to imagine upfront that things have gone wrong by the end and then work backward to find out what might have been missed. They can then use these insights to either prevent problems from happening in the first place or to detect these problems early on before they go off track.[20]

Without mechanisms to pierce an understandable 'can do' mindset, it will often be very hard for those directly involved in a project or programme to say, 'The emperor has, or may have, no clothes'. So, steering groups and project managers with concerns about a project or programme need a humble, questioning, frame of mind and may need to seek independent assurances around what is happening, being prepared to listen to any concerns without seeing these as an affront. Likewise, you need high-calibre auditors to do independent assurance in a way that will be sensitive to its impact on a project but be rigorous. A project management consultant explained:

'There is always pressure in a project environment and therefore lots of scope to get management information that isn't always 100% accurate. So, to get robust assurance, you need people who know what they are doing in terms of project management disciplines, who can dig into the right things and focus on the essentials of what the context demands.

Having the right skill sets matters greatly because even minuscule fractures in critical areas can lead to problems later. For this reason, the more significant and more demanding the project or programme, the more you need to budget for high-quality independent assurance because most project teams are too close to the action to see the importance of certain fractures.'

A few further 'hairline cracks' to look out for:

Megaprojects

The book 'Megaprojects and Risk' by Bent Flyvbjerg[21] provides an excellent, in-depth account of how several large infrastructure projects went off track. There are numerous insightful observations, such as the view that most upfront project proposals are incorrect because:

> '[they] assume, or pretend to assume, that . . . projects exist in a predictable Newtonian world of cause and effect where things go according to plan'.

He argues that various improvements will be needed to overcome recurring issues in the future, including greater transparency, more robust performance specifications, better accountability enforcement and regulatory changes; all themes that readers will recognise from the discussions in this book.

Concerning the Overall Amount of Change an Organisation Can Cope with

It's not hard to find organisations that have initiated one change programme after another over several years. Senior management may be aware, in general terms, of workload and staff well-being risks, but can miss the fact that setbacks in delivering 'business as usual' or certain projects are as a result of other very well-intentioned projects they themselves initiated. The insight from Charlton Ogburn, Jr, years ago is still true to this day:[22]

> 'We tend . . . to meet any new situation by reorganising; and a wonderful method it can be for creating the illusion of progress while producing confusion, inefficiency and demoralisation'.[23]

This theme is discussed in the article 'Too many projects' by Rose Hollister and Michael D Watkins in the Harvard Business Review in Autumn 2018.[24] They make several valuable recommendations, including:

(i) Getting an inventory of all initiatives underway in an organisation;

(ii) Asking senior leadership to agree on a realistic and collective set of priorities across the organisation;

(iii) Recognising that stopping initiatives is not a sign that initiatives didn't matter or were a failure; instead, there will always be a limit on what can be done practically.

The Project Management Triangle

The project management triangle, or triple constraint, concerns the inter-relationship between a project's proposed timeline, its cost budget and the quality of what is delivered (which will invariably affect the benefits it delivers). The fundamental point here is to recognise that budget, time and quality/benefits can be in conflict. For example, a limit on the cost budget of a project now may create a problem 'downstream' where we find the quality of what is built, or the benefits of the project, are not as planned because of the constrained budget earlier.

The role of priorities and dilemmas causing 'spin-off' problems will be discussed in Chapter 11.

Summary

- Building, changing and maintaining is a very commonplace causal factor for problems. However, note it's not the building, maintenance or change itself that is the root cause; *it's the ability to see and manage these risks.*
- Reliability-Centred Maintenance offers a 'gold standard' framework against which to judge maintenance in your organisation, but you can also apply the principles to areas such as 'skills fade'.
- Recognise that there is no such thing as the right project management framework. Prince II has its strengths and weaknesses, and Agile has its strengths and weaknesses.
- Recognise the dilemma when pushing project tasks into the future. It may be necessary to postpone certain tasks in the short run, but they may 'pile up' to create a bigger and more extensive list of issues towards the end of the project. Consequently, contingencies need to be made over the whole length of a project, not just at the beginning.

- Don't assume the most significant risks and issues in a project are down at the operational level; they may be hiding in plain sight at the most senior levels of the project or steering group.
- Be aware of the group dynamics when consulting users on a new project plan or in a project management team, steering group or committee.
- Pay attention to the cumulative number of change programmes and projects in the organisation and across different areas.
- If initiatives are scaled back or stopped, promote the positive aspects of making 'hard choices' and remember the insight, 'In our modern world, it takes courage to slow down, to stop or even to turn around'.[25]

Practical Suggestions

- Have Reliability-Centred Maintenance principles been considered for higher-risk areas to ensure operational factors are kept in good order?
- Consider benchmarking your in-house project management framework (which is a design choice) against other frameworks; how is it the same or different than other frameworks, and what risks might this increase or reduce?
- Clarify when the organisation last got feedback from those working on a project whether the level of project administration was adding value.
- When a big project starts, pay close attention to who was involved in crafting the proposal. Does it have the character of a magic bullet? Were alternative options tested? If so, what were the 'also ran' choices and the reason they were rejected? Pay close attention to 'egos' and the risks of 'tunnel vision'.
- Ensure you are clear on scenarios around how a project or programme might turn out because reality rarely matches the original forecast.

- Have someone independently look at the group dynamics of critical project teams, steering groups and user groups from time to time.
- Clarify how much contingency has been budgeted (time and money) as issues arise – establish whether the use of contingencies is being tracked to avoid the problem of 'too much to do, too little time or resource to fix things' towards the end of a project, which is often a pattern in projects and programmes.
- Be prepared to have a confidential stocktake of views about how things are going, down to the user level, so there is a safety valve for any significant concerns.
- Ensure there are ways to identify areas where staff might be overloaded when working on change initiatives; it's easy for just a few people to get overloaded, but if they have a key role and become stressed or ill or leave, the project can get into great difficulty. These critical staff need to be identified and mechanisms put in place to ensure they are not overloaded.
- Budget for independent assurance, including, if appropriate, for areas that have 'gone dark' for a period but that could be showstoppers.

Chapter 10
Understanding and Adapting to 'Human Factors'

'The fault, . . ., is not in our stars, but in ourselves'.
– William Shakespeare[1]

Human Error and the Evolution of Human Factors Thinking

We have covered many ways to understand why, using examples from the world of aviation: for instance, cockpit and instrumentation design, the importance of understanding the external environment (i.e. the weather), etc. And the significance of each is that they help the captain and crew fly the plane safely; which now takes us to human factors.

If you think about a plane crash in the early days of aviation, one of the things you might have heard on occasion was that the plane crashed because of a 'pilot error'. But if effective root cause analysis (RCA) is about making recommendations that seek to avoid the same or similar problems, what do you say?: 'Next time, choose an even better captain or pilot who won't make any mistakes'?!

Over the years, it became clear that even the most experienced pilot or crew member could make decisions that led to crashes. Going over information from 'black box' flight recorders, it became possible for air crash investigators to say: 'At this point, five minutes before the crash, the pilot should have done X, rather than Y'. But the problem was that such an argument was being made *with the benefit of hindsight after the significance of choosing X over Y was known.*[2]

Thus, we arrive at an important point that has been 'in the mix' in many of the earlier case studies; *human error may arise at any time when people are involved* (i.e. no matter how well trained and experienced you are, you can still make a mistake, have a bad day or just lose your concentration for a few moments).[3] Effective RCA says that human error is a fact of life when people are involved, so you need a working environment that recognises this possibility is always there, but seeks to reduce the odds of a mishap occurring and, if appropriate and possible, put in place measures to stop the worst from happening in the first place, (e.g. by engineering out human involvement).[4]

Human Variability and 'the Miracle on the Hudson'

Recent developments in systems thinking have now broadened the focus from human error to consider *human variability*. The argument is that most people try to do their best most of the time, but what they do can vary depending on the situation. Human variability accepts that people are not the same as clones or robots. It says that without human variability, we would have no creativity, innovation and adaptation as the situation requires. In other words, *human variability is sometimes a part of what we must do to keep things safe. Not every variation in behaviour can be pre-judged as being definitively an error.*[5]

A notable illustration of human variability in action can be found in Flight US 1549 in January 2009. A flock of Canada geese damaged the plane's engines shortly after take-off from the LaGuardia airport, New York City, and Captain Chesley (Sully) Sullenberger made an 'in the moment' and far from obvious decision (and contrary to air traffic control advice) to land the aircraft in the Hudson River, enabling all the passengers and crew to evacuate with no loss of life and few injuries. This was nicknamed 'the Miracle on the Hudson'.[6]

In the extensive air crash investigation led by the US National Transportation Safety Board (NTSB), numerous attempts to recreate the conditions he faced in flight simulators showed how 'Sully's' decision was almost the only choice that could have avoided a catastrophe.[7] In the end, many honoured him for his incredible judgement and skill, especially following such an unexpected and shocking event, with so little time to decide what to do, followed by a nearly flawless landing on water.

A human variability mindset recognises that some people can excel in challenging situations and tough times. Still, it also acknowledges that heroic or superhuman efforts aren't something we can't bank on. Many of us, much of the time, will try to do our best, even if that means a slight deviation from what the official procedures require because of time constraints or other factors. But that doesn't mean we will always get things right. Variability is a fact of life we must recognise, and if we don't want any deviation from a pre-determined formula, this is where an automated procedure may be called for (albeit that it may come with its own problems).[8]

Human Factors

The discipline of Human Factors, developed in earnest after World War II, incorporates human error and human variability thinking. It asks that airlines and other organisations where the stakes are high (e.g. High-Reliability Organisations) should proactively think about the ways they can recognise and optimise human behaviour in the following spirit, spelled out by the Institute of Human Factors and Ergonomics:

'The application of what we know about people, their abilities, characteristics and limitations to the design of equipment they use, environments in which they function and jobs they perform.'[9]

Human Factors thinking recognises, among other things, that people only have a certain 'bandwidth', which is one of the reasons cockpit instrumentation was 'decluttered'. Likewise, Human Factors thinking is central to appreciating why flight simulators are so important; you can hire good people, and you can train them and test them on the theory, but unless you put them in in highly realistic simulations of what might happen, you can't be sure what they will do.[10]

There are many valuable resources concerning Human Factors, but some people find the following analogy to be useful. If an organisation was staffed with personnel such as 'Sully', Mr Spock from *Star Trek*[11] or Superman, you might be confident colleagues would make the right decisions, remember every policy and procedure by heart, not get distracted from the task at hand, share information and cooperate for the organisation's good.

But most people (including those with plenty of qualifications and experience) get tired, forget, don't always think logically and may not always share or interpret information the same way. This may be because they don't appreciate the significance of something or they are tired or demotivated or even because of resentments and rivalries between colleagues.[12]

So, the argument goes, *no matter what Human Resource processes you put in place or what work you do on organisational culture and values, you can't guarantee what everyone in your organisation will think and how everyone will behave.*

Illustration 10.1 tries to highlight the difference between robots, Vulcans, superheroes and human beings. We must recognise the enormous diversity of experiences, capabilities and mindsets that

Illustration 10.1   The Human Factor

people have, which can have both positive and negative consequences for organisations, and which often cannot be eliminated.
*So, with a Human Factors mindset, you need to organise roles, tasks,
etc., so that, even if you get human variation, things will still work
within acceptable limits.*

Just Culture – Balancing Holding People to Account Against Unfair Scapegoating

With a Human Factors perspective, we can look at the critical issue
of whether and how to hold people to account (i.e. to ensure robust
roles, responsibilities, accountabilities and authorities [R2A2]).
And here we have a dilemma:

- On the one hand, we want to accept human variability and recognise that people won't always get things right.

- However, if people have no sense of responsibility or accountability for doing what they should do, there is a risk they might
  behave recklessly or irresponsibly.

To strike the right balance, Professor James Reason developed
the 'just culture' framework.[13] It was identified as a critical ingredient for workplace safety, but its broader importance has been taken
up and evolved in HROs and many other domains (e.g. chemical,
oil and gas, mining, health and safety, aviation and, increasingly,
healthcare).[14]

The essential message is to recognise different types of behaviours and, for each type, to consider an appropriate, fair and
just response if things aren't done as expected. Behaviours can
range from:

- innocent or unintentional lapses, mistakes or errors;
- 'risky' behaviour, but where there was no wilful intention to
  cause harm, and then
- reckless behaviour, where an action or decision was made
  with little or no concern for risks or downside consequences,
  and finally
- malicious, corrupt or fraudulent behaviour, where there is a
  clear intention to cause harm or to break the law.

Appropriate responses to what happened need to consider both
what is appropriate for any individuals involved (bearing in mind
what they did or did not do) as well as lessons for the organisation,
as outlined in Table 10.2.

Reframing What Needs to Be Fixed

So, even if people are reckless or behave corruptly, RCA and systems
thinking demand we understand the root causes that allowed, enabled or failed to stop people from behaving this way, or that failed to
alert others to what might be happening.

Table 10.2   Just Culture – Action Options (illustration of possible responses).

	At an individual level	At an organisational level
Human error	Individuals should be counselled or coached, but not punished.	Processes should be improved (including automation if appropriate). Consider extra training or improved supervision, etc.
'Risky' behaviour	Individuals should be engaged to clarify why they made the decisions they did.	As above, but also taking steps to identify spin-off problems from any stretch targets and to implement measures so staff are less likely to take inappropriate risks (e.g. risk adjusted incentives).
Reckless behaviour	Disciplinary action likely to be appropriate.	As mentioned above, but also work on behavioural risk factors and improve process checks and balances to prevent such behaviour if possible.
Malicious, corrupt or fraudulent behaviour	Disciplinary action, and quite possibly legal proceedings, (subject to evidential questions)	Ensure efforts on anti-fraud activities, anti-bribery and corruption, whistleblowing, anti-retaliation, etc., are fully effective.

It is likely that a 'just culture' framework in the future may evolve.'[15]

Consider the Barings bank collapse, which many people associate with what the 'rogue trader' Nick Leeson did. Such a perspective 'zooms in' on a key person, and clearly he was guilty for wrongdoing. However, if you look at the results of the inquiry into the Barings collapse, you will also find a 'zoom out' perspective, speaking about organisational shortcomings as well.[16]

'Barings' collapse was due to the unauthorised and ultimately catastrophic activities of . . . one individual that went undetected [because] of a failure of management and other internal controls of the most basic kind.

Management failed at various levels and in a variety of ways . . . to institute a proper system of internal controls, to enforce accountability for . . . profits, risks and operations, and adequately to follow up on a number of warning signals over a prolonged period.'

In other words, *even if someone intentionally does something they should not have done, they, the 'bad apple', are not the root cause.*[17]

The power of the just culture framework is that it accepts the possibility of lapses, mistakes, errors and risky behaviour, and reminds us that you can't blame people for being human. However, it does draw a line so that intentionally reckless or malicious behaviour is appropriately punished.

Andrew Wright offers an early experience coming across a just culture approach to a production quality problem:

'I recall an occasion when an audit of work identified quality problems we were doing for a large aviation company. A technician had started using the wrong glue in the assembly of a specific component for the plane's wing. When it was discovered that there was a specific guy who got this wrong, our initial reaction was to discipline him and move him into a less high-profile role.

But when we discussed this with the aviation company we worked with they said: "No, absolutely not! He is the person we want doing this task because he now knows just how big a deal it is if you get this wrong. Our experience in this sort of situation is that it's unlikely he will make such a mistake again. In fact, he can be a quality ambassador for other colleagues, so they realise how much their work can matter".

Of course, we didn't stop our quality control and quality assurance, but I remember sensing a huge cultural difference between us and the aviation company. And I could see subsequently how even this single example created a greater sense of openness with staff working on the factory floor.'

With the just culture mindset, we are wary of rushing to judge the actions of others. This runs contrary to the way many news stories, crime novels and TV detective series discuss 'bad behaviour'.

Often, in the media and fictional accounts, writers take great interest in understanding the motives of evildoers and hunting down the people who should be punished so the rest of us 'good folk' can get on with our lives.

While the desire to single out and punish a 'bad actor' is both understandable and can be wholly appropriate in some circumstances, RCA and systems thinking encourage us to see the context within which people operate that may affect their actions. And it's interesting to note that recent perspectives on the causes of crime and corruption (in the real world and fiction) explore the existence of grey zones (such as apparent inequities) and the way others might look the other way, rather than seeing things in good and evil, black and white, terms.

Indeed, recent discussions about misogyny and racism increasingly draw attention to (i) the role passive bystanders can inadvertently play in supporting bad behaviour, (ii) shortcomings in whistleblowing mechanisms and (iii) weaknesses in investigations intended to get to the bottom of allegations of wrongdoing.

So, *overall, the aim is to deliver appropriate discipline and sanctions at an individual level when it's merited, but also to learn and improve things at an organisational level as well.*

Considering 'Culture', 'Tone at the Top' and 'Behavioural Risk'

As mentioned, Human Factors thinking is mainstream in aviation and other HROs.[18] However, in the financial services sector and some other contexts, you will hear managers and regulators refer to the causes of problems using terms such as 'poor culture',[19] 'a poor tone at the top'[20] or because of 'behavioural risk'.

Thinking of causes in terms of organisational culture encourages us to think more broadly than just what goes on 'at the front end' (e.g. in the cockpit or control room). But I would like to emphasise that it's very easy to think a 'toxic culture' or 'poor tone at the top' can explain the root cause of failings. But, there is more to it than that. *After all, if we have a 'toxic culture', a 'fear culture' or a 'poor tone from the top', do we understand the root causes of why the culture etc. has become like that?*

A systems thinking approach tells us that the behaviour and culture of an organisation don't 'float' freestanding from the organisation and its context. Instead, behaviour 'emerges' from organisational goals, processes, organisational structure, alongside external factors (such as pressure from competition or stakeholders or budget constraints) as well as human factors (such as stress levels, resentments about pay, etc.).[21]

The increasing interest in behavioural science and behavioural risk links closely to the discipline of Human Factors. And the question becomes; did we adequately think about behavioural risks when we were designing systems, policies, processes, roles, responsibilities, etc.?[22] So, *it's an organisational, management-level problem if human factors and behavioural risks are not adequately considered.* W Edwards Deming (Quality Pioneer) sums this up perfectly:

> '94% of the results we experience in the workplace, both good or poor, is a function of the systems and processes in which people work, not the efforts of people.'[23]

Human Factors in Aviation

A former airline captain explains how, even in the world of aviation, the up-take of Human Factors thinking took time, support and encouragement, and a shift in mindset:

> 'There were a series of air crashes, such as US 173, which told us how much the human element mattered.[24] For example, in that case, everyone in the cockpit focused on one problem for the captain, which meant that another factor, the amount of fuel left in the tanks, was overlooked.
>
> As a result, the discipline of "crew resource management" started to become front and centre of what we needed to push

safety to the next level. But I can't stress enough how much of a mindset change this entailed, even among flight crew whose lives depended on learning about and implementing a way of working that said, "anyone can make a mistake, so we need to guard against this". And the tricky bit was recognising that it applied to the most experienced, senior crew, not just the less experienced crew. Some of these older crew members in the early days had thousands of hours of flying experience and had not been involved in a crash and, therefore, thought they knew best.

The traps we needed to overcome included getting rid of the assumption that an experienced crew member knew the correct answer. You only need to read the transcripts of some air crashes where more junior staff are timidly raising their concerns with a domineering captain to realise how serious this problem is. So, you learn to verbalise your thoughts and proactively invite other crew members to test or correct your understanding. I like the Captain Kirk model from *Star Trek*; he was clearly the leader, but he would often ask the other senior crew members for advice.

Likewise, you learn that even the most obvious exchange of information to a person sitting next to you can go wrong. In pilot training and in-flight simulators, you learn about the myriad ways confirmation bias, anchoring, availability bias, etc., can taint what appears to be the most "no-brainer" conversations and assessments of where you are and what you should do. Nowadays, even when travelling with my wife in our car, I have retained a "double-check" approach to programming a GPS or taking down a phone number!

Likewise, when it comes to communicating concerns, pilot training teaches you the importance of early communication and a clear escalation approach with colleagues, from questions, to offering hints and tips, to making suggestions, all the way to giving instructions or taking over control. I sense this sort of discipline in communicating with others would add value in other environments. For example, in a surgical context, I understand it's still not commonplace for surgeons to ask for, and to be content with, feedback from the nursing staff.

The other thing that you understand very clearly in aviation is the bandwidth problem. Crew, and people in general, can take on only so much information and perform only so many tasks in close succession. All too often, when I "swap notes" with those who work outside of aviation, I can see an unrealistic sense of what bandwidth people have. In aviation, you are constantly thinking about workloads and distractions and are hypervigilant about how these factors might get you into trouble.'

I trust some readers will recognise that these insights have a much broader application outside the cockpit. In principle, there should be the opportunity to speak freely (with psychological safety) about the risks of a project, staff workloads or someone who is bullying or misbehaving. However, egos, impatience and fear of what the boss might say can all undermine having the right conversation.

There are many areas you can explore to better understand Human Factors, behavioural risks, etc., and see what role they play in disasters or setbacks.[25] However, for this overview, I have decided to focus on three considerations that are often present when I am involved in RCA work:

- The presence of individual psychological factors (including assumptions and biases).
- Group dynamics that impact team meetings, committees, steering groups and boards.
- Organisational politics.

Psychology 101

Implicit within all discussions about Human Factors, human variability and behavioural risk is a recognition that psychological factors play a more significant role in the workplace than many of us like to think.[26] Dr Mannie Sher, Principal Consultant at the Tavistock Institute, explains:

'Many organisations promote the notion that they are fundamentally professional, rational and serious, doing things for all the right reasons and any decisions that are less rational are the exception rather than the rule. I understand why it's reassuring to have this view. But if you spend time in an organisation and step back, you realise that less rational behaviour is more common than you think.

So, I start with the position that organisations, as with many social structures, want to appear to be rational when, in fact, they are not fully rational. There are individual personalities of many types, from extroverts to introverts, from ambitious people to less ambitious people, those with big egos and thin skin, etc. And beyond this, there are better and less good working relationships, friendships, networks, rivalries, empires, silos, etc.

In other words, every organisation has a range of deep, underlying, irrational forces influencing them; whether it's in their behaviour, decision-making, implementation, relationships, etc. And until we have a better understanding of the irrational factors that are in play at work, whether at the individual level, in an operational team, a senior committee or at the board level or even in a strategic body that regulates others, you are always going to get dysfunctions and surprises, based on the mysteries of organisational and inter-organisational behaviour'.[27]

The challenging thought is that we cannot fight, conquer or overcome 'the human factor'. It's baked into who we are. Following policies and procedures, receiving training on cognitive biases or using checklists does not mean you will overcome those biases.[28] Most pervasive of all, in my experience, are 'self-justification' and 'confirmation bias', and the role of 'obedience to authority'. These mean, among other things, that 'self-assessment'-based mechanisms to report problems may not work.

Trying to eliminate human factors by using automated processes, or Artificial Intelligence, may help, but there are still people and organisations 'behind the scenes' who fund, design and oversee these activities.[29]

RCA and systems thinking tell us that we must accept that people have their fingerprints on what appear to be even the 'cleanest' environments. Amilcar Zambrano illustrates what he sees:

'I come across people who are highly skilled from a technical perspective; they love machinery and equipment, circuit boards and all of the engineering know-how you would expect them to have given their role. And their bosses are often quite similar; they are technical, practical "no nonsense" people. The culture is highly professional and process and data oriented.

However, on more than one occasion, I've noticed that if something goes wrong involving an engineer and even their supervisor, you can see sometimes it's because of people thinking too much "inside the box". You'll discover something has or hasn't been done because of what it says in a procedural document, but without those involved thinking about, or checking, the context in which that procedure was envisaged or how it might fit in with the bigger picture.

You can say all you want about "they ought to have realised there might be a wider question to consider", but these people are good at their jobs 99% of the time precisely because they like detail, can stay focused and don't get distracted. But sometimes "out of the box" thinking is needed and may be important to see a problem at the fringes.

In any event, sometimes engineers face challenges requiring decisions to be made at short notice to keep a piece of equipment working. They do their best but may, unknowingly, be storing up a problem for some time down the line.'

Amilcar's observations could be expanded to consider how different personalities, qualifications and experience levels and mindsets can impact organisational effectiveness. This can include the way in which some people can find it difficult to think in terms of complex, systemic, problems preferring to think in more simple, linear, ways. However, recognising the overview nature of this book, I do not propose to go into all of these aspects in more depth, recognising these topics have been explored extensively elsewhere.[30]

Group Dynamics

We all understand the importance of collaborative ways of working (e.g. working on cross-functional projects). Still, staff and managers are often expected to pick up these skills 'on the job', sometimes with limited in-depth training or coaching.

As a result, it's not hard to find situations where unhelpful group dynamics can occur in meetings. This can include the impact of dominant personalities, who can quickly crowd out other team members' views. Different group dynamics can arise, such as 'fight/flight' where essential issues are scheduled, but time is used up for less important matters, leading to no, or only a cursory, discussion on the crucial topic (see Illustration 10.3).[31]

This is why professional and independent effectiveness reviews for teams, steering groups and committees can be so critical and why some organisations engage psychologists and facilitators to observe meetings, call out the group dynamics in play and offer interventions to enable more constructive working in the future.[32]

Charlie Hendry offers the following illustration concerning group dynamics following a serious incident and what a leader did to improve things:

'In my career working in the Fire Service, I have seen some very tragic things, both in terms of members of the public who get

Illustration 10.3 Group dynamics – fight flight

caught in a fire and firefighters who die in the line of duty. The death of a firefighter is a rare occurrence, thankfully, especially since firefighters can be, by the very nature of their role, in very hazardous situations. Nonetheless, when a firefighter dies, there is going to be a thorough investigation of what happened and why the firefighter died.

Sometimes, an investigation will provide insights concerning well-established, well-intentioned policies and procedures, as well as flaws with training, and the way things are executed in practice, which is absolutely as it should be, nothing should be "off the table". In one case, I remember the investigation revealed there was a misguided view of what should be happening on the ground and a questionable decision at the level of the "incident commander".

Now incident commanders are very experienced personnel who "calls the shots" and will know the appropriate decisions to make to handle a difficult incident effectively and keep everyone safe, often under extreme time pressure. Incident commanders can change during the evolution of an incident depending on its severity and the duration of the incident. So, despite your best efforts, there will be moments when decisions are made with incomplete information.

The outcome of our inquiry was to create a simplified model for firefighters to make decisions in the field by distilling down the big-ticket risk issues into simple chunks that they could process under pressure at pace. Before that, the guidance firefighters got for making decisions came from what I would call the "laboratory model", gathering all the information, sifting it, prioritising it, implementing it and then reviewing it. But that is not what can happen in an emergency because it takes too long.

As we worked on a new way of making decisions under pressure, we started to see that, even though there was no overt blame culture, there was still a culture where firefighters were afraid of being blamed for not making the "right" decision. Here accountability for a task became accountability for taking the blame rather than doing your best. I can't go into all the details, but we realised there wasn't enough challenge from the front line to say, "I can't make this work, this doesn't work for me, I can't remember this. People glossed over it, avoided it and didn't talk about it".

Through these insights, we encouraged firefighters to raise concerns during incidents, and we also developed a "review of command" process, which was implemented after large incidents. Here there might be three or four commanders of escalating seniority, and they would meet afterwards with a facilitator to look at what decisions were made, why they were made and what happened as a result.

At first, several incident commanders went into these review meetings with the mindset: "I'm not going to say anything because if I say anything, I will be blamed and I may get into trouble". The people facilitating these reviews came out of the first two or three and said, "We are going nowhere with this; they are not learning anything because people won't talk about what really happened. They seem to be conceding points in vague, impersonal terms and avoiding personal responsibility".

What changed things was that one of the most senior operational officers in the fire service happened to be involved in an incident. He decided he would participate in the review process, and he sat there at the beginning and opened it up by saying he thought he had made some mistakes and wanted to talk about what happened. He was brave enough to admit he probably rushed one decision and should have checked something else. This changed everything because it gave permission for others in the room to be open. Following this, we took great care to make sure learnings were shared in a positive spirit with senior staff, and I made it clear this was what I was looking forward to seeing in the future. It wasn't perfect, and we had to work at this on an ongoing basis, but it set a tone that encouraged people to be open and honest, to admit mistakes and to want to learn.

No matter what people say about openness and honesty in the workplace, unless they see senior leaders admitting mistakes, expressing doubts, asking questions sincerely and taking on board difficult feedback, you will mostly have people paying lip service to the needed behavioural change.'

One final point about a healthy group dynamic, and contrary to much 'received wisdom', healthy group behaviour does not mean meetings run smoothly; in fact, often, it's a lack of challenge and questioning that is the problem. As Andy Stanley says, 'Leaders who don't listen will eventually be surrounded by people who have nothing to say'.[33]

Organisational Politics

If you want to do justice to the totality of all that is involved in human factors, in its broadest sense and how it can play into things going wrong (and going right), you must consider organisational politics. By organisational politics, I mean the strategies and tactics (involving influence, power, etc.) that people in an organisation use to

- achieve favourable outcomes for the organisation and themselves, and
- avoid unfavourable consequences for the organisation and themselves.

We can see how organisational outcomes (e.g. a new zero-carbon strategy or launching a new product) can be closely linked to personal outcomes (e.g. where you personally might play a vital role in the new strategy or in launching the new product). Note also how politics is not just about getting things done, it's also about being able to stop things from being done; so, if you think drilling a new oil well will conflict with a zero-carbon goal, you might try, and perhaps succeed, in stopping it.

Consequently, there are two fundamental points that I regard as a 'base camp' in some of the training courses I run and when coaching clients about organisational politics:

1. *Organisational politics will take place around you, whether you choose to engage with it or not;*[34]
2. *Although many people associate organisational politics with Machiavellian plotting for personal gain, it is also quite possible to use politics for an organisation's good.*[35]

A useful model for thinking about organisational politics was developed by Simon Baddeley and Kim James.[36] It uses an animal analogy to illustrate the types of characters in an organisation. They posit two animals who don't think much about organisational politics: the 'innocent' lamb and the 'stubborn' donkey; and two animals who operate politically: the 'wise' owl and the 'cunning' fox.

The difference between the two types (lamb and owl, and donkey and fox) is that the former are primarily oriented towards what is good for the organisation. In contrast, the latter are primarily oriented towards self-interest. The different types are summarised in Illustration 10.4.

In an ideal world, you would hope there weren't too many foxes (or Machiavellian managers) in senior roles; however, you do find foxes in senior positions in most organisations. Based on my experience and work with clients, this can happen because many have learned to hide their self-centred behaviour from others. As Machiavelli says: 'Everyone sees what you appear to be, few really know what you are'. Indeed, some managers may hide their self-serving

Illustration 10.4   Political animals (after Kim James & Simon Baddley)

behaviour from themselves, thinking they aren't Machiavellian, just 'mature', 'flexible', they 'know how to play the game' or they 'naturally know the pragmatic thing to do'.

On the receiving end of Machiavellian behaviour, managers' report how some foxes won't reply to emails unless their boss is copied in or how they change their views depending on the way the wind is blowing in a meeting. They also cite examples of 'silo behaviour' and 'empire building' and good people 'being thrown under the bus' if things go wrong. As the saying goes: 'Having a scapegoat in mind is almost as good a real solution to a problem'.[37]

The Consequences of Machiavellian Behaviour and What to Do About It

So, with Machiavellian managers in an organisation, you have an extra human factor to contend with that can cause problems. At the most extreme end of the spectrum, you hear about psychopaths and sociopaths in senior roles.[38] And (sadly) you may find bullies and managers who are racist, misogynistic, etc., and while these corrosive behaviours are being called out more often, they are still not always dealt with as many would like.[39]

But let's not forget 'plain' self-serving (foxy or Machiavellian) behaviour, which can nonetheless be a key factor when understanding why things didn't go to plan, for example:

- *Projects where the goals were always thought to be unrealistic,* and – with the benefit of hindsight – stakeholders recognised was more of an 'ego project';
- *Where concerns and risks were ignored or downplayed* – so that 'inconvenient truths' were kept from senior decision-makers;
- *Where the budgets of risk, compliance, controlling, auditing or assurance activities are constrained,* ensuring independent and objective challenge is kept to a minimum;
- *Ensuring the responsibility for things going wrong will be attributed to others* (you sometimes hear of 'Teflon' managers, where 'nothing sticks').

Andrew Wright highlights the importance of being on the lookout for Machiavellian behaviour and some of the factors that can make things worse:

'My default expectation for staff and managers is that they will work to their best for the organisation's good. However, if I spot that someone is doing something that isn't that or get any sense of silos or factions, I will call out my concerns in no uncertain terms because it leads to all sorts of problems.

The senior managers I especially watch out for are the ones who appear to be unable to take on board feedback and change accordingly or who operate inconsistently upwards compared to more junior staff. Likewise, I am on my guard for senior managers who seem primarily motivated by their career advancement, self-aggrandisement or greed.

In this latter case, bonus schemes can get in the way. The problem is that the more you "turn up the dial" on bonuses to "make things happen" that no one else could achieve, you start to encourage them to take risks they shouldn't. The pattern is simple and predictable – ask people to move mountains in the short run, pay them a big bonus and then find this has created an enormous avalanche risk in the longer term. It's depressing to see how often boards overlook this only to find, a few years later, "chickens coming home to roost".'

Mindful of these sorts of risks, and a few years after the financial crisis of 2007–2008, the CPA Canada issued a director's briefing on board oversight of risks.[40] It does not directly refer to politics but makes several statements highlighting that even at the most senior levels of an organisation, self-interest, bias and lacunae can exist:

'There are valid circumstances in which boards must take a leadership role in assessing risk. For example, a primary risk might be an ill-advised strategy or a failure to execute strategy. How does management critically evaluate the very strategy it developed or objectively assess its ability to execute?

Similarly, the quality and effectiveness of an enterprise's leadership, including the chief executive officer, can pose a major risk. How is it possible for management to assess itself?'

It is interesting to note, but not surprising, that these insights have not spread very far to date. And the UK Walker review after the 2007–2008 financial crisis highlighted a related problem: board discussions being dominated by a successful CEO/CFO, making it hard sometimes for the board to slow down and think through the risks of different proposals. This is why the review highlighted the importance of independent board effectiveness evaluations.[41]

Also, the UK code for internal auditing has highlighted for several years that *assurance over the information presented to the board and executive* should be seriously considered in the audit planning process.[42] This requirement also has a deterrent effect; if a senior manager understood that a project forecast would be 'pressure tested' before it went to the executive or board, any attempt to 'finesse' forecasts or downplay risks might be thought about more carefully. However, from my vantage point, it appears only a few organisations have used this and similar techniques as a means of systematically 'cleaning up' what is presented to the executive and the board.

So, when regulators and managers refer to 'a poor at the top' or 'a toxic culture', they may be speaking about organisations where foxes may occupy senior leadership roles *but also recognising there may not be adequately robust and progressive governance checks and balances to keep the worst excesses of Machiavellian behaviour in check.*

Silence in Many Quarters About Organisational Politics

In the workshops I run, we discuss why organisational politics is such a sensitive topic in many organisations. There are multiple explanations, for example:

1. Some managers and staff like to think of their organisation primarily in logical, rational terms and don't want to spread gossip about as 'minor political squabbles';

2. Some managers and staff see Machiavellian behaviour in the workplace that is subtly harming organisational performance and may raise concerns informally with trusted colleagues (e.g. during a coffee break or after work). Still, this often won't be shared further because:

    (i) they can't provide any 'hard evidence' for their concerns and

    (ii) of a fear of being accused of being disloyal or political.

3. For foxy managers, the last thing they would want to do is alert innocent lambs (or more savvy owls) to the tricks they get up to!

In other words, we have a serious, corrosive human factor that can lead to significant setbacks and problems *that is hard to name in many organisations.*

The absence of serious discussion and training on this topic in many organisations should, therefore, not be a great surprise. Nonetheless, it represents a considerable threat to organisational effectiveness. I liken the training, workshops, and coaching that would be needed to address these problems to the 'defence against the dark arts' classes in the *Harry Potter* series by JK Rowling.[43] She calls out the profound truth that the dark side of human behaviour cannot be eradicated or definitively 'put in its place'. Professor Snape says:

> 'The Dark Arts are many, varied, ever-changing and eternal. Fighting them is like fighting a many-headed monster, which, each time a neck is severed, sprouts a head even fiercer and cleverer than before.
>
> You are fighting that which is unfixed, mutating and indestructible. Your defences must therefore be as flexible and inventive as the arts you seek to undo.'

Thus, in the wizarding world, it is recognised that unless you equip children with the skills and know-how to deal with these challenges as adults, they will be 'lambs to the slaughter'. Likewise, the popularity of TV series such as *The Office, Mad Men, In the Thick of It,* etc., can be explained – in part – by the way they show the workplace as it is. From this perspective, many corporate 'visions', 'values statements' and 'codes of conduct' are fiction, and some fiction is a lot more like the truth.

It's interesting to note that Machiavellian behaviour (and organisational politics more generally) is rarely, if ever, explicitly tackled in governance, risk and compliance (GRC) circles or in RCA literature that – supposedly – should be free of the shackles of political forces. This is even though good corporate governance promotes speaking openly about difficult issues and that political machinations may undermine GRC and RCA budgets, etc.[44] One hypothesis is that these areas are not immune from politics either (whether that is externally or internally).

And while you can hear many organisations and regulators talking about culture change initiatives and 'behavioural risk' initiatives,[45] and the progress they have made, the presence of politics and human factors tells us progress may only be true in certain areas or that it may not last.[46]

Again, it's outside the scope of this book to discuss organisational politics in greater depth (e.g. how to recognise it, the role it has played in disasters and setbacks, and what to do about it). But it's vitally important that *those who have an interest in RCA and systems thinking to recognise the full spectrum of human factors that are at play in the workplace, not just those prescribed in some Human Factors literature.*

And for the avoidance of doubt, my message is not that Machiavellian behaviour is a root cause of problems; it will be an immediate or contributing cause. But, unless we can recognise it, talk about it and try to equip organisations to better deal with this phenomenon in all its various guises, we cannot be surprised if things go wrong for this reason.

If we are lucky, we might be able to punish the fox for their self-serving behaviour, but we still have the question of the factors that allowed the fox to roam freely and kill the hens in the coop.[47]

Here are some books I would recommend about detecting and trying to manage political behaviour, but I would recommend getting personal support and advice if this is a serious concern:

- '*Confronting Company Politics*' by Beverly Stone – which is an inspiring book that discusses the many corrosive effects dysfunctional politics can have, the defence routines[48] that exist to downplay their effect and the need to take some personal responsibility to do something about its harmful effects.
- '*The Drama of Leadership*' by Patricia Pitcher – which is an insightful, forensic book that discusses power struggles between 'artists', 'craftsmen' and 'technocrats' and the asymmetrical ways each sees one another.
- '*Political Savvy*' by Joel R DeLuca – which is a 'game-changing' book in which he speaks clearly about the need to acknowledge and deal with Machiavellians ('Machs', who I would equate with 'foxes').

Summary

- Remember, a person is not a root cause, even if they deliberately did something wrong.
- People make mistakes for all sorts of reasons, many of them quite innocent.
- The fact that a person's response to a process step or procedure is not 100% in line with the process or procedure is not always a problem; processes and procedures are not always perfect and they may not address every eventuality that can arise in practice.
- Human variability is part of the human condition because we are not robots or clones. Sometimes human variability has positive outcomes.
- It's the inability to identify and adjust to human factors that is a causal factor (something that management needs to consider and address appropriately), not the human factor itself.
- The 'just culture' framework seeks to balance holding people accountable and disciplining them with an acceptance of potentially innocent human variability where people should not be scapegoated.

- Aviation and other High-Reliability Organisations embrace Human Factors thinking and just culture. Still, it takes ongoing effort to make sure this is properly understood and applied in practice.
- The identification of 'cultural' and 'tone at the top' problems can be useful to ensure Human Factors thinking examines all parts of an organisation. However, a 'poor culture' and a 'poor tone' are not root causes in themselves.
- Despite the importance of many standard HR activities (selection, performance management, and training and development), there can still be critical cracks in, for example:
  - Recruitment – in relation to cognitive diversity;
  - Senior leader knowledge and understanding of certain technical areas;
  - Senior management understanding of 'the basics that matter' in finance, governance, IT, and other compliance and control-related matters.
- The 'fit and proper' tests for senior managers that have become mainstream in financial services are likely to be worth considering in other contexts and sectors.
- Group dynamics in meetings is an area that can be easily neglected in organisations.
- Organisational politics is another area that is overlooked in many organisations. Unfortunately, political animals are often present and work hard to stay 'below the radar'.
- The Canadian CPA document on the oversight of risks at the board level is to be commended, as is the Walker review on board effectiveness (notably the discussion on group dynamics).
- Political behaviour often seeks to find scapegoats, a mindset that runs entirely contrary to an RCA and systems thinking mindset.

Practical Suggestions

- If stakeholders do not understand the 'just culture' framework, strive to encourage the adoption of this way of thinking, explaining its importance to get to the real roots of problems rather than find scapegoats.

- Do values and culture surveys ask staff about political behaviour, unhealthy group dynamics and work overload? (They often do not.) Is there free text for staff to expand on their concerns?
- Is there any capability in behavioural science in the organisation to look in depth at the effectiveness of meetings or how different departments work (or don't work) together?
- How strong is the notion of 'leadership at all levels' so that staff feels safe to call out risky behaviour, especially if more senior managers are involved, without fear?
- How much work has been done on 'psychological safety' in the workplace?
- Do recruitment and staff appraisal processes address cognitive biases?
- How much work has been done on diversity and inclusion, including the benefits of cognitive diversity?
- How often should teams, steering groups and committees conduct effectiveness reviews, and what standards apply?
- What workshops or training are there on organisational politics? What mechanisms are in place to detect and address Machiavellian behaviour?

Chapter 11
Addressing Resources, Priorities and Dilemmas

'First, have a definite, clear, practical ideal; a goal, an objective. Second, have the necessary means to achieve your ends; wisdom, money, materials, and methods. Third, adjust all your means to that end'.

– *Aristotle*[1]

Safe Staffing

Human Factors and just culture perspectives have been critical to airline safety, and by the late 1970s, a concept called 'crew resource management' (CRM) developed. It looks at many of the behavioural factors that can arise between crew members in a cockpit alongside an even more fundamental point, viz. if you want a safe flight you need to ensure (i) a minimum number of crew members (in the cockpit and the cabin) and (ii) crew with the appropriate training to fly the particular aircraft and even certifications to land on certain runways (e.g. Lukla in Nepal).[2] These expectations in aviation are not 'advisory'; *if you don't have the correct number of crew with the right amount of experience, you will not be allowed to fly the aircraft.*

You will see the equivalent requirement in a maritime context with 'bridge resource management' and 'engine room resource management', as well as in other high-reliability contexts (e.g. railways and nuclear), with minimum staffing levels addressed in specific laws and regulations.[3]

In this vein, in healthcare, the 1999 landmark report in the United States, 'To err is human', demonstrated the link between the number of nurses and trained medical staff on a ward with better or worse patient outcomes.[4] Thus, an intensive care ward has patients with a certain level of need and if you want to treat them effectively and reduce the number of adverse events, you will need a minimum number of staff to cope with the workload you are likely to get. In a general ward, you will most likely need less staff to keep everyone safe, but there will still be a minimum 'staff staffing' level.

Illustration 11.1 summarises the safe staffing concept and highlights that if there is a limitation on staff numbers, there is an increasing chance of less good outcomes for patients depending on the type of workload the staff will have (often linked to the type of ward).

In many other countries (UK, Canada, Australia, etc.), 'safe staffing' guidance has been developed in a healthcare context to recommend or require a minimum number of staff for a given type of ward.[5] It also applies to other contexts (e.g. in operating theatres).

Organisations such as the UK National Institute for Clinical Excellence (NICE) have also set out 'warning indicators' indicating inadequate staff levels (e.g. delays in giving medicines at the right time).[6] The results of required staff vs. actual staff should then be reviewed regularly, to address gaps. The idea is that *adequate resource acts as a preventative measure to stop bad things from happening. Conversely, a lack of resource creates cracks or stress points that can result in incidents, especially at peak times.*

The topic of 'safe staffing' has become a national news story in the UK and other countries since the COVID-19 (CV19) pandemic

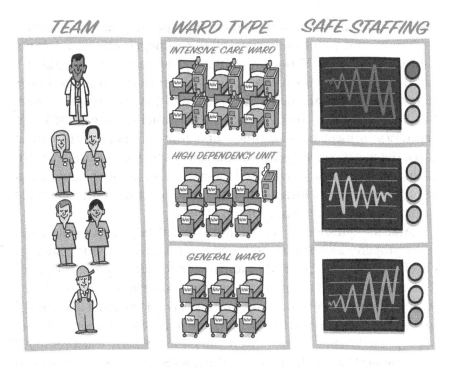

Illustration 11.1 Safe staffing

because of the increased healthcare demand, and the sometimes-limited availability of doctors and nurses.[7]

Sadly, you can also see this issue clearly when there is a war or conflict zone; an absence of ambulances and safe, working, hospital facilities, and qualified doctors and nurses will inevitably lead to worse outcomes for those caught in the crossfire as well as those just needing routine healthcare treatment. Likewise, in relation to other humanitarian goals (shelter, food and water), if you don't have the correct quantity and quality of resources for a relief programme, you will inevitably find worse outcomes for those in need despite the heroic efforts of staff and communities on the ground to do all that they can to help them.

The same thing applies in relation to more conventional project management. Suppose you plan to deliver something by a given date. In that case, you will need an appropriate level of resources, materials, personnel and contractors (numbers, skills and experience) to succeed. However, unlike getting ready for a flight, it's not unusual for senior managers to start projects and programmes knowing that not all the needed resources have yet been secured, but hoping there is enough slack in the timeline to get sufficient resources to meet key deadlines. Sometimes organisations put in place the necessary steps to make this work (e.g. expediting recruitment), but often you will find organisations getting caught out because 'lead times' turn out to be beyond what was either planned or required by the demands of the project.[8]

And the question of the appropriate staffing levels to carry out tasks properly also applies to 'business as usual' activities, such as checking payments before they are made or ensuring product quality. Too often, I have seen organisations where something has gone badly wrong. Then, everyone turns around and says, 'How did it get so bad?' to discover either (i) there were no 'guide rails' to keep resources at an appropriate level or (ii) there were only limited 'early warning signs' that standards were slipping or (iii) requests for extra resources had been made, but securing this was – literally – 'too little, too late'.

This then takes us to the question of prioritisation because whether or not there are adequate staffing levels, sometimes you will still encounter short-term pressures that will demand appropriate and disciplined prioritisation. This area is addressed in aviation, medicine and many High-Reliability Organisations (HROs).

Prioritisation in Aviation

CRM techniques help pilots prioritise what is most important in the cockpit and – beyond that – approach decision-making in a disciplined way when under pressure. An airline captain explains the TDODAR framework:[9]

> 'One of the most valuable acronyms I learned as a pilot was TDODAR:
>
> *Time* – How much have you got before you need to decide, one way or the other? You can have all the ideas you

like about analysing things in detail, but sometimes you just need to act.

Diagnosis – What exactly is the concern? Can you triangulate instrumentation with other data to understand where you are and what's happening? Any assumptions to check?

Options – This will depend on time; as you think about options, you need to consider their likely impact and pros and cons.

Decide – Come to some agreement, summarising the basis for making the decision. Recognise it can change after review.

Assign Action – Who is doing what? Confirm the way actions will be executed. Cross-check what's just been done.

Review – Anything arising from the action taken? Anything important changed? Keep an eye on the time and the what-ifs.

It's a framework that's easy to follow, and these steps are second nature to most pilots.'

Prioritisation in Other Contexts

Triaging and prioritisation protocols exist in a medical context.[10] And you will see various other tools and techniques to help with prioritisation so that resources and attention can, ideally, be focused on the things that matter the most:

- *In supplier management*, the identification of key, critical or single-source suppliers, so attention is focused on the areas that might have the most significant impact on the organisation.[11]
- *In process execution*, the use of Lean techniques to expedite high-priority items of the most value to key customers.[12]
- *In financial controls and compliance*, the identification of critical controls that must be kept running for the accounts to be up to date and accurate and for fraud to be kept in check.[13]
- *In business continuity planning and crisis management*, prioritisation mechanisms for keeping contingency plans up to date and testing them.
- *In cyber risk management*, understanding the mission-critical IT 'crown jewels' – to make sure data and information is kept secure, and system operability is sustained'.[14]

However, even though we know resourcing and prioritisation is a crucial area to get right, it's still quite usual to encounter difficulties that cause a host of knock-on problems.

Change Overload and Too Much Firefighting

Bruce Sherry (Senior Audit Manager, Tesco Bank) offers this insight about keeping track of the aggregate workload staff have:

> 'Most organisations nowadays need to deal with changing customer requirements in an Agile way. This is something we have developed an increasingly strong capability in, for example, learning how to "pivot" when the COVID-19 pandemic arose. And the good thing with Agile is that, at a project-by-project level, it helps you to tackle one thing at a time over a short timescale, so every time you complete a "sprint," you have something tangible to show for your efforts.
>
> But you need to keep a close eye on the number of things you are doing, the interdependencies between those and the number of times staff must switch from one task to another. This is often problematic because of the time and effort it takes to catch up with what you were last doing and with what everyone else has been doing.
>
> Some organisations can get caught out by this subtle but essential detail. However, to its credit, most Agile projects don't like too much staff switching, precisely because of this problem.'

Andrew Wright outlines how he thinks about the workload of colleagues and how they approach work tasks:

> 'You want an organisation to be productive and efficient. But you don't want managers to be too busy. This is something I look out for. The tricky bit is unpicking whether people are really overloaded or just not so good at prioritising, managing their time and delegating. This is where Lean techniques can help. You can say you are productive all you want. But you can't be sure unless you are using tried and tested methods to prioritise and squeeze out effectiveness and efficiency.

I think the other part of this is that people need some capacity to step back from day-to-day tasks at regular intervals. Being good in a business is about having the capacity to review management information and then dig into things, such as minor variations in production costs or potential market changes thoughtfully, rather than just operating in firefighting mode.

I admire managers who are good under pressure and who can firefight. But too often, I have seen instances where staff and managers pride themselves on their heroic efforts fixing one thing after another as if it's a badge of honour. I know this is commonplace, but this is a warning sign for the organisation around strategic thinking, prioritisation, capability, and resources. A manager who mostly does firefighting may be a hero for a while. Still, in the long run, they can be a liability. Modern business should be about more intelligent ways of working, not just working harder.

I'm not saying that I dislike managers who can get things done quickly under pressure, this is important, and it can be better to act quickly in some situations than to overanalyse and overthink. But it's about finding a balance.

One way to think about this is to clarify what is driving the pace of problem-solving and decision-making. If there is an external factor that means you must respond to something immediately, that's understandable. But often, I see people rushing at things out of habit to get things off their desk and show they are decisive and busy. But this is a huge mistake if you are a senior manager because rushed decisions at the top can generate chaos and stress elsewhere in an organisation.

My view is that if you have got some time, why not take it? A bit of time and effort to think things through at a senior level has a multiplying effect when it's translated into what goes on at an operational level.'[15]

Dilemmas and Trade-Offs

Even with 'safe staffing' and 'good prioritisation', managers may still encounter dilemmas in what should be done. Here, decisions may need to be made based on the 'least bad' choice. For example, the airline captain I spoke to explained some of the dilemmas you can encounter when flying a plane:

'Although there is absolutely no doubt about the safety culture in aviation, there are still many ways in which the pilot needs to have "their wits about them" because, like it or not, there are dilemmas you need to work through from time to time. Here are a few examples:

1. You are flying over Canada in wintertime, and you get an engine warning. You are supposed to land as soon as practicable, so your co-pilot suggests an airfield nearby that is just long enough to take your plane. But you know there will be ice on the runway which may affect your ability to brake safely and, therefore, the landing distance. So, do you land or keep flying?

2. You urgently need to land, which should demand that the passenger cabin is made secure, and everyone is in their seat. But someone is in the toilet. Do you go around until the person is out of the bathroom and back in their seat, or take action to land anyway, even though the passenger may not return to their seat in time?

Even air traffic controllers can face dilemmas in what they are supposed to do. Their prime responsibility is to maintain separation between aircraft. But there can also be an implicit pressure to get planes landing so that delays don't build up. Experienced pilots see cultural differences concerning this, and I have, on several occasions, declined an air traffic control request to catch up with another plane while making an approach because I am the one accountable for flying the aircraft safely and wanted more separation for my peace of mind.

This is where the whole flight simulator regime is excellent. You simulate the flight from being in the briefing room to landing and unlocking the cabin doors, so it's very realistic. It tests how you make decisions in as natural a context as possible and confronts you with "hard choices".'

Norman Marks (Author, Speaker and Thought Leader)[16] provides the following observation concerning supervision:

> 'There is an interesting practical question about what you believe is a suitable level of supervision. On the one hand, we know that a lack of sufficient monitoring by a manager can mean that a staff member might make a mistake that gets missed.
>
> On the other hand, staff can feel disempowered, even micromanaged, if everything they do is checked. People sometimes won't check their work if they know it will be double-checked by someone else anyway. So, strangely, you end up confused between responsibility and accountability through what appears to be the very best of intentions.'

Here are a few other dilemmas to look out for because, like human factors, these can often be found to be implicated in incidents and setbacks:

- Sharing data and information.

  On the one hand, we want to share information within an organisation to get data and ideas to help us overcome problems and develop products and services that our clients might want. But on the other hand, we may be prohibited from sharing information, even within the same company, because of specific data privacy laws (such as the EU GDPR legislation).
- Whether grey zones in compliance with laws, regulations and policies are recognised?

  It's understandable that some laws, regulations, policies and procedures can take a 'hard line' spelling out they want to be done (e.g. EU procurement standards can require some organisations to seek bids from suppliers for contracts over a particular value). However, for practical reasons, it may appear appropriate to grant an exception to proceed (e.g. because there is time pressure to move forward, the supplier is known and it is extremely unlikely there is a credible alternative supplier).

So, do policies and procedures, etc., recognise why people might take 'shortcuts'? And offer advice on what to do when faced with conflicting requirements? If not, shortcuts may still take place, but this time, 'under the radar'.[17]

- Concerning the scope, schedule, cost and benefits forecast for a project.[18]

As mentioned in the chapter on change management, it's common to find the costs of projects and programmes can turn out to be higher than planned. In these circumstances, it can be very tempting to 'scale back' the project scope (e.g. build an IT system with just basic functionality at first), to save money. However, such a change in the functionality of the new system might mean the benefits from the project won't be as much as planned until all the needed functionality of the system is in place. *Thus, the decision to save money on project costs in the short-term is one of the causes why the project benefits will not turn out as hoped for in the future.*

- Concerning efficiency, and cost-saving programmes.

Cost savings programmes may be required because an organisation is under pressure to meet its financial goals. As a result, these programmes can look at whether cost savings, headcount reductions, efficiency gains, etc., are going to plan and what other things can be cut or scaled back.

Often back-office roles, such as quality, compliance, finance or administration, are considered an overhead, and this may be the case on occasions. However, I have seen several instances where efficiency programmes have cut back-office activities too much, weakening an organisation's control skeleton, impacting product quality, customer service levels or the basic checks and balances needed in financial controls and compliance. Even where a process is being automated, it is not uncommon to find (i) a dilution of control in the design of the new system or (ii) an underestimate of the staff needed to manage the new process.

So, *we may create a cost savings and efficiency programme that's meant to be a solution to high costs. However, it's essential to see that such a solution may create 'spin-off' problems and make other issues more likely.* And often managers can feel uncomfortable to accept the 'shadow' in what they are doing, meaning they may not want to acknowledge 'spin-off' risks. But if the risks of a cost savings or efficiency programme are not made visible with appropriate metrics, warning flags and a means to rapidly carry out 'course corrections', you cannot be surprised if you get a surprise because you have cut 'too close to the bone'.

This is an area where I have even seen senior managers and board members overseeing cost savings programmes but somehow (i) assuming that standards would not slip (i.e. not asking questions about this risk) and (ii) accepting management assurances they were not slipping without much challenge. Here, some timely checks or audits of what was happening on the ground would have revealed a growing number of gaps that would eventually culminate in a much bigger problem.

Addressing Dilemmas and Managing Trade-Offs

I worked with an international organisation trying to get to the heart of some problems they had experienced in customer services that had not been resolved satisfactorily.

In summary, we looked at how call centre staff were measured and some of the dilemmas that call centre staff faced. We agreed there needed to be a more explicit framework to allow for trade-offs between one choice and another. For example, there was a general desire that staff should 'stick to the call script' (which was in place to encourage consistency) and to 'clear the call quickly' (to drive productivity), but this sometimes conflicted with the need to take time to tailor the right solution for a customer who had had a significant or unusual complaint.

In the end, we recognised that (i) time targets for clearing calls quickly needed to be matched to the difficulty of the call that was being handled, not just a 'one size fits all' time target, and (ii) sometimes it was preferable to 'fail to meet' some targets, to deal with a difficult complaint (that might otherwise escalate internally and or even externally).

Finally, changes were made to how metrics were set, and extra guidance was given to call handlers so they could feel empowered to do what was suitable rather than being made to operate like robots. This also had the benefit of creating a more enjoyable working environment and reducing staff turnover (which is a massive issue for many call centres and essential for customers).

Dilemmas can be found when you are making an outsourcing decision; on the one hand, you may want to save money, but there may be a risk of more variable quality from the third party, along with a range of other risks. Diagram 11.2 illustrates, through a 'spider diagram', how to capture different requirements and illustrate how different suppliers may be more or less expensive but also vary in their product quality or environmental track record, etc.

So, when you make an outsourcing decision, you must understand trade-offs explicitly, i.e. if you go for the cheaper supplier, you need to know that extra attention will be required to check product quality and oversee environmental risk management.

The exact elements included in a spider diagram can vary, and these diagrams are not yet mainstream. But they can make an enormous contribution towards having the right conversations about dilemmas and trade-offs between one choice and another. After all, in day-to-day life, we think nothing of weighing up pros and cons when buying a new washing machine or car (e.g. we consider the cost, reliability, etc.), and recognise the cheapest option isn't always the most sensible choice. And here, we may see a contrast between the conversations we have in daily life and what might be said at work, where in some contexts, the cheapest choice will invariably be the preference, ignoring or downplaying concerns about quality. This contrast in what gets said and how decisions are made between the home and work environments *illustrates how systemic factors (such as goals, budgets, and politics) can constrain or warp what would otherwise be common-sense conversations and choices.*

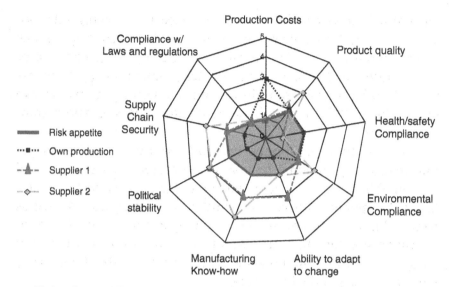

Choices between Suppliers etc. may involve trade offs and dilemmas, which are best made explicit.

Diagram 11.2   Outsourcing – tensions in what is wanted

To Write It Down or Not

The final dilemma I want to cover concerns what should be written down. Think about a committee meeting or a steering group. When it makes decisions, you might expect to see a report or presentation sent to its members beforehand, discussing the pros and cons of a course of action and then a minute recording what was decided.

But there may be several things that were said 'behind the scenes' that won't ever make it into the written record of the proposal or the final decision. Many of the points discussed before, during and after a committee meeting may be unimportant, but you may have a situation where some managers had grave concerns about a proposal and expressed these concerns in the meeting, but the meeting minutes don't reflect this.[19]

To counter this, managers with concerns may decide to put their reservations in writing. However, the written expression of 'dissenting' views can have a consequence for working relationships and may constitute a risk because the document might make its way into the public domain (whether through a legal process or an unauthorised leak), creating another problem for the organisation.[20] In other words, committing things to writing seems to solve one problem. Still, it may, in some circumstances, create a spinoff problem.

In many countries around the world, you will see 'freedom of information' legislation.[21] Its goal is to promote transparency and accountability in government and other organisations so that members of the public, journalists and other interest groups can access data and information of interest. In many instances, this has been a positive step forward, but – as a result – it's an open secret that many organisations are now much more cautious about what they put into writing in the first place.

The same applies to risk management activities. Some risks are embarrassing, such as 'the senior project manager is out of their depth and needs to be replaced', or risks that may be sensitive from a regulatory perspective. Therefore, they may not be written down at all or perhaps only in vague, coded terms. This doesn't mean the organisation will be doing nothing on these issues, but it's important to recognise this happens.

So, the question 'What are the "off the record" risks? And what is being done about them?' needs to be faced by senior managers from time to time. Otherwise, you might see a major project setback and uncover that the steering group was not adequately resolving problems with the project manager, who was out of their depth. *This is a classic example of an 'open secret' which could be addressed but often is not until it's too late.*

In conclusion, to head off significant disappointments or setbacks, organisations need to face the fact that they will have resource constraints and prioritisation challenges and accept and resolve some of the dilemmas they face.[22]

The CV19 pandemic provides a powerful illustration of this; a 'lockdown' in some countries was seen to be a solution to avoid the scenario of, inter alia, queues building up outside hospitals, with patients waiting for a bed and gasping for oxygen, as we saw in India.[23] However, this solution created a whole host of knock-on effects, separating friends and families, impacting children's education, leading to safeguarding risks, causing mental health problems, increasing alcoholism and adversely affecting businesses and workers, with global economic impacts on top of this. At the time of writing this book, we are still dealing with 'Long COVID', not just in terms of health impacts on people, but in terms of all the societal impacts we are now trying to address, where this is still possible.

So, as we start to plan for other challenges facing us in the future (e.g. other pandemics, environmental and climate challenges, the impact of AI, etc.), I hope to see more explicit discussions regarding short-term versus longer-term trade-offs. Then, we might be able to have more in-depth conversations about how we might strike the 'least bad' outcome at a given point in time. We may also become clearer on what basis we might re-evaluate decisions as things unfold, although recognising that sometimes when you open Pandora's box, there is no going back.[24]

Thus, resources, priorities and dilemmas is another root cause that profoundly impacts the other cause types. After all:

(i) You may not be able to identify the optimal design you need for a new building, facility, process, crisis management plan, etc., without engaging the right operational staff and using expert help (which takes time and costs money).

(ii) You are unlikely to have an optimal build quality or a resilience capability, if you don't have the resources and materials to invest in building, materials and supplies, keeping things in good order, etc.

(iii) You are unlikely to be able to optimise the organisation's human resources unless you can pay competitive salaries and invest in staff training and development, etc.

And it should be no surprise that political behaviour is often closely associated with budget and resource discussions, after all, 'Politics determines who has the power, not who has the truth'.[25]

Summary

- The disciplines of crew resource management and 'safe staffing' remind us that having the correct number and type of resources is fundamental to avoiding accidents and setbacks.
- Even if you have an adequate staff complement for a given area, you will always need a robust way of prioritising what you tackle first. The TDODAR framework from the world of aviation provides a valuable checklist for making decisions when time may be limited.
- Other prioritisation techniques in supplier management, Lean production, cyber security, financial controls and compliance can help us distinguish more clearly between what is critical and the things that are a lesser priority.
- It's very easy to have initiative overload, with staff losing time 'switching' between tasks and spending too much time firefighting.
- Dilemmas arise in many ways in organisational life, e.g. data privacy, cost savings programmes, project management trade-offs between short-term costs and longer-term benefits realisation, and outsourcing decisions.
- Multi-dimensional risk appetite frameworks are rare but are helpful in making dilemmas more transparent.
- Despite the many benefits of writing things down and freedom of information legislation, there remain pros and cons concerning putting things in writing. The world of unwritten risks is always worth understanding because sometimes key risks lie in this area.

Practical Suggestions

- Establish which areas in your organisation have a safe or minimum staffing framework. Are there any higher-risk areas (in operations or projects) where clear minimum requirements would reduce the risks of a gap in the level of operations or service(s)?

- If there is no minimum staffing framework, are there any other warning signs (key risk indicators [KRIs]) that are used to highlight staffing problems?
- How explicit is the workforce and budgeting process in relation to staffing and resourcing decisions? If there is a gap between resources wanted and what is provided, what decisions were made concerning how to prioritise or work on efficiency opportunities?
- What are the priority categories for suppliers, systems, activities and business continuity planning? How do these practically help those working in these areas to ensure the most critical risks are addressed?
- How do organisations judge whether areas are, or are not, inefficient? Are specific tools, such as Lean SIPOC or DMAIC, used?
- Is there a clear understanding of the totality of change activities going on? For example, is there visible evidence of programmes and projects being aligned, combined, rescheduled and 'killed' (in a constructive manner)?
- What evidence is there that the culture of the organisation can identify and process dilemmas: for example, policy exceptions, cost savings programme downsides and project costs vs. project benefits?
- Do risks get the same attention as financial information?
- What are the key issues not being written down? What is being done about them?

Chapter 12

The Titanic Tragedy and Parallels with Modern Disasters

'If you look in your dictionary, you will find Titans – a race of people vainly striving to overcome the forces of nature. Could anything be more unfortunate than such a name, anything more significant?'

– Captain Arthur Rostron (RMS Carpathia*)*[1]

Having discussed the eight ways to understand why in earlier chapters and some of the connections between causes, this chapter examines the Titanic tragedy of April 1912 to:

- illustrate how root cause analysis (RCA) and systems thinking can clarify its root causes, and why the two Titanic inquiries made the recommendations they did, and
- provide some parallels with more recent disasters and setbacks, e.g. 9/11, the 2007-2008 financial crisis, Hurricane Katrina and the COVID-19 pandemic.[2]

In relation to the Titanic tragedy, I won't recount every twist and turn of what happened (e.g. why binoculars were locked in a cupboard, a possible fire in the coal bunker and the actions of each crew member and passenger)[3] because there are plenty of other books, films and TV programmes that have done this.[4] But I will recount some details that deserve to be better known and point to extra material in the notes for those who want to verify or dive deeper into the points that follow. That said, fact-checking this tragedy is not straightforward, but – as much as has been possible – I believe the key points that follow can be corroborated at this point in time.[5]

Some Basic Facts About the Titanic Tragedy

On 10 April 1912, the largest ship ever built at that time, the SS/RMS Titanic[6] set sail from Queenstown Ireland,[7] bound for New York, USA. Her captain was Edward John Smith, RD, RNR, 62 years old and one of the most experienced captains of large ships at that time. The Titanic carried around 2240 passengers and crew,[8] 1300 fewer than her full capacity of around 3500.[9] She crossed the Atlantic on the 'southern track', a winter route intended to avoid icepacks.[10] However, as she got closer to Newfoundland, she received numerous warnings of ice.[11]

At 11.40 p.m. on 14 April, lookout Frederick Fleet spotted an iceberg around 400 metres away and cried out, 'Iceberg, right ahead!' First Officer Murdoch requested the Titanic be steered hard starboard, which she did as best she could.[12] Still, there were only 40 seconds before she received a glancing blow from the iceberg below the waterline. The resulting damage to the hull affected 5 out of 16 watertight compartments.[13] Despite closing the doors on the bulkheads and efforts to pump water out of the hull, the Titanic rapidly filled with water.

An SOS message was sent by radio just after midnight, and several ships replied to the request for help and set sail towards the Titanic. By 2.20 a.m., just 2 hours and 40 minutes after the iceberg strike, the Titanic sank some 595 kilometres (370 miles) off the coast of Newfoundland.[14]

While there were 1178 lifeboat places for the 2240 passengers and crew on board, loading the passengers on board was challenging.[15] At first, passengers were reluctant to get into the lifeboats, in part because the damage to the Titanic seemed to be minimal.[16] Later, when the ship's plight became clear, passengers struggled to get into lifeboats, posing difficulties for safe loading and putting them to sea. In total, around 700 passengers went into the lifeboats.[17] Many crew and passengers went down with the Titanic, but it is estimated hundreds fell into the freezing cold sea.[18]

The first ship that arrived at the scene was the RMS *Carpathia*. It had travelled some 91 kilometres (57 miles) in 4 hours and rescued all the passengers and crew in lifeboats. Unfortunately, no one who was still in the water survived. Around 1500 out of 2240 on board died. This amounted to a death toll of around two-thirds, which could have been even higher if the Titanic had been full.

Given the scale of the disaster, there was a public outcry concerning what had happened. This was heightened by pronouncements about the ship's safety before its maiden voyage, such as those of Phillip Franklin (VP of the White Star Line), who said: 'There is no danger that Titanic will sink. The boat is unsinkable, and nothing but inconvenience will be suffered by the passengers'[19] and 'I thought her unsinkable and based my opinion on the best expert advice'.[20]

The Scope and Boundaries of the Two Titanic Inquiries

On 17 April 1912, a resolution was passed by the US Senate which stated that the Committee on Commerce, or a subcommittee thereof, '[should] investigate the causes leading to the wreck of the White Star Liner Titanic, with its attendant loss of life so shocking to the civilized world'.[21] The investigation commenced almost immediately,[22] and a transcript of witness statements, and the conclusions made, is available online, comprising some 1000 pages.[23]

A British Wreck Commissioner inquiry started in May 1912. It was asked to address 20+ key questions relating to what happened to the Titanic, its crew and passengers, including:

- Compliance with the requirements of the Merchant Shipping Acts, 1894–1906, and the rules and regulations regarding passenger safety.
- Questions about the design and construction of the Titanic, arrangements made in the event of collisions, etc.
- The adequacy of manning.
- Telegraphy installations and whether they were in good working order.
- Whether the route (track) taken was usual for voyages to New York in the month of April.
- Warnings of ice, lookout arrangements and directions concerning speed.
- Was ice seen and reported? Were measures to avoid it adequate?
- Was the Titanic's speed excessive?
- The way in which messages were sent by the Titanic and how these were received by other vessels?
- Were lifeboats filled, lowered and moved away appropriately? Were the boats sent away in seaworthy condition?

The concluding points for the British inquiry to examine were:

'What was the cause of the loss of the Titanic and of the loss of life which thereby ensued or occurred? Was the construction of the vessel and its arrangements such as to make it difficult for any class of passenger or any portion of the crew to take full advantage of any existing provisions for safety?'[24] and

'. . . to report upon the rules and regulations made under the Merchant Shipping Acts, 1894–1906, and the administration of those Acts, and of such rules and regulations, so far as the consideration thereof is material to this casualty, and to make any recommendations or suggestions that it may think fit, having regard to the circumstances of the casualty with a view to promoting the safety of vessels and persons at sea.'

The British inquiry concluded in early July. It is over 2000 pages long, and the full transcript is also available online.[25]

The Essential RCA Questions and Reflections on the Rigour of the Inquiries

As with all inquiries or root cause investigations, it is essential to recognise the question you are asking and answering.[26] The Titanic inquiries were not simply looking at the question: 'What happened and why did the Titanic sink?'; instead, they were also asking, *'Why did the Titanic sink so quickly, and why did so many people die?'*

By *paying attention to the consequences of what happened, you can appreciate why prevention, detection and recovery measures might all be relevant.*

If you read just a few pages of either inquiry, you get a sense of the diligence with which they tried to find out the 'what, where, when, who, how and why' through witness testimonies.[27] However, several caveats need to be added:

1. The public and newspapers at the time were looking to find someone responsible for the Titanic tragedy, and you sense, during the inquiries, a great deal of focus on who did or did not do what.
2. The plight of the third-class passengers was not a significant focus of either inquiry,[28] even though this is where the bulk of the passenger casualties occurred (along with the crew members).[29]
3. The inquiries were expedited quickly for understandable reasons, but that meant the significance of some issues (such as the condition of the hull and rivets and optical effects due to the freezing water) were only fully understood many years later (and even now several mysteries remain).[30]
4. Whether the British Wreck inquiry could be completely unbiased since it was under the authority of the Board of Trade, which was responsible for the relevant maritime laws and regulations at the time, and had overseen the Titanic's design, construction and sea trials.[31]

Recognising that the inquiries were not perfect, they nonetheless resulted in a set of 'game-changing' insights, specifically:

- There was no compelling evidence any of the crew of the Titanic did anything deliberately to damage the ship or harm the passengers.[32]
- The root causes of the Titanic tragedy went far beyond what happened that night.
- There were a range of problems with maritime customs and practices and relevant laws and regulations, and how these were supervised at that time, that needed to be addressed.

I will now outline some further details relevant to these conclusions, referring to various RCA tools and techniques as I go. If you are unfamiliar with this story, be prepared for some inevitably tragic 'twists and turns' and consider how misleading many 'urban myths' about the Titanic tragedy are. I also hope this brings home what it means to have a root cause and systems thinking frame of mind and how some modern disasters bear uncanny similarities to some of the things that happened to the Titanic, its crew and its passengers.

RCA Starting Point: The Goal and Its Risks: How Much Risk Was the Titanic Taking?

With any RCA analysis, you usually start by considering the relevant objective, the key risks to achieving this and tolerance for failure.

The objective of the Titanic was to cross the Atlantic safely, and we can be sure there would have been little appetite for the loss of the ship or any loss of life.[33] This appears to be a realistic goal because many ships were crossing the Atlantic then, but it was clear this was not a risk-free 'walk in the park'.[34] In terms of the scale of the risk that the Titanic faced, we can use the Failure Mode and Effects Analysis (FMEA) framework.

Here, we can ask: what is the worst-case scenario for crossing the Atlantic? Clearly, it would be to lose the ship and many, or all, of the passengers and crew. Using the FMEA scale, from the perspective of the captain and crew, the risk for the Titanic crossing the Atlantic would be 'extremely high' (9/10) or 'dangerously high' (10/10).[35]

Some might think, 'That's too high a rating; we should adjust the impact for the mitigations in place', but the FMEA mindset says: 'One thing at a time. If you cross the Atlantic, you could lose a ship and all the passengers. It's incredibly unlikely, but *you have safety measures precisely because of all that is at stake*'.

Using the Bowtie Technique to Unpick the Key Causes of What Happened

To avoid a disaster at sea, many measures should be (and were) designed and put in place to prevent damage to the Titanic, its passengers and crew. These included:

- *Preventative measures* – e.g. travelling in a designated shipping lane intended to avoid icepacks, with an experienced crew;
- *Detective measures* – e.g. lookouts;
- *Recovery measures* – e.g. bulkheads to compartmentalise any water ingress, water pumps and lifeboats.

Diagram 12.1 sets out, using the Bowtie format, many of the measures or lines of defence in place to maximise the chances of a successful, safe crossing of the Atlantic.

Thus, contrary to some urban myths, *the Titanic was designed and built with an eye on safety.*[36] There were multiple measures put in place to avoid a disaster, and these were signed off by the Board of Trade.[37] Yet we know that despite putting multiple measures in place, these were not enough to stop the tragedy.

Let's now consider the question of detective measures.

Detective Measure: What Could the Lookouts See?

If you are a lookout up in the crow's nest, and it is daylight, you might see many kilometres into the distance. And with the Titanic travelling close to its top speed (37 kilometres per hour (20 knots)), she covers 600 metres in a minute. So, at face value, in clear

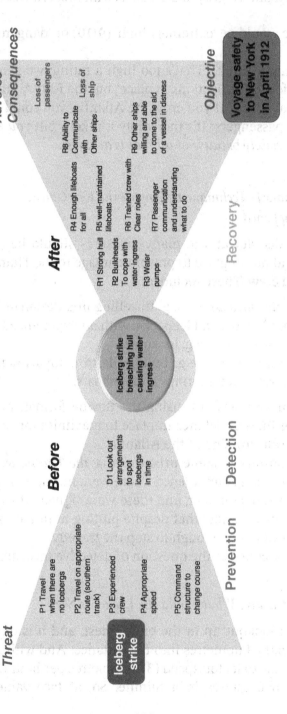

Diagram 12.1 Bowtie diagram applied to the Titanic/Iceberg strike

conditions, a lookout should have plenty of time to see an obstacle several kilometres away and react to it.

But the further away you are from something the smaller it seems, so you need to recognise that even though theoretically you might see several kilometres in the distance, the object needs to be big enough to be visible. So, if we dig into the question of detecting icebergs, there are a range of scenarios relevant to the Titanic's crossing, each of which would affect the chances of seeing it.

To illustrate the point, consider the chances of spotting an iceberg in the following situations:

1. a 75-metre-wide iceberg in daylight in clear conditions from, say, 3 kilometres,
2. a 3-metre-wide 'growler' (broken iceberg) in daylight, from 3 kilometres,
3. a 75-metre-wide iceberg at night when it is clear, with a full moon, from 1 kilometre,
4. a 75-metre-wide iceberg at night when it is clear, but with no moonlight, from 1 kilometre.

We can see the odds of spotting an iceberg will depend on its size and are likely to reduce as we go from day to night, and at night depending on whether you have moonlight or starlight. Note the circumstances closest to 14 April 1912 were scenario 4.[38]

There were other factors that we now know will have affected the lookouts' ability to see the iceberg that night, including:

- The calmness of the sea (which would have reduced the 'cue' of waves splashing against an iceberg);[39]
- The colour of the iceberg (witnesses said it appeared to be dark, almost black);[40]
- Significant distortions, even mirage effects, at the water's surface were caused by freezing air adjacent to the ice-cold water of the Labrador Current (which had brought the icebergs south onto the 'southern track').[41]

Thus, we have a series of 'external factors' that were outside of the control of the crew of the Titanic that almost certainly made an enormous difference to the chances of seeing an iceberg.[42]

So, saying 'it was obvious the lookouts should have seen the iceberg sooner' *is based on a high-level analysis that isn't recognising the very particular circumstances that night.*

Here, we see a classic 'hairline crack' problem; you have something that seems a simple question in relation to the ability to detect a threat, and then you realise (as the inquiries did) that 'the devil is in the detail'. The lookout arrangements were, of course, a significant contributing factor to what happened on the night. However, they were not a root cause, given the uncertainties of what could be seen at a distance at night and given the specific atmospheric conditions present.[43] This takes us to the question of the speed of the Titanic that night (and more).

Preventative Measure: The Speed of the Titanic and Its Ability to Avoid an Iceberg

The Titanic travelled on the customary 'southern track' route for shipping across the Atlantic during winter. This route was intended to avoid icebergs that might be encountered on a more northerly route, but in April 1912, ice packs had travelled very far south,[44] meaning there were multiple warnings of ice en route. Consequently, Second Officer Charles Lightoller ordered that the crow's nest be told to 'keep a sharp lookout for small ice and growlers'.[45]

With lookouts in place and on notice of ice, *it was not the custom and practice of mariners to slow down in the presence of ice in clear conditions, even at night.* This was because, until that time, there had been no suggestion that taking evasive action would be problematic (ships did not have the speed or momentum to mean this was seen to be a problem in mid-ocean).[46] However, the Titanic was the largest ship ever built at the time, with considerable momentum, meaning she did not handle like most other ships.[47] This is another crucial detail because if someone had been able to 'put two and two together', it could have triggered a thought to be more cautious. Suppose the Titanic had travelled more slowly that night. In that case, it might have (i) avoided the collision entirely or (ii) not breached five watertight compartments. In both scenarios, the Titanic would most likely have stayed afloat.[48]

You could argue there was 'nothing stopping' Captain Smith, or First Officer Murdoch, from slowing the Titanic that night, even if this wasn't the custom and practice. But there can be no doubt the passengers on board were asking questions about the progress of the ship and when she was going to arrive in New York.[49] Furthermore, there was a high-pressure area above and clear skies, which would have encouraged Captain Smith to travel without delay, lest they encountered fog (which would then have caused him to slow the ship).

Thus, you have the human factor in relation to the question of going slower and a dilemma. The captain could have ordered her to travel slower, but many on board might have wondered why he was being so cautious. And note that the Titanic was not a cruise ship as we might think of her today. She was a working passenger ship, the equivalent of a scheduled train or plane nowadays, so crossing the Atlantic without delay, especially when the conditions were clear and calm, was the customary manner of crossing and an expectation of the passengers.[50]

Consequently, the Titanic crossed without slowing down that night. And as a result, with just 40 seconds notice of the iceberg, she was unable to avoid the iceberg in time, which resulted in damage to her side.

However, as readers will undoubtedly appreciate, this is by no means the end of the story. The Titanic and its passengers were provided with a range of recovery measures to mitigate against a disastrous outcome if it hit something. So, we will now turn to the numerous means by which the Titanic, and its passengers and crew, should have been saved from the worst but were not.

Recovery Measure: The Design of the Titanic's Bulkheads

There were many aspects of the Titanic's bulkheads that were state of the art, including electrically operated doors that could be (and

were) closed in the event of a breach of the hull (to stop water passing from one watertight compartment to another). The Titanic was
also designed so that, if it was damaged, it could stay afloat with four
compartments breached.[51] The decision about the number of bulkheads that could be safely breached without the Titanic sinking was
based on a *reasonable worst-case scenario* that there might be damage to the hull because of a strike from another ship.[52]

This takes us to the problem of a 'failure of imagination', an
expression coined after the 9/11 attacks of 2001, where it was noted
that no one had seriously thought about an attack from within
the USA, using commercial aircraft as weapons.[53] Understanding
human factors tells us people can block out thinking about worst-
case scenarios. But the result of this is that you might be inade-
quately prepared as a result. You can see this problem when you
look at the financial crisis of 2007–2008 and before the COVID-19
pandemic. And this is precisely why flight simulators in aviation
often involve unusual challenges, sometimes in combination with
one another, to keep a full spectrum of unlikely but perilous possibilities 'alive' in pilots' minds.

One more design point about the bulkheads is worth highlighting (which played a role in the rapid sinking). The bulkhead
design did not extend all the way from the keel to the outside deck
but rather to decks D and E instead.[54] This was because having
15 bulkheads, rising upwards all the way to deck level, would have
cut across key passenger areas, especially the first-class lounge,
smoking room, dining room, etc.

So, we have a dilemma in the requirements for the bulkheads; on
the one hand, we want watertight compartments to protect against
flooding, but on the other hand, we need to meet the expectations
of first-class passengers who are looking for unrivalled luxury and
space, not smaller rooms separated by heavy metal doors.[55]

Recovery Measure: The Number of Lifeboats

Early designs of the Titanic by Alexander Carlisle proposed a lifeboat for most onboard, but as these plans were discussed with
William Pirrie (for the White Star Line) and Francis Carruthers (for

the Board of Trade), it was eventually resolved to have 16 lifeboats plus four extra collapsible boats.[56] This was more than the 16 lifeboats the laws and regulations required at the time and allowed for up to 1176 passengers and crew in lifeboats at the same time.

So, why did the regulations allow fewer lifeboats than the simple formula 'one person, one lifeboat?' It was thought that lifeboats were primarily there to ferry passengers and crew from a stricken ship to another rescue vessel. Therefore, it did *not make sense to plan to put all the passengers and crew at the same time into lifeboats after an incident, especially since this might be in the context of stormy weather if the ship was in difficulty.* Furthermore, the Board of Trade was keen to encourage vessels to be built with watertight compartments, so they could 'be their own lifeboat' rather than having less well-built ships with more lifeboats. And the Titanic had state-of-the-art bulkheads for the time.[57]

This highlights that laws and regulations are not always a 'gold standard' to follow, and therefore, *being compliant with laws and regulations (as the Titanic was) does not mean you are inoculated from something disastrous happening to you.*

Recovery Measure: Lifeboat Trials and Crew and Passenger Behaviours

There were problems loading passengers into the lifeboats (especially in the early stages of evacuating passengers when it was not obvious the ship was in real jeopardy).[58] Some explain these shortcomings by highlighting that there was no full test of all the lifeboats before the maiden voyage. Others note that Captain Smith cancelled a lifeboat drill on the morning of the day that the Titanic struck the iceberg. However, numerous tests of the lifeboat cranes were carried out before the maiden voyage, including lowering several lifeboats down to the sea. The seaworthiness trials and some lifeboat tests were observed by Francis Carruthers, granting the Titanic approval to sail. With the benefit of hindsight, it became clear that these trials, and the level of regulatory oversight, were insufficient. However, this was not identified as a serious problem until after the Titanic disaster.

On top of these 'internal' measures to protect the Titanic and its crew and passengers, there were additional external recovery measures, that were not under the direct control of the Titanic, but that were nonetheless vitally important factors concerning what happened in the end; in particular, assistance from other ships in the vicinity.

Recovery Measure (External Factor): The RMS Carpathia and Captain Rostron

After the iceberg strike, Thomas Andrews (build supervisor of the Titanic from Harland & Wolff, who was on board as a passenger)[59] went down to inspect the damage to the hull. He ascertained that five watertight compartments had been damaged and realised that it was inevitable that the Titanic would sink.

He informed Captain Smith what was going to happen, and stressed the importance of starting an evacuation immediately, so Captain Smith initiated steps to launch lifeboats and, in parallel, asked the wireless operator, Jack Phillips, to issue a distress signal, explain the situation and position of the Titanic, and request assistance.[60] Several ships responded and began to head towards the Titanic; however, many were some distance away.

By 12.26 a.m., the RMS Carpathia, with Captain Rostron, set a course for the Titanic and travelled at full speed to rescue the passengers. The SS Mount Temple also set a course for the Titanic, but her progress was slow, hampered by ice floes.

The Carpathia was the first ship to reach the location of the Titanic at around 4.00 a.m., just over two and a half hours after the Titanic sank. She then spent the next few hours recovering passengers from the lifeboats. She was the only ship to collect survivors.

The Mount Temple arrived later that morning and picked up dead bodies in the water.

More distant ships that had been contacted that night eventually abandoned their rescue attempts after the Carpathia reported that she had picked up all survivors.

Recovery Measure (External Factor): The SS Californian and Captain Lord

The only other ship that came to the site of the sinking later that morning was the SS *Californian*, which, by most accounts, was the ship closest to the Titanic. So, why didn't the Californian come to the aid of the Titanic?

The Californian, captained by Stanley Lord, was en route to Boston. It encountered icebergs on its passage and had sent several warnings to other vessels about ice. Eventually, Captain Lord decided that there were too many icebergs surrounding the Californian to continue, and he decided to stop the ship where it was on the evening of 14 April. Shortly after this, at around 10.50 p.m., Cyril Evans, the radio operator of the Californian, sent out a message that it had stopped and was surrounded by ice. This message was received by Jack Philips, the radio operator for the Titanic.[61]

After sending other warning messages about ice, with the Californian stopped, Cyril Evans switched off the ship's radio equipment and went to bed. As a result, the Californian did not receive the radio distress messages sent by the Titanic later that night.[62]

After striking the iceberg and sending SOS messages to be rescued, the Titanic could see a ship on the horizon that had clearly not replied to the radio SOS messages. As a result, the crew of the Titanic sent up flares at intervals to signal she was in trouble.[63] The Californian crew's testimony was that flares were seen, and the sight of flares was relayed to Captain Lord. There was some confusion about whether these rockets were a distress signal, and attempts we made to clarify what was happening by Morse lamp,[64] the usual means of ship-to-ship communication at that time, which did not get a clear response.

One can reasonably ask why Captain Lord didn't ask the radio operator, Cyril Evans, to get up, turn on the radio set, and find out whether there was a problem with the ship. However, Captain Lord's testimony was that he would have ordered additional steps to be taken if he had thought a boat was in distress. From what he had seen earlier that night and later heard from his crew, he had no impression that the rockets were a distress signal. Furthermore, the crew of the Californian was convinced that the ship they could see was not the Titanic because it appeared to be a much smaller ship.[65] Also note that, at that time, radio was just coming into use, so it would not have been the only, or usual, means of communication between ships at that time.

It was not until the morning of 15 April, when Cyril Evans switched on the radio of the Californian, that it became clear what had happened to the Titanic. The ship made its way through the ice to the location of the sinking and arrived shortly after the Carpathia had picked up all the survivors.

The two inquiries disapproved of Captain Lord's conduct that night, and there were reports of his brusque style and the evasive manner in the inquiries. The outcome of the inquiries was that the lack of proactive action by the Californian may have caused more lives to be lost, but neither inquiry pressed charges against Captain Lord.[66] Furthermore, after these tragic events, fundamental changes were made to the way distress messages should be sent and received in future, highlighting there were shortcomings in the rules governing maritime communications.[67]

Recovery Measure: Missed Opportunities to Rescue Those in the Water

We know that many passengers and crew went down with the Titanic. Still, hundreds fell into the sea wearing lifejackets, and we know that there were a number of spaces available in several lifeboats because of how they were loaded, especially at the beginning. A few of those in the water were able to get into the collapsible lifeboats, but after that only a handful of those who fell into the water were hauled into the rigid lifeboats. Jack Thayer was one of the lucky ones who was rescued from the water; he said: 'The most heart-rending part of the whole tragedy was the failure, right after the Titanic sank, of those boats which were only partially loaded, to pick up the poor souls in the water. There they were, only four or five hundred yards away, listening to the cries, and still, they did not come back. If they had turned back, several hundred more would have been saved'.[68]

In the book '*Unsinkable*', the plight of those who had fallen into the water (in total darkness most of the time), hoping for rescue, was called 'the saddest act of the entire tragedy'.[69]

Accounts of what happened in the lifeboats suggest that while some wanted to go back to rescue those who were in the water (and at least one did), most passengers in the lifeboats appear to have been afraid that their lifeboats would be overwhelmed by desperate survivors in the water toppling the lifeboats, so they held back. And there is a heart-wrenching story of a man in the water being turned away from a lifeboat, saying 'Goodbye. God bless you all!' to the passengers; then sinking below the water.[70]

There is something very poignant about this final twist to the tale. Where spaces were available in a lifeboat, do we want to blame the passengers and crew for not acting? Or can we accept the human factor that many in the lifeboats were tired, traumatised and afraid of capsizing? Viewed from this perspective, it's not a complete surprise that not all were keen to act.

Here readers might be reminded of something discussed earlier in this book; you start an RCA expecting to find a problem in one direction, and then – like a boomerang – the causes rebound, calling into question the actions of those who are in so many ways blameless; in this case, some of the survivors.

Whatever your own perspective on this final question, it should be clear by now that the root causes for the Titanic tragedy put the simplistic 'blame the captain', 'blame the lookout', 'blame the design', 'blame the ship owner', 'blame the number of lifeboats' and 'blame the regulator' into a completely different light.[71]

However, I do appreciate that when you come up with this account of what happened, where no one has been identified as responsible, you can be left with a feeling that 'perhaps someone has got away with it?' This is always a possibility when you do an RCA; you can't look into the souls of all of those involved and know whether, deep down, malice (conscious or unconscious) was present. But, in any event, this would still not amount to finding a root cause but rather a contributing cause.

The Titanic Tragedy – Overall Root Causes

So, having considered many of the key elements of the Titanic tragedy, we can reframe what happened by looking at Illustration 12.2.

It wasn't just those 'in the thick of it' that fateful night who were the cause of the sinking of the Titanic and the terrible loss of life. You could say many involved that night were 'actors on the stage' of a Greek tragedy. A whole number of elements contributed to the death toll: the southern track route, the atmospheric conditions, the number of lifeboats, the design of the bulkheads, the regulations at the time, etc. Thus, to properly understand the root causes of the Titanic tragedy, you need to recognise many of the ingredients that led to this tragedy go back weeks, months and even years before April 1912.

Illustration 12.2   The Titanic tragedy

So, *don't just look at the actors on the stage; look at how the whole stage has been set.*

The Outcome of the Two Titanic Inquiries: SOLAS 1914

The key outcomes from the two inquiries were:

1. Many of the fundamental measures you would design, and put in place, to ensure the Titanic could make a safe voyage, were in place.
2. A series of what seemed to be relatively minor shortcomings ended up causing the loss of the Titanic within just a few hours and a catastrophic loss of life.
3. Although prepared to some extent, the captain, crew and even the passengers could not cope with a crisis of these proportions in such a compressed timescale.
4. Expectations for rescue by another ship were not sufficiently clear to compel a different response from the SS *Californian.*

As a result of the inquiries, it became clear there were more fundamental reasons why the Titanic tragedy turned out as badly as it did. Thus, the US Senate inquiry concluded with the following observation:

'We must change the admiralty and navigation laws of this country. They consist of an incongruous collection of antiquated statutes which should be repealed and re-enacted to meet the necessities . . . of the present day'.[72]

And the British Board of Trade inquiry proposed:

'Steps should be taken to call an International Conference to consider and, as far as possible, to agree upon a common line of conduct in respect of [Safety of Life at Sea]'.[73]

The Titanic tragedy was a wake-up call for the shipping industry, regulators, the public and politicians concerning maritime safety. As a result of the US and British inquiries, an international Safety of

Life at Sea (SOLAS) convention was held.[74] And afterwards, the first SOLAS treaty was published in January 1914, transforming the way maritime safety was managed across the world.[75]

Key areas addressed in the treaty included:

- A change in the southern track route and a new international ice patrol to look out for ice that might impact shipping;
- Mandatory speed limits when ships were in the vicinity of ice;
- New requirements around the design and construction of vessels (including sub-division arrangements and double-bottomed hulls);
- A requirement to have enough lifeboats for everyone on board and mandatory training exercises and inspections of both equipment and training records;
- New requirements around communications (including protocols concerning how information was conveyed and disciplines around the use of red flares and radios);
- More explicit expectations concerning the need to come to the aid of another craft (specifically addressing the problems that arose between the Titanic and the Californian);
- Improved safety certification regimes.[76]

SOLAS (with associated codes updated since the first treaty) is still in place to this day. It is managed by the International Maritime Organisation (IMO), its requirements evolve as maritime practice, and its associated risks change over time.[77]

Such a substantial change in laws and regulations is based on a mindset that says, 'We don't want to see the same or similar things happen again'. The Titanic tragedy is a reminder of how weaknesses in a regulatory framework, and its enforcement, can create an environment in which a catastrophic event can occur. But even the regulatory framework and regulator was sitting within the context of commercial, public and political expectations.

One analysis is that there was a clear systemic failure, and as a result, that night, the consequences were terrible. Another analysis is that the regime of maritime safety had hairline cracks and vulnerabilities that wouldn't merit the label of a systemic failure by most but were nonetheless important enough to require a fundamental reappraisal.

Other inquiries that have led to step changes in laws and regulations offer insights about what it really means to adequately address the root causes of something that has gone wrong; often setting new benchmarks around the design and operation of activities.[78] The history of construction, shipping, aviation, railways, etc., is defined by this sort of learning over decades. Inquiries that I have found to be illuminating from a general knowledge perspective are listed below. However, readers with an interest in other domains would undoubtedly have their own list of inquiries that are essential reading for anyone wanting to better understand root causes. Notable inquiries include:

- New London Texas Gas explosion (1937) – which made decisions to reform the rules around gas installations and gas odorants;[79]
- The Exxon Valdez oil spill (1989) – which was a game changer around the need for a double-hull design for most oil tankers, also highlighting numerous coordination, resourcing and preparedness matters to be improved as well as bridge resource management improvements;[80]
- 9/11 (2001) – with the overhaul of US homeland security arrangements and a range of what were, quite clearly, systemic-level changes (going far beyond just changes to aviation security);[81]
- Enron (2003) – with the Sarbanes Oxley regime for disclosure and financial reporting controls;[82]
- The financial crisis (2007–2008) – with updated capital adequacy, stress testing arrangements and a range of other regulations (e.g. the regime for senior officials), which I have already touched upon.

Each of these is worthy of note because of the way they kept 'the rules of the game' (i.e. the regulatory regime) within the scope of the inquiry and were prepared to make 'game changing' recommendations. And this is one of the reasons why regulators in aviation, transport, health and safety, medicine, etc., sometimes get directly involved in investigating serious incidents or ask to be notified of the outcome of any investigation.[83] That way they can, among other things:

(I) be confident that the correct root causes have been identified and

(II) consider whether changes in regulatory rules, guidance or their enforcement are needed.[84]

The Titanic Tragedy, in Summary: An RCA and Systems Analysis Perspective

The complexity of what happened in the Titanic tragedy is such that a complete causal loop diagram would be very elaborate (and too much to be contained within a single chapter in a book).

However, if we primarily focus on the question of preventing the Titanic from encountering icebergs, we can provide a high-level analysis by saying (1) it was known there needed to be a winter and summer track because (2) the southern track was needed avoids icebergs at certain times of year; however, (3) the southern track was affected by icebergs in April 1912, but even knowing this, (4) there was no mechanism at the time to alter the southern track, so (5) we had to rely on the crew to look out for ice (and in particular in April 1912) and (6) pass on the message to other ships, etc.

So, one way of 'seeing' what happened is to think of the preventative, detective and recovery measures that were put in place, which were supposed to act as 'lines of defence' to stop a disaster (i.e. as shown in Diagram 12.1), and see how these were undermined.

Diagram 12.3 illustrates how the Swiss cheese perspective (or a hairline cracks perspective) can explain what happened. As we can see, so many measures were in place to stop the worst from happening, and yet we still ended up with a terrible disaster.[85]

This illustration of all the measures that nearly worked, but didn't, highlights how little it would have taken to – most likely – drastically reduce the death toll. It is a powerful reminder that doing lots of good things does not prevent something terrible from

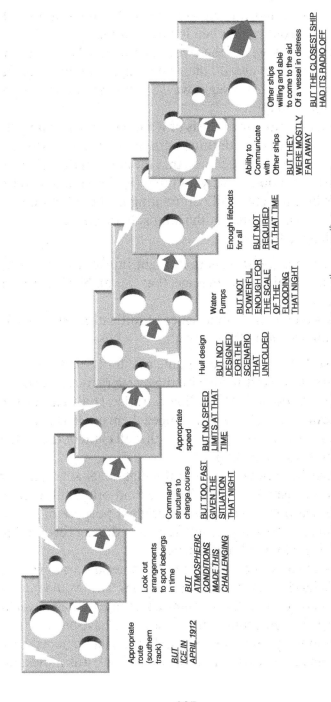

Appropriate route (southern track)
BUT ICE IN APRIL 1912

Look out arrangements to spot icebergs in time
BUT ATMOSPHERIC CONDITIONS MADE THIS CHALLENGING

Command structure to change course
BUT TOO FAST GIVEN THE SITUATION THAT NIGHT

Appropriate speed
BUT NO SPEED LIMITS AT THAT TIME

Hull design
BUT NOT DESIGNED FOR THE SCENARIO THAT UNFOLDED

Water Pumps
BUT NOT POWERFUL ENOUGH FOR THE SCALE OF THE FLOODING THAT NIGHT

Enough lifeboats for all
BUT NOT REQUIRED AT THAT TIME

Ability to Communicate with Other ships
BUT THEY WERE MOSTLY FAR AWAY

Other ships willing and able to come to the aid Of a vessel in distress
BUT THE CLOSEST SHIP HAD ITS RADIO OFF

Holes or 'hairline cracks' were revealed on 14th and 15th April 1912.

Diagram 12.3 The Titanic tragedy – many lines of defence in place happening – it all depends on what you did or did not do and how useful this turns out to be when it really counts.

But for all the power of the Swiss cheese model in Diagram 12.3, it still doesn't explain *why all these holes, or cracks, lined up the way they did*. This is where the eight ways to understand why, with connections, can be helpful.

So, if we pick up our analysis of what happened, from point (6) (just discussed), we can continue with more reasons for what happened, such as (7) the expectation that the crew on the bridge would take the needed action quickly and that (8) the Titanic will be able to turn her in time, etc. – all culminating in the difficulties seeing the iceberg sooner because of the atmospheric effects.

And what we find is that:

- it's sometimes the threats that might impact us the most, that are the most painful to envisage, that we can block out,[86] and for this reason,
- there is – inevitably – an absence of mitigating defences for the very thing we didn't think about.

As a result, it can often be a 'home run' for the catastrophic outcome, unless we are fortunate with the recovery measures available.

To illustrate how such a 'fault line' can arise, I have chosen some of the salient causes and effects and mapped them out in Diagram 12.4.[87] It should not be a great surprise to see that all eight of the eight ways to understand why were 'in play'.

What also becomes clear, from the high-level analysis, is to see how much the risks facing the Titanic (and other shipping at the time) increased hugely because the original purpose of the southern track (to provide a largely ice-free route during certain times of the year) was no longer holding true.

However, to alter the southern track route so it was even further south would have resulted in a longer journey. This would mean extra time at sea, extra cost for the shipping companies and an even longer journey for passengers, something most would have been reluctant to agree to without a good reason. So, sadly, the Titanic tragedy became the 'good reason', after which the southern track was moved further

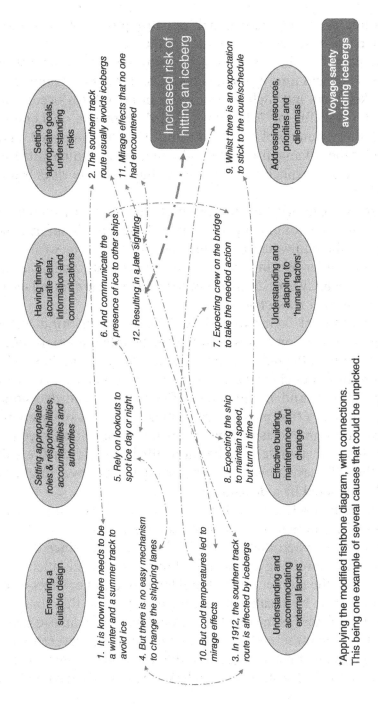

Diagram 12.4 Titanic tragedy – reducing the risk of encountering ice

*Applying the modified fishbone diagram, with connections.
This being one example of several causes that could be unpicked.

southwards, with the international ice patrol providing extra information to mariners about the location of the ice.

The parallels with what happens today should not be lost on readers. Time and time again, it takes a disaster to bring home that a low-likelihood, but high impact risk can nonethless occur. The Grenfell Tower fire of 2017, which killed 72 people, in London, was another example of this happening. The fire happened eight years after the Lakanal fire of 2009, also in London, which killed six people and gave explicit warnings about high-rise fire risks before Grenfell.[88]

Here, we can see that the mindset that says 'It's incredibly unlikely that this could happen; what we have done is surely good enough' is the equivalent of saying 'We don't need to wear seatbelts in the car' or 'We don't need fire insurance'. But, again, *the fact that the probability of an incident occurring is very low does not mean something terrible cannot happen.*

An additional factor that should be borne in mind is the asymmetry that often arises between the people who make decisions and those affected by their decisions. Very often, those who make important decisions are not the same people as those who will be directly and immediately affected by those decisions. This is not to say that most decision-makers do not sincerely try to make the right decisions based on the information given to them. However, people may be more likely to 'err on the side of caution' if they know that they, or ones they love, might be directly impacted by a decision.[89]

And, going back to what happened in April 1912, there was a mindset (i.e. a human factor) at the time that said: 'Why should ships go slower when there is ice? It's been decades since the last major disaster involving a passenger ship across the Atlantic!'

However, the momentum of the Titanic, or another super-sized ship, could have been calculated at a given speed at that time. So, the Board of Trade (as the regulator) would have been able to establish that if it did hit something at speed, it could have severely damaged the hull and breached many of the watertight compartments. As a result, through a stress test analysis, such as this, it could have been determined that the speed of the ship really did matter, especially in the vicinity of ice.

To highlight that it really didn't need to turn out this way, note that the Titanic was not the White Star Line's only super-sized passenger ship at that time. A sister ship, almost identical to the Titanic, the RMS *Olympic*, was built just before the Titanic. After the Titanic sank, she was refitted between October 1912 and April 1913, implementing a range of extra safety measures, including:

- Increasing the number of lifeboats from 20 to 68;
- Adding an inner watertight skin between the boiler and engine room;
- Extending five of the watertight bulkheads up to B-Deck;
- Adding an extra bulkhead to subdivide the electrical dynamo room, bringing the total number of watertight compartments to 17;
- Improving the ship's pumping equipment.

The Olympic was in service until 1935. Thus, the urban myths that the Titanic was too big or poorly designed and built are not a fair characterisation of what Harland & Wolff and the White Star Line did.

It's for this reason, and the memory of Captain Edward Smith and the crew and passengers of the Titanic and Captain Stanley Lord and those on the Californian, that I feel sad about simplistic, blame-oriented, accounts of the Titanic tragedy, which I still hear and read. Worse still, while you might understand a blame mindset in the days, weeks, months or early years after the tragedy; to have a relatively poor popular understanding of the root causes of the Titanic tragedy more than 100 years after highlights the step change we need to see in people's mindsets around root causes, which is why I have written this book.

The Titanic tragedy teaches us that no matter how many marvellous things we have done, no matter how new and bright and splendid a new creation is, if you encounter the wrong risk, at the wrong time, in the wrong place and the wrong conditions, all may be lost. And this even holds true even on a first attempt.

Risks are like wild animals; they don't wait their turn, and they don't give you the benefit of the doubt. If you turn your back for a second (and even if you don't), you are rolling the dice and may suffer catastrophic consequences.

The Titanic tragedy is an archetypal example of many things that were well done. Still, regarding some critical factors, a key, catastrophic type of risk was underestimated for a host of what seemed to be understandable reasons at that time.

While the world in which we now live seems relatively remote from 1912, I hope this explanation has provided a helpful reminder of why the Titanic story still has such a powerful hold on our collective imagination and why the lessons to be learned are still relevant in the twenty-first century. As discussed, the 9/11 attacks, the 2007–2008 financial crisis and the COVID-19 all highlight the problems that can arise when you think, 'That'll never happen'.

Time and time again, people prepare for a 'reasonable worst case' that is undercooked. This is why 'stress testing' techniques are so important. They are, rightly, a cornerstone of regulations in building and construction, engineering projects, financial services, etc.[90] However, stress tests, and reverse stress tests (where we test things to breaking point), are needed in a wider range of contexts because, too often, we see organisations run into problems and then hear, 'No one thought that something that bad could happen'.

Alongside this, as mentioned, there can be shortcomings in how accountabilities work when decision-makers say, 'We have done enough', when they may not be impacted by the consequences of their decisions. There are also questions about the role of regulatory frameworks and regulatory oversight because there is a growing list of examples where insufficient regulatory attention has been a factor in crises.

Of course, 99% of the time, the 'nightmare scenario' you plan for won't arise, and there are cost/benefit trade-off decisions to be made. Still, if we don't do realistic, thought-provoking, scenario analysis from time to time, we are increasing the chances of those in power making irreversible choices under pressure that they may end up sorely regretting with the benefit of hindsight.[91]

If Captain Smith had had the opportunity to be in a realistic but challenging bridge simulation in advance of the Titanic's maiden voyage, one can wonder what might have happened in April 1912. Sadly, that is in the past. However, future tragedies and setbacks that will arise after I have written this book are not.

We will never be able to stop all future disasters, surprises and setbacks, but I sense, and believe I detect a growing sense in the zeitgeist, that many people are tired of seeing the same old problems recurring. Given the scale and complexity of issues likely to be at stake in the future, we need more 'flight simulator' equivalents for business leaders, managers, politicians, regulators and others, so that they, and we, can be better prepared. We must 'step up our game', working smarter not just harder, to avoid 'deja vu all over again'.[92]

Section 3

Taking Action, Now and In the Future

I f you have come this far reading the book, I sincerely hope you have found some valuable insights from all the case studies and the discussions about their root causes. Clearly, however, in each case there is more that could have been unpacked, and many other case studies, covering different domains and different aspects of the eight cause types that I could have chosen.

But just because you know what the root causes are for a given problem that does not mean you will be able to address those causes. So, in this final section, I discuss:

In Chapter 13: The factors that are likely to be involved in terms of planning actions after a root cause analysis (RCA) or inquiry.

In Chapter 14: Reflections on the application of RCA and systems thinking to perennial and new challenges facing organisations and society.

This concludes the book for most readers. However, Appendices A–C may be a helpful resource for those with specific needs or in particular roles:

Appendix A: Offers more detailed advice around effective action planning.

Appendix B: Is primarily written for board members, executives and managers who want to upgrade their current RCA efforts. Therein I have provided more information about different RCA and systems analysis techniques.

Appendix C: Is primarily written for those in audit, internal audit, quality or supervisory roles.

Chapter 13

The Challenges
with Action Planning

Diagnosis, Then Treatment

When you think about significant disasters, such as the Titanic tragedy, 9/11, the 2007–2008 financial crisis, etc., you expect decision-makers will agree on actions to address the root causes. The magnitude of what has happened creates a clear 'burning platform', so, usually, decision-makers will support time and effort to address the root causes to avoid similar problems recurring. Put another way, a cost/benefit analysis is in favour of taking remedial action, even if this entails additional costs in the short run and disruption to the status quo.

Of course, root causes may be identified when less serious things go wrong. In these circumstances, there can be a debate about what action, if any, should be taken. In High Reliability Organisations (HROs), you would normally expect to see a small incident serve as an 'early warning sign' to galvanise decision-makers to act.

In other contexts, even regulated environments, if there is a minor incident, there can be tough negotiations about what action, if any, should be taken. The sort of argument and counterargument you might hear goes along the following lines:

'It's obvious we should act now; the near miss is an early warning sign that something much bigger could have gone wrong.

We should do something; otherwise, we have an accident waiting to happen', versus 'Perhaps there was a problem, but it was just a minor setback. Budgets are tight right now, and we have other, more pressing, goals. So, we can't embark on a costly remediation exercise to address something unlikely to result in a big problem in the near future'.

And, even when there have been significant problems, you can find some decision-makers reluctant to act. For example, in the United Kingdom, there have now been two reviews concerning the actions taken after various public inquiries (into a range of substantial issues). These reviews of public inquiry action proposals have identified that a number of the proposals were not implemented, with a relatively opaque understanding of why this is so. As far as I can tell, at the time of writing, the two reviews into action implementation and the additional actions they proposed have not demonstrably secured a 'step change' in what is done in the United Kingdom.[1] This raises questions about the value for money from inquiries and the risk of an element of 'theatre' with a limited appetite, or ability, to take determined action to address issues raised.

So, even if there are major setbacks, and especially if there appear to be just minor problems, you should not expect the process for agreeing to actions to be straightforward:

- First, there may be questions about whether the right causes have been identified.
- Second, there may be questions about the importance of the issue or risk.
- Third, there may be discussions about the likely cost/benefit case for different courses of action.
- Fourth, there may be questions about who will act.
- Fifth, there may be practical choices to make to track progress in fixing things.

A medical analogy might help: We have a diagnosis stage; why is the patient ill?; then we have the treatment options stage, and what course of treatment will the patient agree to take? etc.

Seen this way, we realise that a patient is entitled to say: 'No, I don't want that treatment; it's too disruptive, too expensive'. It also reminds us that the patient might start a course of treatment and then give up. And finally, we should remember that, despite our best efforts in diagnosis and treatment, the disease may evolve or the treatment may not work.

Diagram 13.1 highlights the various stages that follow a root cause analysis (RCA) investigation or inquiry. Phase 1 covers the core RCA; Phase 2 highlights the options for action; Phase 3 illustrates implementing actions; Phases 4 and 5 reminds us we should ensure the risk we were concerned about is now appropriately 'under control'. Thus, even with a *good RCA or inquiry, this does not guarantee the proper actions will be taken and sustained or that they will work.*

RCAs and inquiries, done well, may 'reach the parts other problem-solving techniques cannot'. However, they still won't solve the stakeholder management and influencing challenges that can arise. This is one of the reasons I spend time working with clients on political savvy and influencing skills.

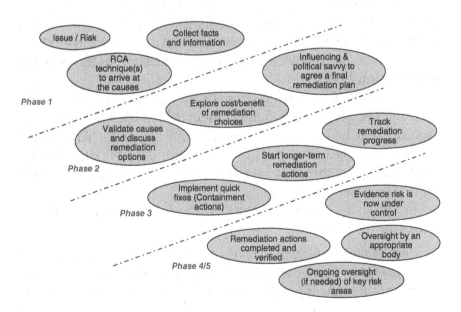

Diagram 13.1   RCA does not ensure everything will get fixed

Be Prepared for Not All Root Causes to Be Addressed

You only need to think about some of the case studies in this book to recognise that 'there's many a slip twixt cup and lip' when it comes to achieving the goals you want, and this applies equally to agreeing and sustaining remedial action after an RCA investigation or inquiry.

Here is an account of an incident investigation that I was involved in where we could not agree on what seemed to be an 'obvious' action,

One of my clients had a serious health and safety incident involving two relatively inexperienced members of staff who were hospitalised because of underestimating a risk, combined with the fact that their supervisor was called away to attend to another urgent and important matter. Initially, the head of health and safety set up a team to look at what had happened, but the chief executive recognised a potential conflict of interest – after all, could a head of health and safety carry out a wholly unbiased and objective review in an area where the role and actions of the health and safety team were, potentially, something that needed to be considered? As a result, the Chief Audit Executive (CAE) was asked to get involved, and he contacted me to support the investigation.

The health and safety department led the investigation, but the CAE and I played a role in helping them 'widen their horizons' and capture what had happened (positive and negative). This helped explain a complex story relatively simply; it gave the organisation credit for many things it had done well while highlighting the 'cracks' that had let it down.

In summary, the RCA identified the following key facts and causes for the incident:

- Despite the temptation to blame the supervisor, given all the circumstances, there was no deliberate intention by them to cause any harm to the injured members of staff or neglect their work.

Likewise, the members of staff involved thought they were showing some initiative doing some preparatory work ahead of schedule, but – for a range of reasons – this was unwise and triggered the accident.

- While the injured staff had been trained on health and safety basics when they joined the organisation, they should also have had refresher training through a new e-learning course. This would have covered, in general terms, the sort of risk that led to the accident.

- However, the staff concerned had not done their additional e-learning training at the time of the accident, although they had been reminded to take it by their depot manager. This happened for several reasons, including the workload of the staff and the fact that the depot manager did not have access to the e-learning system to check what training had been completed by their team members.

- The question of who should check that staff had been trained resulted in an argument between health and safety (the policy owner), HR (who managed the e-learning system) and the depot manager; a typical roles, responsibilities, accountabilities and authorities (R2A2) problem at an operational level.

- We also established that even if the staff had done the e-learning training, its contents did not spell out, in detail, the scenarios that could lead to an incident.[2] It also did not sufficiently explore which tasks needed to be 'actively supervised' by a manager (such that the staff should probably not have acted until their depot manager returned). And, while it's impossible to be sure, the CAE and I thought that the health and safety team would have been unlikely to identify this shortcoming in the e-learning without some independent challenge.[3]

At the end of the investigation, five actions were proposed:

1. The creation of a framework for the implementation of the health and safety policy (i.e. the practical steps to make sure the policy

would be operational) – a design and change management recommendation;

2. More explicit roles and responsibilities concerning the supervision of staff training and enabling depot managers to have access to the e-learning training system to see who had been trained – an R2A2 recommendation, with a human factors aspect;

3. Manager targets to make sure their staff had been trained by a deadline – an information recommendation with a human factors component;

4. A new face-to-face training programme for managers and staff working in higher-risk areas (to cover higher risks in more detail than would be possible in an e-learning training) – another human factors recommendation, with resource implications;

5. Using the insights from the health and safety incident, we identified the need to improve the implementation of a range of other policies, e.g. data privacy, information security, etc. (where there was no e-learning training at the time, nor timely tracking of training and staff understanding) – a change management recommendation with R2A2 and resource implications.

Actions 1–4 were accepted and implemented, with the additional face-to-face health and safety training requiring a substantial amount of time, cost and effort, but agreed upon without any significant resistance. However, regarding the wider learnings for other policy areas (point 5), we were told that although there might be broader lessons to learn, it was felt there was no 'burning platform' to justify these changes straight away.

At the time, I was somewhat taken aback by the decision to reject our fifth recommendation; but over the years, I have come to expect this when doing an RCA. No matter how 'obvious' it seems that broader lessons should be learned, decision-makers will not always prioritise the issues you think are important. They have other challenges and priorities, and you should expect the outcome of an RCA and recommended actions to be subject to the same cost/benefit thought process as other proposals.

A Paradox at the Heart of an RCA or Inquiry Scope

So, if you reflect on the depth and breadth of an inquiry or RCA and the actions you might take afterward, you can face the following dilemma:

- If you know you have a limit on the resources for an RCA and remediation actions, you can focus the scope of any RCA work and do it quite quickly, but you may miss other important improvement opportunities;
- If you have an ambitious scope, this should maximise the chances that all the principal root causes will be uncovered so that numerous improvement actions will be proposed.[4] But this (i) increases the time, effort and cost required, and (ii) increases the chances that a more comprehensive set of actions may not be taken up.

The more significant the issue that is being looked at, the more this will suggest you should have a 'gold-plated' RCA or inquiry; and this is why air crash investigations (e.g. by the US National Transportation Safety Board) and public inquiries into major disasters can be very high quality, with a sufficiently broad scope to get at crucial causal factors, wherever they are located. However, if resources are constrained or there are other priorities or there are political dynamics in play, it is not unusual to be disappointed with inquiry scopes, and getting proposed actions agreed and implemented.

Some Strategies for Overcoming Barriers to Action

The steps required to overcome resistance to action will be many and varied, but the following accounts are offered to illustrate some of the challenges that can arise and how they might be overcome.

Before Doing an RCA, Clarify with Stakeholders What Level of Commitment (and Budget) There Might Be to Taking Action

On a couple of occasions, I have been involved in 'calling out' the danger of an RCA as 'theatre', with conversations along the following lines: 'Before we spend a lot of time and effort doing the RCA, and raising expectations things will be improved, are you prepared to follow-through? Because there are many who strongly suspect this problem is associated with old systems and poor cooperation with Department X. So, unless you are prepared to act on the findings, it is highly likely that those involved will end up being demotivated if nothing changes. Worst still, they may see the RCA shift into a blame game. So, are we OK to proceed with a commitment to just culture principles, investing in systems changes, etc., if the evidence merits this?'

This sort of questioning has sometimes surprised managers but has usually yielded a greater appreciation of the downside effect of just seeing RCA as a necessary evil, leading to little change. Most of all, you want to avoid a culture in which those involved in RCAs or inquiries, who might be hoping for meaningful improvements, become disenchanted with the gap between rhetoric and reality.

When Decision-Makers Argue That a Problem Doesn't Deserve to Be Addressed – Consider Potential Impacts

Here it's important to remember *the difference between actual problems and potential future problems*. Here, good practice can include extrapolating what has been found to overcome resistance to change.

For example, Project X went $50,000 over budget against a total budget of $2.5 million (i.e. 2% over) because expenditure commitments weren't tracked. To solve this required, among other things, a cost tracking tool that would cost $50,000 to build. But management thought it was not worth implementing the change because the cost of developing the new tool and the benefit were the same.

However, we took the 2% overspend and asked the question; what if this issue was repeated across other projects? And we established that there were projects with a cumulative budget of $50 million. So, with a potential error of 2% error across all the projects, this could mean we might save as much as a $1 million (i.e. 2% of $50 million) for an investment of $50,000. In this light, the new tool to track commitments was recognised to be worthwhile, not least because it would also follow project commitments each year into the future.

Consider External Sources of Information and 'Killer Facts'

We discovered a problem with data privacy that required $200,000 to fix (IT system changes, training and monitoring). This needed to be approved at a committee meeting involving various senior managers, and there was a clear message that funds were limited. So, we looked at some of the data privacy fines levied recently on other companies. One was several million dollars for a similar problem. We used this information about the penalty on other organisations to make the risk and potential loss more real (sometimes called a 'killer fact' because it kills off arguments). As a result, we got approval for most of the extra budget we wanted. The theoretical risk became tangible and quantified rather than generic. Also, management could see, in terms of a potential news headline, how much greater the downside would be if they didn't act.

So, if decision-makers don't seem to be taking an RCA issue seriously, consider the following: 'Perhaps the reason they are not acting isn't that they are being stubborn. Maybe it's because they don't think the problem is that big.' Unless you can join up the dots, and make an issue, near miss or risk more pointed, more real, *decision-makers will just make their typical cost/benefit trade-off decision, in which the issue you are raising doesn't seem that significant; unless you show otherwise.*

Other Considerations

There are many other matters concerning effective action planning, such as:

- Tools and techniques for determining good action plans;
- The importance of going beyond staff briefing sessions and training courses;
- Addressing dependencies on third parties;
- How quickly actions should be completed;
- How actions might be tracked.

However, to keep this discussion focused on key messages, I have added further guidance in Appendix A, at the end of this book, for those who want to learn more.

I'll leave a closing thought on action planning to Stephen Foster (holder of SVP positions in Finance, Audit and Compliance) who highlights the need to balance robust solutions with practical considerations:

'There is an interesting line to tread when it comes to thinking about the improvement actions after an RCA investigation. On the one hand, the RCA team needs to discuss ideas for remediation with the people who are managing, or operating, an area to understand what they think about different options. That way, you should understand the detailed practicalities of what might be involved to effect change and sustain it over time.

But on the other hand, talking to the people closest to the current situation can also be a limit on the options that will be preferred. This is because people often work in a role, a structure and a culture they are used to, and see as being the norm so, understandably, and with no sense of malice, they can't always be relied upon to give you a completely neutral perspective on what actions to prioritise and what will work for the long term. They will want their problems solved as a priority.

In this context, you must bear in mind that no matter how much you think you know the "right" solution to a problem, you still must understand and question how much you can push the organisation to take action it doesn't want to, or is unable to take at that point in time – a common dilemma of prioritisation.

I'm all for high standards in RCA, but I'd generally counsel making progress with genuine buy-in and then move on from there, rather than "over-egg" something and end up with the organisation becoming fatigued with implementing solutions. Though not always appropriate, progress rather than perfection should be the initial goal of change.'

Chapter 14

Where Are We Now and Looking Ahead

'. . . problems are solved, not by . . . new information, but by arranging what we have known since long'.

– Ludwig Wittgenstein[1]

To conclude this book, a few final comments concerning:

- Where are we now;
- Advice if you want to make improvements in your working environment (if applicable);
- Other areas to watch out for, as we look to the future.

Where Are We Now: Going Beyond the Five Whys

Everything I have been able to share in this book is a testimony to years of hard work and dedication to root cause analysis (RCA) and systems analysis by countless professionals in High-Reliability

229

Organisations and elsewhere (e.g. engineering, quality, medicine, internal audit, etc.).

I hope this book makes it clear that the 'pure' five whys, searching for just one root cause, is a technique that we seriously need to think about retiring in the twenty-first century. I say this because although asking why is central to any RCA, the notion that there is a just one root cause, or a main root cause, can be problematic because of the way it effectively 'turns its back' on systemic considerations. In my experience, it often constrains and limits the thinking of those who get attached to the idea of finding a 'main root cause'.

Fortunately, a narrow understanding of the five whys technique has been left behind by most experienced RCA practitioners, who use the five whys two legs, three-way five whys, the Bowtie, the fishbone, fault tree diagrams or other techniques. This is why this book has been entitled *Beyond the Five Whys*. In each case, these other RCA techniques take the power of asking why but provide a much richer sense of why things can go wrong and what we might do to avoid problems in the future. So, the saying, 'The future is already here – it's just not evenly distributed'[2] rings true when it comes to RCA.

Having said this, my RCA work with clients over the past decade tells me that RCA techniques without a clear and explicit systems thinking perspective can be limited when seeking to get a full understanding of what has happened. This is why I developed the 'eight ways to understand why, with connections' (modified fishbone, with causal loops) technique outlined in this book.

And there are many other systems analysis tools and techniques (such as FRAM, SEIPS, STAMP, etc.) that I have not been able to cover in detail, but which are worth learning about. So, to this end, I have included, in Appendix B, a range of materials and links that can be a springboard for learning about other RCA and systems analysis techniques.

I want to stress, however, that readers should be mindful of getting attached to any particular RCA or systems thinking tool or technique, or combination thereof. And this includes the 'eight ways to understand why, with connections' in this book. I think it's a powerful technique and hope readers have found it to be a helpful 'entrée' into this topic; but neither it, nor any other technique in my opinion, represents 'the last word' on RCA and systems thinking.[3]

My firm view is that as we consider opportunities and threats, in organisations and the wider world, we should use, or pilot, whichever RCA and systems analysis tools and techniques that might help us. Thus, I strongly advocate being 'multilingual' in terms of different RCA and systems analysis tools and techniques. If you don't do this there is a chance you will stay in a single-loop learning comfort zone, using what you like and what seems to work, but not necessarily getting fresh perspectives that may challenge and evolve your preferred approach.

Making Improvements in Your Working Environment (If Applicable)

For those in managerial, governance, risk, compliance (GRC), or internal audit, supervisory or inspection roles, I hope there is sufficient that is fresh and new that you can calibrate, or recalibrate, where your organisation sits in relation to RCA and systems thinking. Having done this, it should be possible to apply some of the insights from this book as follows:

- To proactively improve what is currently done on projects, policies, processes, etc., to head off potential problems.
- To improve current RCA practice in your organisation or team, either spreading good practice more widely or building new RCA capabilities (hopefully with a systems thinking component).

Because the detailed steps to build RCA and systems analysis capabilities in an organisation or team may only interest some readers, Appendix B contains guidance for managers and GRC professionals, and Appendix C contains guidance for internal auditors and those in supervisory or inspection roles.

Things to Consider, Taking a Broader Perspective, and Looking at Current and Future Challenges

RCA and systems thinking tools and techniques can be used to give us some fresh perspectives on the challenges we face in the twenty-first century. Some readers may already have their own views on specific areas where things might be improved, but here is a summary of points you might want to look for, and perhaps even call out, if the circumstances arise.

Think Twice About Magic Bullet Solutions

Many of us like the idea of simple solutions to complex problems, but history teaches us that there are many reasons why 'magic bullet' solutions (e.g. programmes, projects, policies, etc.) can disappoint.[4] So, be prepared to ask:

- What has been done, or will be done, to test the feasibility of proposed solutions, especially if there is an 'overarching goal' (e.g. with AI, climate change, etc.)?
- What dilemmas and constraints might be underestimated (e.g. a cost savings programme but a desire to keep standards high; or green energy plans [such as wind farms and dams] that may damage natural habitats if they are built)?
- At what points will we get any early warnings any plan might be harder to deliver than we thought?

Remember, as well, that solutions, tools, techniques, etc., proposed by consultants, service providers and even academics, may, consciously or unconsciously, downplay costs, risks and limitations.

Look Out for Human Factors, Including Games Regarding Progress Updates and 'Rabbit Out of the Hat' Excuses

Remember that it's inevitable to hear the message 'look at all the progress we have made' but also pay attention to the question of 'how much we still have to do'. This is important to bear in mind when we hear broad brush messages that suggest a homogenous picture, such as 'We're winning the hearts and minds of people'. Human Factors thinking tells us that people do not respond like clones, there will be enthusiasts, detractors and then those in the middle. And there will be others who try to bypass, or game, rules or new initiatives.

Watch out for the classic 'rabbit out of a hat' excuse when things don't go to plan, i.e. 'We could never have foreseen this reason for a setback'. For example, in early 2023, some Central Banks said, 'We could not have foreseen that inflation would be high; this is due to external factors that no one could predict'. [5] To which the RCA and systems thinking response might be, 'Of course, you could not have predicted the COVID-19 (CV19) pandemic or the war in Ukraine. Still, you could have recognised *something* might come along that would knock things off track. So, what stress testing had you done to prepare for something unexpected, and do you think it was adequate?'

Also bear in mind the way in which past 'solutions' may be playing a role in current problems. Continuing the example of inflation rates in 2023: Is it possible that action, or inaction, by Central Banks in previous years has played a role in what we are seeing now (e.g. quantitative easing)? Is it possible Central Banks underestimated how difficult it might be to 'turn the ship' with interest rate rises as well as the spin-off consequences on some financial institutions if rates were changed quickly?'[6]

Are Managers and Leaders Claiming Short-Term Success at the Expense of the Long Term?

Reliability-centred maintenance tells us that if we don't carry out regular inspections, maintenance for things that we build and invest in capability and skills on an ongoing basis, we are likely to be storing up problems down the line.[7]

So, if you are looking at the performance of a manager or leader, consider how much of their short-term success might be at the expense of problems in the future? For example, at the time of writing this book, in mid-2023, it was established the UK Environment

Agency in England has allowed several dams not to be repaired for up to eight years.[8] I am not suggesting the UK Environment Agency is to blame for this since it might say, if it could speak freely, it is constrained by government policy, priorities and budget commitments, and – voila! – we see systemic factors are in play again. Nonetheless, a lapse in a regular repair programme is a ticking time bomb.

In addition, safe staffing principles tell us we need minimum staffing levels for areas that matter, both customer facing and with back-office staff (e.g. in finance, compliance, quality and audit, but also research and development and staff capability building). So, when leaders and managers' report progress in meeting budgets, and meeting efficiency goals, do we really understand the difference between modest 'belt tightening' and 'cutting to the bone'? There are far too many examples of people reporting successes (and being rewarded for this) while fraud risks, quality issues and environmental issues build up 'off the books' due to a lack of checks and balances.[9] Likewise, there are too many organisations suffering from skills and capability gaps and a dearth of innovations in products, services and processes because these areas are neglected, often with no warning signs until, sometimes, it's too late.

So, ask what 'warning mechanisms' have been put in place to detect whether standards are slipping or long-term opportunities are being lost? And ask how reward and recognition programmes do not incentivise the wrong sort of short-term behaviour by managers or leaders?

Beware of Leaders and Narratives That Won't Entertain Doubt

As I have tried to stress throughout this book, the human factor is incredibly pervasive and impacts many things. This explains how we can sometimes deceive ourselves and thus look at facts and evidence selectively, thanks to 'confirmation bias'. So, we need to have a 'Scout mindset' that is curious and prepared to seek alternative perspectives on complex issues.[10]

However, some leaders behave as if they have no doubts and some even believe they have all the answers. They often feel this very sincerely because they have convinced themselves they are right. For this reason, they can be great at persuading others. But, if you find yourself thinking that you, or someone else, or some organisation has a definitive formula that resolves all doubts and has solutions for everything, you need to recognise this as a warning sign since it may reflect a single-loop learning mindset. In these circumstances, 'inconvenient truths' are dismissed, and you can find increasingly bizarre excuses for things that are happening.

Embracing double-loop learning (and RCA and systems thinking) will mean you are prepared to see some valued ideas and paradigms challenged, refined, changed or even overturned. And I can say that, in the process of writing this book (and sharing the draft manuscripts with others), I have been forced to fundamentally rethink a range of points that I thought were 'sorted' several years ago (e.g., the exact number and types of the eight ways to understand why).

So, despite my passion for the eight ways to understand why, and the tools and techniques I have been sharing, I know this book is just part of an ongoing conversation with others, hopefully helping us to better tackle the challenges we face now and will face in the future.

Expect Higher Standards from RCA Investigations and Inquiries and Watch Out for the Blame Game

Much time and effort can go into investigations and inquiries when things go wrong or nearly go wrong. However, unless we ensure that they are conducted to the highest standards, incorporating RCA and systems thinking good practices and conscious of conflicts of interest (which are much more prevalent than many like to believe), they may not correctly tackle the 'why' questions to support meaningful change.[11]

Especially watch for:

- Clarity around how the scope in and out was established?
- How the ingredients of time, cost and quality for the RCA or inquiry were determined?[12]

- Whether there is a clear, robust, just culture framework, so people don't get scapegoated?
- How operational level accountabilities were managed and will be improved?
- Even if someone was found to be responsible for a problem, how broader lessons around prevention, detection (supervision), recovery, etc., will be learned alongside this?

Pay More Attention to How 'The Stage Is Set'

Beyond the physical and material world that we live in, there are structures, customs and norms that 'hide in plain sight' that we often barely notice.[13] These structures and norms impact our ability to see and engage with forces that may be pulling us off track. These become more obvious as you develop a mindset that thinks systemically.

For example, even radio and TV panel discussions intended to get to the bottom of issues and hold people to account can be inadvertently 'staged' in a way that may limit getting to a deeper understanding of critical issues.

The obvious point is when interviews on serious topics are repeatedly constrained to just five or ten minutes of discussion. The very format of the programme acts as a limit to what is discussed and not discussed. A notable example of this came on a radio programme a few years ago, when an interviewer asked, 'What's the one thing we should do to address climate change?' to which the response was 'Stop thinking the solution to climate change can be found in just one thing!' Of course, as we appreciate, there is a dilemma here, because not everyone will want to hear half an hour devoted to a given topic. But the key thing is to *see the choices, constraints and dilemmas* being made, reflect on whether they are helping or hindering, and be prepared to call them out on occasion.

Other areas for improvement in relation to news and current affairs include:

(I) how fact-checking does or does not work as statements are made (it's encouraging to see this is improving in various media organisations, e.g. the BBC);

(II)   the need to be more precise about the difference between immediate, contributing and root causes;

(III) whether human factors thinking and just culture principles are operating;

(IV)   the absence of explicit root cause and systems analysis discussions or showing causal loop diagrams (e.g. how much inflation is caused by which factors?).

Of course, these points apply even more strongly to social media, online forums and some news media, which have – rightly – been highlighted as areas of concern by many.

Beyond radio and TV there are other bodies and factors that play a significant role in defining our lives, including local and national governments, educational institutions, commercial and not for profit organisations, laws, traditions, customs, practices, etc. Some of these will be serving us well and some less so; which is why healthy, open, debate and discussion about a range of topics and institutions has such an important role to play.

Moreover, we must watch for the risk that open systems (and constitutional arrangements for government) are not eroded or undermined by Machiavellian forces, President George Washington predicted this risk clearly in his farewell address, 'However [political parties] may now and then answer popular ends, they are likely in the course of time and things, to become potent engines, by which cunning, ambitious, and unprincipled men will be enabled to subvert the power of the people and to usurp for themselves the reins of government, destroying afterwards the very engines which have lifted them to unjust dominion'.[14]

Has the Thinking and Level of Discussion About Strategic and Endemic Problems Got to the Right Level?

Where countries have experienced long-standing challenges with crime, drug taking, illegal immigration, habitat destruction, etc., consider whether a systems-based analysis has been carried out to understand why it's proving hard to make progress. The chances are that assumptions are being made or factors are being excluded, which means it will be impossible to achieve any wanted step change. This takes us back to a fundamental truth that *trying to solve complex problems as if they were complicated ones is almost guaranteed to result in frustration and more problems.*[15]

Looking at the infrastructure investments we will need to make to help prepare the world for the inevitable climate changes that are already (sadly) baked in: Are enough steps being taken to design resilience (e.g. thermal properties of buildings, solar panels, EV charge points, avoiding the risk of flooding, etc.)? After all, if we don't think about these issues now, think of the cost and disruption we will face in the decades ahead upgrading, rebuilding or relocating facilities.

For poorer nations, there are starker challenges just feeding, housing and educating their populations, never mind addressing resilience issues. However, the consequences of this are that longer-term risks are building that we know about in general terms (e.g. deforestation and dependency on fossil fuels), but that few people, if any, have properly got their arms around. Partly this may be because of the time and effort it would take to collect the data, but it may also be due to a fear that this data will show the problems we face on a far greater scale than anyone wants to see.

There is interesting work going on in various institutions (such as Cambridge, UK, and Stamford, USA) and a range of international bodies, including in the UN, looking at some of the existential threats that we face.[16] However, it's worth noting that, generally, *they tend to highlight 'tangible' threats* (e.g. climate change, pandemic risks, AI, etc.) *rather than the underlying causal factors in play* (e.g. resource and skills constraints, role gaps, conflicts, etc.) that span across domains. This may be because we currently think of expertise in pre-defined domains rather than in a more 'free range' cognitive diversity terms. And, again, the human factor of our mindsets is likely to be involved, highlighted by Thomas M Nichols in his book *'Our Own Worst Enemy'*.[17]

Alongside all of this, we should be encouraging more explicit sharing of causal loop diagrams with one another, as an aid to discussion and debate. Fortunately, at the time of finishing this book in summer 2023, there are signs systems analysis tools are being increasingly used to understand 'complex and wicked' problems:

- Concerning CV19: 'Developing a preliminary causal loop diagram for understanding the wicked complexity of the COVID-19 pandemic'.[18]
- Concerning climate change and bioenergy: 'Using systems thinking and causal loop diagrams to identify cascading climate change impacts on bioenergy supply systems'.[19]
- Concerning child poverty in Scotland: 'Child poverty system map'.[20]

No Organisation or Person Should Be 'Above' the Need to Learn

As we look forward, it should be evident how important it is to have a fact-based learning frame of mind if we are going to address future challenges. Thus, all of us need to accept (i) we may have only a partial perspective on significant issues and (ii) we may have a bias around who we think needs to act, which may act as a barrier to improving things. Mannie Sher (Principal Consultant, the Tavistock Institute) explains:

> 'When working with an organisation where things haven't gone to plan, remember there is a context in which blockages have arisen. Organisations don't operate in a vacuum. They are subject to rules and regulations created by others and regulated by others as well as their internal policies and procedures. So, regulators, and other bodies, may be an important part of the context in which problems arise.
>
> However, it can be tempting for regulators, politicians or others to want to stay above the fray. Consequently, they may want to stay outside any review evaluating past performance. They are consciously or unconsciously avoiding responsibility for what happened. They sometimes have projected into them the role of persecutor, as in the recent case involving OFSTED and a school

head, Ruth Perry, who is believed to have taken her own life after an adverse OFSTED review.[21]

Here a specific shortcoming in record keeping was rated as highly significant, thus "wiping out" many good aspects of the way the school was run. As a result, the school was given an unsatisfactory overall rating which created a dynamic that was experienced as an unfair judgement. In this situation, people have claimed that the regulator was responsible for what happened by virtue of distilling a complex organisational process into a single rating, and therefore OFSTED should be reformed or disbanded.[22]

Understandably, people are concerned when things don't go well, but we need to be mindful of a blame mindset in all the parties involved. Otherwise, we will never resolve the challenging problems of society. You need a mindset that is open to the possibility that while each stakeholder, including the school board of governors, the government, which sets the OFSTED terms of reference, etc., may hold a valuable perspective on potential solutions, and equally, each may also be part of the problem.

In my experience, it's getting all the parts (or representatives) of an extended system into the same room at the same time, to review, evaluate and debate as equals, that offers us the greatest hope of solving perennial problems.'

If we follow this line of argument, it means that *some of the organisations that exist to help the world solve its problems* (e.g. the United Nations, World Economic Forum, Non-Governmental Organisations, regulators and even charities, etc.) *need to consider the way their own roles and objectives, etc., may need to be 'in' the scope of any diagnosis of the perennial problems we face.*

'The Journey of a Thousand Miles Begins with One Step' – Lao Tzu

I started conceiving this book in earnest four years ago at a writer's workshop.[23] And I hope that what I, and the others who have contributed to the book, have shared has been enough to encourage some new thinking and offered some practical steps to take.

Perhaps it may encourage those working in schools, universities and business schools to cover these topics in more detail.[24] As I hope I have shown, many of the insights from these techniques can be used in a range of contexts and should not be left only to specialists.

I hope individual efforts to address critical areas of concern, whether in our role as citizens or as managers and leaders in organisations, may cumulatively help to shift things in a better direction. However, I appreciate individual action may seem to be just a 'drop in the ocean' and not amount to much. Indeed, the temptation to 'get on with our lives' or 'get on with business', leaving systemic problems to be solved by politicians and other leaders, is understandable. But if we do this, we are likely to find ourselves disappointed with what others have, or have not, done and say, 'How on earth did *they* get us into this mess?' In this case, we have the blame game again, and we are not going to learn to address the many challenges facing the world, some of which are existential in nature. Illustration 14.1 illustrates, in simple terms, the choice that lies ahead.

Illustration 14.1   The choices ahead

I hope we will remember the words of all those who have reminded us not to succumb to a fatalistic frame of mind. As Susan Scott said, 'Remember that what gets talked about and how it gets talked about determines what will happen. Or it won't happen. And that we succeed or fail, . . . , one conversation at a time'.[25]

In conclusion, I want to share something I learned at a leadership development workshop that I have often found to be helpful: 'Managers work in the system, whereas leaders work on the system'. Now is the time to ask ourselves what we can do to make a positive difference. The clock is most certainly ticking.

Appendix A

Practical Advice on Action Planning

'Most of the problems in life are because . . . we act without thinking, or we keep thinking without acting'.

– after Zig Zaglar[1]

As explained in Chapter 13, the factors that can impact action planning include:

1. Accepting that the scope of a root cause analysis (RCA) or inquiry may impact the root causes found.
2. Recognising there are invariably choices around what actions to take after an RCA or inquiry. This often involves some cost/benefit assessment.
3. Being mindful that *'near misses' and risks need to be considered in terms of what might have happened, not simply what just happened.* Otherwise, minor issues that are early warning signs of something much bigger will not be heeded.

This appendix provides additional, practical advice concerning:

- The types of actions that are more and less likely to address root causes.
- The importance of going beyond just training courses.
- Agreeing timescales for remediation and tracking progress.
- Validating the closure of action plans.

The Types of Actions That Are More and Less Likely to Address Root Causes

Some actions are more likely to address root causes than others. Table A.1 sets out some pros and cons of different types of actions.

Table A.1 The Pros and Cons of Different Corrective Actions

Examples of corrective actions	Pros and cons
Remind staff what to do by email, newsletter or via an intranet	May be quickly forgotten, especially when the workload is high.
Regularly train staff on what they need to do	It is more likely to be remembered, but staff may find it boring after a while (which needs to be checked).
	It may not address practical challenges. However, case studies of real, interesting events can significantly improve the impact of this sort of activity.
Run workshops or coaching sessions to discuss real world challenges	It may provide specific, tailored help, but great care is needed around the dynamics of any group meetings so people can speak openly.
Offer tools and checklists to guide better decision-making	It may help if staff have the time and have said they would find this helpful. These short checklists need to be a living document where users are engaged in the design, use and how they are updated.

Examples of corrective actions	Pros and cons
Implement double-checks or reviews on occasion with a supervisor	Essential to be clear whether double-checking is going to be preventative, detective or recovery. Role clarity and understanding of what the second check is doing will be necessary. If selected, preventative checking should be based on materiality or risk (e.g. payments above X or certain medical procedures or reviewing critical installations).
Offer incentives/penalties for better or less good performance	Shows the matter is being taken seriously, creates an incentive for others to call out poor behaviour, but may also encourage suppression of problems (e.g. due to no breach targets). Incentives for proactive openness about issues and timely action can work well.
Discipline or remove staff	Unless implemented in the context of a 'just culture' framework, it may lead to a fear culture. Also note that if disciplinary action is kept 'below the radar screen', relevant staff will not know what has been done. Therefore, there may be no deterrent effect in practice.
Conduct ethical phishing, mystery shopping or other 'real world' checks on what is happening (Also CCTV or body cams)	It shows what staff do in the real world when they are working under pressure and provides detective control, but the right lessons need to be learned and privacy concerns need to be thought through.
Modify or redesign the equipment/tools/devices in use	It starts to address the environment in which staff operate and may address human factors (e.g. better labelling of medicines) if staff is engaged in the proposed changes.
Redesign the overall policies, processes or systems impacting the area	Starting to become more systemic, provided all aspects are considered (systems, policies, processes, human factors and resources). This may include the automating of controls and even decision-making algorithms, but biases and gaps in information may none the less remain a risk.

Thus, *there will be a hierarchy of 'weaker' and 'stronger' actions you might take.*

And, quite often, if remedial actions come together in a package, working on the system rather than in the system, there will be a greater likelihood of lasting change.

Going Beyond Training: Sustaining Interest and Vigilance

Summarised hereafter are some reflections highlighting the importance of sustaining improvement efforts as part of 'business as usual'.

Amilcar Zambrano (RCA Practice Lead DNV) explains:

> 'Of course, you must deliver quick-fix solutions when things go wrong. But to stop things repeating, you need to address the underlying causes. This may involve equipment redesign, process changes and training programmes. But very often, it involves some sort of behavioural change. And when the human factor is involved, you mustn't equate that to being solved only by training.
>
> You should recognise that changing behaviour can require one-to-one coaching and other guidance and support. And even after that, effort will be required to maintain discipline over time. You need to be imaginative in how you "keep things alive" for staff because few people announce they have started taking shortcuts.'

John Bendermacher (CAE Euroclear) sums up the challenge:

> 'When you're doing root cause analysis, it's possible to highlight "the emperor has no clothes" on certain issues. But this means you need to be acutely aware of the sensitivities politically and culturally of the things you're going to say and the actions you are going to propose.
>
> Good root cause analysis is just the start; then, you need to work with the organisation to find practical "streetwise" solutions that stakeholders will support. And after that, there is the need to sustain effort and interest over time, which requires diligence and imagination, especially as people move on.'

Farhad Peerally (Associate Professor, University of Leicester) reminds us:

> 'Remember the fundamental purpose of good RCA is to be able to propose better controls and measures over risks. This is why it's important to understand why things go right and keep sharing good practices. So, the practicality of what you suggest for improvement, and its long-term sustainability in the organisation, must not be forgotten.'

Rolling out new policies and procedures and running training events have their place, but *none of these will guarantee that people will do what they should.*

A range of techniques provide further guidance on action planning after an RCA. These include:

- Root cause corrective action (RCCA).[2]
- RCA2 (RCA and action).[3]
- The Ford 8D framework.[4]

The value of these techniques is the way they emphasise:

(i) the necessity of timely action if you want to address root causes;
(ii) the difference between quick-fix solutions, compared to the measures that address longer-term causal factors;
(iii) the need to sustain effort and track implementation progress;
(iv) ensuring improvement activities have had the desired effect on an ongoing basis (i.e. their effectiveness has been validated as much as is appropriate given the risk).

Timescales for Remediation and Tracking Remediation Progress

Clearly, if there is an immediate problem of concern, managers and stakeholders will likely agree to deliver a 'quick fix' as soon as possible. This may also include 'containment' and 'recovery' actions to undo any immediate adverse impacts. This is a territory that many organisations will be familiar with.

But once the damage has been repaired and a quick-fix improvement implemented, key questions to consider afterwards are: (i) how robust are any quick-fix measures? (ii) How quickly should a longer-term solution be put in place?

Suppose we need to change a process, improve staff training and automate certain activities in a system. On the one hand, we would like to fix things as quickly as possible. Still, on the other hand, we mustn't fix things in such a rush that we make mistakes in the way any new processes and systems are updated.

A good practice is to create a framework within which the dilemma between (a) the speed to act and (b) the time to ensure actions are robust is considered and addressed.

Some organisations specify remediation timeframes. So, for high-impact areas, they might specify: 'These should usually be fixed within (say) 1–3 months if action just relates to simple process changes and (say) 4–6 months if an IT system change is required. And suppose there isn't enough resource to do this in the time specified. In that case, this should be escalated to an operations committee or risk committee to ask them to decide whether an additional resource should be allocated or whether they are going to accept risk for a longer period'. Diagram A.2 illustrates the sort of remediation framework that can be adopted.

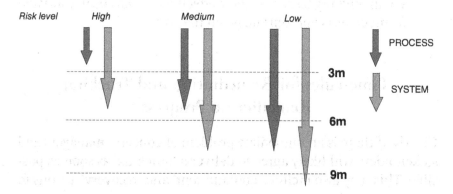

Diagram A.2 Recommended remediation timescales

This framework is helpful because:

(i) It encourages consistency across different areas about what should be done and by when;

(ii) It seeks to normalise the process for determining whether there will be additional resources (or not);

(iii) It ensures that accountability for any risk exposures sits with budget holders who have the authority to expedite actions or not or gets escalated further if they do not have the authority to act (e.g. when a cross-functional initiative is needed).

In terms of tracking progress, a good practice is to set SMART targets at intervals.[5]

Thus, for a new IT system to be in place in, say, 24 weeks, it might require a plan along the following lines:

- 6 weeks: new, approved process, with critical new IT system requirements clarified;
- 8 weeks: commencement of systems upgrade;
- 16 weeks: system built and tested;
- 18 weeks: staff training starts;
- 22 weeks: staff training ends and go-live decision made;
- 24 weeks: new IT system go live.

In this scenario, any problems with resources or priorities would become transparent within weeks and can be escalated quickly, reducing the chances of last-minute surprises.

Validating Closure of Action Plans

There are two important points concerning how to validate the agreed actions after an RCA or inquiry has been effectively completed: (1) is there evidence to show that the agreed remediation actions have been completed and (2) have the actions resulted in the needed change in the risk profile in accordance with any specified risk appetite?

For the first point, good practice involves agreeing, upfront, the verification (or evidence) requirements that should prove an action has been completed, using SMART principles. That way, later, you should have a more straightforward, less contentious discussion about whether (i) action steps are on track and (ii) they have been completed.

For the second requirement, operate on something other than a 'no news is good news basis', which is what often gets organisations into trouble in the first place. Instead, think about the likely leading and lagging indicators that would tell you, actively, that the risk is now being managed to a better level and in accordance to the necessary tolerances specified by senior management, and ensure that there is an active process to monitor these measures, with agreed responsible and accountable roles.

Beyond this, it is essential to have an oversight process for key RCA action points, with timely management information.[6] This should involve senior managers and – if necessary – the board, so they can understand progress against key milestones. Management information should always be presented based on the importance of each area being fixed; if three medium-risk actions are on track, that usually won't compensate for one higher-risk point that has stalled.

Appendix B

Practical Advice to Improve RCA in an Organisation

'There are two main dimensions to bear in mind with root cause analysis. The first is the physical, practical and technical side. But then there are the reasons why, which is what you will need to find to get a lasting solution'.

– Andrew Pal

This appendix is written for executives, managers and other professionals in an organisation (e.g. in GRC, IT, quality and ESG, etc.) who want to strengthen their root cause analysis (RCA) practice. It is intended to complement other, more detailed RCA guides and manuals that you can find.[1]

To move forward, there are several critical choices, and steps, to consider:

- Where to focus your improvement efforts?
- Making the most of existing RCA expertise.
- Building a case for change with relevant stakeholders.

- Practical details to address, including the use of appropriate RCA tools and techniques.
- Sharing the results of RCA work, including RCA themes.

I have also included some reflections from managers who have improved their RCA practice recently.

Where to Focus Your Improvement Efforts

We know that RCA is a powerful tool to 'get to the heart' of organisational problems and opportunities. The typical areas where implementing or upgrading RCA will be of value include:

(i) Areas where there have been *significant unexpected surprises* in business performance or major setbacks compared to plan.

(ii) Areas where there have been *recurring problems* in the same process or unit that have not been satisfactorily resolved.

(iii) Instances where there have been *similar problems* across different units, projects, etc.

(iv) Areas where there is, or may be, regulatory interest in the quality of RCA.

Process Improvement First or RCA Improvements?

However, there is an important choice to make:

- If you and other colleagues are unsure why a problem keeps recurring, then a robust RCA analysis might help clarify the reasons for the problem, so you have a more focused way ahead.
- However, suppose you and other colleagues *already have a good idea (or working hypotheses) of why a problem is happening*. In that case, *it may be better to work directly on the following:*
  - validating the facts and evidence for the causes, and then
  - proposing changes to improve relevant organisational processes, projects, etc., rather than working on RCA first.

Here, we see a fundamental point about RCA: RCA tools and techniques are there to improve organisational performance and avoid setbacks but need not be an immediate top priority unless there is – for example – a specific regulatory requirement or there is a good case for improving this capability in certain areas.

Of course, if you encounter resistance to taking action to improve a process or project this may require you to understand better the human factors and other reasons (e.g. budget constraints or interdependencies on other activities), why is this the case.

Whether or not you can take 'direct action' improving business activities based on RCA insights, you may still want to improve RCA practice in your organisation.

Working on Improving RCA Practices: There Are Still More Choices

If you believe that RCA should be improved in your organisation, then there are other choices to be mindful of:

1. Improve RCA in areas where it is already being used but is perhaps not having the impact it should be.
2. Implement RCA tools and techniques in areas where there is no or limited application to date.

Choosing option 1 or 2 will involve considering where the organisation will most likely benefit from an improvement in RCA alongside the question of which is the most achievable first step. What you decide may depend on the role you are in and the influence you have.

Making the Most of Existing RCA Expertise

Suppose you want to deploy RCA in a new area. In that case, it's essential to clarify whether there are any RCA subject matter experts (SMEs) in other parts of the organisation (e.g. in health and safety or quality control). Because even if they cannot give you a significant amount of help, there may be perspectives they have on conducting RCA in your organisation that are of value. Further, it should ensure that anything new that is done is not regarded as a 'breakaway' activity or a waste of resources.

Unless there is already a strong 'burning platform', I would advise progressing RCA in new areas or using new techniques through a piloting approach because it may be necessary to adapt what is needed according to what works for your organisation.

I generally encourage building 'RCA centres of excellence' across an organisation. Thus:

(i)   use existing RCA SMEs to offer some practical guidance on fact-finding, timelines, evidential good practices, statistical techniques (e.g. for causation questions), etc., but

(ii) don't automatically 'copy paste' tools and techniques from one area (e.g. IT) to another (e.g. finance and compliance), and

(iii) encourage a cross-functional approach to RCA so that there is a diversity of perspectives and thinking styles (e.g. consider a 'buddy' from an area not directly involved in the domain being examined)[2], and

(iv) share information, cause theme types, etc., between areas, so that underlying, systemic areas of concern can be more clearly identified and the case for change made.[3]

Building a Case for Change

Whatever role you are in, and whatever your level of competence in RCA, making progress in RCA and systems analysis will entail utilising appropriate change management techniques:

- First, have a 'good enough goal, vision or direction of travel', so stakeholders understand how these fit into organisational plans and priorities.
- Second, consider how your work will link to a recognised problem area so there is a 'burning platform' for action.
- Third, determine practical first steps to take, whether that is communicating with others and/or carrying out a pilot exercise.

- Fourth, clarify roles and responsibilities and consider the skills and resources that must be mobilised, for example, to deliver training or for a pilot exercise. This may include getting support from those who must free up time, staff and budgets.
- Fifth, determine the likely reward that those involved will receive; this could be as simple as giving recognition for problems they have worked to better understand. Also, how you will demonstrate the impact of your efforts to prove it was worthwhile and will be worth continuing in the future?

Diagram B.1 sets out the key ingredients in a tabular format. It reminds us that unless you can 'line up' many, or all, of these elements, change will often not progress at the pace you might want (or at all).

Selecting Appropriate RCA Techniques

If you are just starting to do RCA in earnest, I would start with either three-way five whys, the Bowtie or the modified fishbone (with or without causal loops), but always recognise that there will be simplifications and limitations.

As you become more sophisticated in your approach to RCA, a more comprehensive barrier analysis approach, fault tree technique

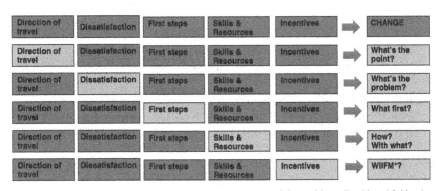

Adapted from Beckhard & Harris

*WIIFM -What's in it for me? (Incentives and penalties)

Diagram B.1   Change management – key ingredients

Table B.2 Summary of various RCA tools with potential pros and cons[4]

Technique	Potential pros	Potential cons[5]
Five whys and two legs	Simple, but not too simple[6], contains prevent and detect	It may miss multiple other causes and does not include systems thinking
Three-way five whys	Simple, contains prevent, detect and other (e.g. recovery, risk identification or design) Popular with many clients	Misses the systemic dimension
Bowtie	Simple and has prevention, detection and recovery Considers impact Useful to assess risks and the design of control measures. Can show hairline cracks	More of an indirect RCA tool; it takes skill to link RCA data gathering with the diagram A systemic dimension is not usually present
Fault/issue tree Logic tree	Popular in various sectors with software tools available; also, many instructional materials are online	Depending on the tool, it can take time to master Systems thinking approach and causal loops are not always present[7]
Fishbone	Simple and often has 6–8 causal categories to encourage more holistic thinking	Popular categories can be misunderstood (e.g. people) The systemic dimension is often not included
Modified fishbone with causal loops (eight ways to understand why (connected)	Relatively simple Causal loops encourage a systems analysis approach	The eight high-level cause types may need to be further analysed
FMEA	Tool for RCA as well as risk management Useful rating system because of its emphasis on higher impacts first and focus on detection	Sometimes needs tailoring; it takes time to become skilled. A systemic dimension is not usually present

Technique	Potential pros	Potential cons[5]
FRAM	A systems thinking approach that explicitly considers human variability	It takes some effort to become skilled and to communicate with stakeholders
SEIPS	Systems analysis approach – simplified by some	More descriptive, so some effort is needed to draw out causal factors
STAMP Business Dynamics (MIT)	Systems thinking approach	It takes some effort to become skilled and to communicate with stakeholders

or systems analysis technique may be useful. A summary list, with some indicative, high-level, pros and cons, is provided in Table B.2.

A fuller list of RCA and systems analysis techniques, accident investigation frameworks, etc., is provided in Supplement B1 at the end of this appendix. *Please note this list of pros and cons is not intended to be a definitive assessment of each approach, so readers should always carry out their own due diligence or pilot studies to determine appropriate tools and techniques and appropriate ways forward.*[8] *Further, whatever tools and techniques you use, remember that there will always be simplifications, assumptions, and pros and cons; there is no 'one best' approach to RCA or systems analysis.* As Alfred Korzybski said: 'The map is not the territory'.[9]

Thematic Analysis – Utilising RCA for Insights at an Organisational Level

Typically, RCA improvements will be sustained if stakeholders or decision-makers can see results, for example:

- Where processes and systems run more smoothly or projects deliver more reliably.
- Where there is evidence (which might be a combination of objective and subjective data points) that RCA improvements

in specific areas have 'headed problems off at the pass' (e.g. in cyber security or project delivery).

- Where there is a sense that RCA and systems thinking are highlighting 'system-wide', cross-functional improvements, Diagram B.3 illustrates a 'what' and 'why' analysis that can reveal themes to be worked on.

Initiatives I have seen at an organisation-wide (or regional or divisional) level have included:

- Improving data and information quality.
  - Improve management information so that there is a more 'balanced scorecard' approach (with key performance indicators [KPIs] and key risk indicators [KRIs]).
  - Much more clarity about how metrics, issues, incidents and near misses are filtered and reported upwards and – even – where 'questions' need to be fast-tracked upwards for a resolution (e.g. who is accountable for an emerging risk).
- Accountability mapping for the executive team and their direct reports (i.e. who oversees the quality of business continuity plans for critical areas).
- Frameworks determining the way processes and policies are written, approved and 'joined up' with other activities (including

Issue and risks causing concern - **what** is happening

Area	Key problem areas
Contract Terms & Conditions	Non-standard terms
Procurement / Vendor Selection	Absence of multiple bids / too many exceptions
IT access controls	Leavers not up-dated

Root cause themes - explaining the reasons **why**

Area	Goals	Information	R2A2	Design	External	Change Maintain	Human factors	Resources / dilemmas
Contract Terms & Conditions		X	X		X		X	X
Procurement / Vendor Selection	X		X		X	X		X
IT access controls	X	X	x	X	X	X	X	

Diagram B.3 A new type of thematic analysis

policy streamlining and establishing key control objectives across the organisation).

- More good practice sharing around the management of third parties and more scenario planning around forecasts.
- Improving the management of human factors, including: Overhauling training and development; Testing whether those on the receiving end find the training relevant and realistic for the 'real world', and ethical hacking/phishing, mystery customer exercises and exercises to bypass security – to reveal behavioural risks.[10]
  - Changing incentive and bonus schemes to better reflect risk and control requirements.
- More clarity on staffing baselines and productivity measures – as someone said to me recently, 'If the knights on horseback are off to war, you need a good team behind the scenes, ensuring they are fed, watered and looked after. Success only comes through a team effort'.

There is a further important point to be made when you attempt to analyse root causes into different categories across an organisation. Bruce Sherry (Senior Audit Manager, Tesco Bank) explains:

'Of course, with RCA, you will always have the specific facts of what you have found. That's always central. But when it comes to categorising cause types for thematic analysis, you must get the balance right around the number of categories you use.

If you have a team who like detail, it's understandable that you might want to break down causes into particular cause types. But the more I have worked with this over the years, the more I can see that people can get drawn to specific cause types based on their background and personal preferences, and so it's entirely possible to 'lose the wood for the trees'.

I think for many teams, a high-level categorisation of cause types is best until you are very confident categorisation is being done effectively and consistently.'

It is beyond the scope of this book to discuss all the various organisation-wide or end-to-end process changes that are possible through RCA and systems analysis. However, the usual outcome is to (i) learn lessons from one area (including sharing of good practices) and spread this rapidly to other areas where this is needed and (ii) create more consistency around 'the basics' and resilience at an organisation-wide level.

Reflections from Managers Who Have Improved Their RCA Practice

Ian Brimicombe (SVP, Specialist Finance, and Projects, Burberry):

'Improving RCA in areas such as finance and IT requires a few key ingredients. First, you need to train and coach staff. Second, you need to recognise the time it can take to do a good RCA. Third, you need to be prepared to dig into small details from time to time, especially when there can be a cumulative impact from minor errors. Fourth, you must have a culture that accepts openness and speaking up about issues and doesn't blame staff for raising issues.

The goal should be about process excellence and continuous improvement and "fixing forward".'

Sandeep Das (Head of Internal Audit, St John Ambulance):

'When you are involved in an emergency or crisis, don't expect to start a full-blown RCA first thing. In situations like this, you often need to implement some "quick-fix" solutions. So, as long as stakeholders know that this is step one, then you can turn to an RCA review when things have calmed down.

But don't let the fact that the fire has been put out stop you from turning to the RCA stage. If necessary, remind everyone how much time and effort it took to deal with the crisis and the value of heading off problems in advance.'

Martin Falck-Hansen (Former Head of Internal Audit, KMD A/S – an NEC Company):

'Never forget how often people will fear getting the blame. So, always engage the sponsors of an RCA investigation to establish whether this will be a "point the blame" review or a learning RCA. Show them the just culture framework if you need to.

The more people know that the RCA is for learning, the more likely you are to get all the facts and angles and a robust RCA.'

Nancy Haig (Principal, PIAC LLC):[11]

'I would expect any risk or compliance team to have looked at RCA and to have trained key personnel involved in monitoring how to understand the difference between cause types. You also need to recognise that RCA may highlight gaps in policies and training that were previously thought to be unimportant.

You may find that pragmatic "concessions" that were agreed to in the past have come back around and need to be addressed. Don't be reluctant to have the discussion. Saying that "We discussed this in the past, and I gave you the benefit of the doubt, but now I can see that it's led to issues, so we need a resolution" shows flexibility and builds transparency and credibility.'

Jerome Lobet (Audit Director, Euroclear):

'My advice is don't over-engineer your RCA methodology or RCA cause categories. Some colleagues I know are using the Bowtie framework, it's basic, but it does seem to be yielding results.'

Norman Marks (Author, Speaker and Thought Leader):[12]

'When you're doing an RCA, you need to go deep down enough to get a decent understanding of what individual people are doing because if you don't get to this level of detail, you won't understand what it's like from the perspective of the person who's carrying out specific tasks. Getting to this level means you must be disciplined in gathering evidence during any investigation or inquiry.

(a) You need active listening skills.
(b) You need to exhaust the information that person can give you.
(c) You also need to understand any problems from their perspective.

RCA is about adopting a childlike perspective on things, asking why, why, why, why, and why.'

Andrew Pal (Leadership Coach and Organisation Consultant):[13]

'When you are thinking of the team who will carry out the RCA, make sure that they, and the key stakeholders, are mentally ready for what they come up with.

Make sure you are tuned in to the cultural and political sensitivities that may be in play. Don't do the RCA in a technical silo ignoring this side of the equation.'

Dr Mohammad Farhad Peerally (Associate Professor, University of Leicester):[14]

'Improving RCA should be part of a bigger learning journey for an organisation. It should also be about the positive benefits of improvement actions, not just the negatives that have been avoided.

Don't be surprised if you uncover key improvements at the point where different systems and processes interact.

Remember the importance of the "just culture" framework when working on RCA. If this framework isn't understood and accepted, an organisation can easily get pulled into a "blame game" mindset.

In a healthcare context, the "just culture" mindset is especially important when someone has been impacted negatively when being cared for (directly or by a family member). In these situations, you may need to provide an apology on behalf of a care provider, explaining what has been learned and giving assurances that improvement actions will be implemented, so the same thing can't happen again. Here it's crucial that stakeholders recognise that the person responsible for apologising on behalf of the institution *is not the same as them personally accepting blame.*

Interestingly, when you speak to people who have been badly affected by a medical incident, many recognise that the medical staff will have been trying to do their best. So, very often, their main concerns are (i) to get an acknowledgement that things went wrong and (ii) to be confident that lessons have been learned.

This is where there is an interesting link between root cause analysis and the whole "restorative justice" movement.'

Richard Taylor (Audit Support Director Aegon Investment Management):

'Don't underestimate how easy it is for everybody to say, let's do root cause analysis, but to find that it's not that high quality. Recognise that ingredients such as the maturity of the team involved, the maturity of the organisation and cultural factors all play a part.

The people aspect to root cause is often underestimated; if you don't have a sponsor and a team lead with the right mindset, you may have very basic RCA.'

In conclusion, if you implement RCA in a step-by-step manner, my experience is it is an initiative that many senior executives and board members will support (recognising there may be some political headwinds sometimes), especially if the right 'success stories' are found and shared.

Supplement B1: List of Different RCA and Systems Analysis Techniques[15]

Examples of RCA guides	Useful links/references
Accimap	https://en.wikipedia.org/wiki/AcciMap_approach
Affinity diagram	https://www.mindtools.com/axm7sxc/affinity-diagrams
Aerospace (survey)	https://apps.dtic.mil/sti/pdfs/ADA626691.pdf
CAA (Aviation)	https://www.caa.co.uk/commercial-industry/aircraft/airworthiness/approval-information-and-guidance/root-cause-analysis/
Causal loop analysis	https://thesystemsthinker.com/causal-loop-construction-the-basics/
DUPONT SAVANNAH	https://www.osti.gov/servlets/purl/6069992
Fault Tree – Apollo/NASA	https://ntrs.nasa.gov/api/citations/20000070463/downloads/20000070463.pdf

(continued)

Examples of RCA guides	Useful links/references
Fault Tree – MORT	https://www.osti.gov/servlets/purl/5254810/
FMEA	https://www.ihi.org/resources/Pages/Tools/FailureModesandEffectsAnalysisTool.aspx
FRAM	https://www.functionalresonance.com/FRAM-1_understanding_accidents.pdf
HAZOP	https://pqri.org/wp-content/uploads/2015/08/pdf/HAZOP_Training_Guide.pdf
RCA2	https://www.ihi.org/resources/Pages/Tools/RCA2-Improving-Root-Cause-Analyses-and-Actions-to-Prevent-Harm.aspx
SHELL model	https://www.skybrary.aero/articles/icao-shell-model
STAMP	http://psas.scripts.mit.edu/home/wp-content/uploads/2014/04/File_1_Poster_UNIVANCE_Corporation.pdf
Six Sigma – DMAIC	https://asq.org/quality-resources/dmaic
PRISMA (incl. Eindhoven classification)	https://cmapspublic.ihmc.us/rid=1HVP2STJD-1KVJMC3-10YR/PRISMA_Medical.pdf
SAFETY 1 and SAFETY 2	https://www.skybrary.aero/sites/default/files/bookshelf/2437.pdf
SEIPS	https://www.ncbi.nlm.nih.gov/pmc/articles/PMC3835697/https://www.england.nhs.uk/wp-content/uploads/2022/08/B1465-SEIPS-quick-reference-and-work-system-explorer-v1-FINAL.pdf

Examples of software-based RCA[16]	Useful links/references
BSCAT	`https://www.wolterskluwer.com/en/solutions/enablon/bowtie/expert-insights/barrier-based-risk-management-knowledge-base/bscat`
Causelink	`https://www.causelink.com`
Think Reliability	`https://www.thinkreliability.com`
	`https://root-cause-analysis.info/`
Taproot	`https://www.taproot.com`
KELVIN TOP SET	`https://kelvintopset.com`
NASA root cause analysis RCAT	`https://software.nasa.gov/software/LEW-19737-1`
Sologic	`https://www.sologic.com`
TRIPOD Beta	`https://www.wolterskluwer.com/en/solutions/enablon/bowtie/expert-insights/barrier-based-risk-management-knowledge-base/tripod-beta`

Incident analysis guides[17]	Useful links/references
Aviation (Skylibrary)	`https://www.skybrary.aero/sites/default/files/bookshelf/3282.pdf`
CIAF	`https://www.ismp-canada.org/ciaf.htm`
Department of Energy Accident investigation manual	`https://www.standards.doe.gov/standards-documents/1200/1208-bhdbk-2012-v1/@@images/file` (contains an excellent summary of the reasons for non-compliance)
	`https://www.standards.doe.gov/standards-documents/1200/1208-bhdbk-2012-v2/@@images/file`

(continued)

Incident analysis guides[17]	Useful links/references
EU Accident investigation	Old but comprehensive: `https://www.nri` `.eu.com/SSDC27.pdf`
EU Agency for Cyber Security	`www.enisa.europa.eu`

HSE Investigations	Human Factors section: `https://www`
	`.hse.gov.uk/humanfactors/topics/`
	`investigation.htm`

HSIB	`https://www.hsib.org.uk/investigations-`
	`and-reports/never-events-analysis-`
	`of-hsibs-national-investigations/`

Marine (MAIIF)	`https://maiif.org/wp-content/uploads/` `2017/08/MAIIF-Manual-2014.pdf`
NTSB	`https://www.ntsb.gov/investigations/` `process/pages/default.aspx`
OSHA (Oregon)	`https://osha.oregon.gov/edu/Documents/` `workshop-materials/1-110i.pdf`

Sentinel events	`https://www.jointcommission.org/-/`
	`media/tjc/documents/resources/`
	`patient-safety-topics/sentinel-`
	`event/camh_24_se_all_current.pdf?db=`
	`web&hash=835C25502A3AC075F6602B1372`
	`6CB958`

Appendix C

Practical Advice for Internal Audit and Others in an Audit or Inspection Role

This appendix is written for those who work in internal audit (IA), or who carry out other assurance activities/ inspections, and who want to (i) offer more insight from audits, reviews or inspections; (ii) better judge root cause analysis (RCA) activities they encounter; and (iii) make a more significant impact.

Before I set out some of the practical steps to follow, I want to reiterate how important RCA is to effective audit work. Here are the reflections of Nancy Haig:

> 'It is impossible to be truly effective and insightful when auditing without the identification of root causes. Chief Audit Executives (CAEs), and everyone in the IA team, must be prepared to discuss the "how" and "why" issues occurred and, consequently, how the underlying causes of issues or problems will be addressed and resolved. This should be a routine way of doing business for all IA professionals.

RCA skills are important because without them, how can you provide insight on governance, risk and compliance (GRC) processes, comment on the quality of the root cause analysis being done by other functions or what is being missed by them not doing it?

It's encouraging that RCA will be included in the new Institute of Internal Auditors (IIA) Global Internal Audit Standards. And, not surprisingly, regulators across a range of domains are taking an increasing interest in RCA.'

This appendix covers various critical aspects of RCA in an IA context:

- Getting your bearings,
- Thinking about RCA when preparing audit plans,
- Considering root causes at the start of an assignment,
- Incorporating RCA thinking into the audit methodology and work programmes,
- Using root causes to consolidate observations and improve action plans,
- Being prepared to 'look in the mirror',
- Applying RCA to day-to-day challenges the audit team encounters,
- Outlining other materials that may be useful,
- Seeing RCA improvement as a journey and remembering mindset change takes time.

Getting Your Bearings

To make progress in RCA, it's essential you are clear about where you currently are:

- Clarify the 'state of the art' of RCA practice in your organisation.
  Which functions in your organisation use RCA, and how sophisticated are their RCA methodologies, analysis of causes and themes, and tracking of actions? In particular, understand the position for critical functions such as customer relationship management, product quality, health and safety, finance, IT, risk and compliance.

This context should help your RCA efforts in IA to be appropriately linked to and build on what is being done elsewhere.

- Determine the level of maturity of RCA in current audit practice, methodologies, tools and techniques.

For example, Is RCA covered in the audit methodology? Are there any recognised tools and techniques used during assignments beyond the five whys (e.g. the Bowtie, the fishbone diagram or causal loop analysis)? Is there any reporting of thematic analysis (not just 'what', but 'why')?

Note RCA is not something that an audit team should start only when they have an audit observation. It is far more important than that:

Start Thinking About RCA When Making Audit/Inspection Plans

When considering the audit plan, you need to consider critical objectives, risks, past incidents and issues, and emerging themes (externally, or from earlier work, which may include RCA insights).[1]

The full impact of how RCA can improve the audit planning process is a big topic and outside the scope of this appendix. However, the fundamental message is that many stakeholders (and regulators) are interested in seeing thematic reviews. RCA insights should be key when considering thematic assignments. This takes us to the question of how you determine the scope of an assignment.

Consider Root Causes from the Start of Any Assignment

Nancy Haig explains her 80/20 approach to audits utilising RCA insights:

'RCA thinking should start as an engagement is conceived, utilising the "working hypothesis" concept spelled out in the "*Lean*

Auditing" book. Otherwise, you miss many opportunities to focus your work and add value by waiting until the end of the assignment to do your RCA.

This is part of my "80/20 rule" for the successful completion of IA engagements, which means that approximately 80% of time should be spent on planning and approximately 20% on execution. While the percentages may not be exact, they clearly demonstrate the focus on planning and critical thinking rather than "test" work just in detail, without seeing the bigger picture.'

So, with a given assignment scope, there are innovative ways to focus on the key objectives (or 'exam questions') using RCA tools, such as the Bowtie, modified fishbone or the eight ways to understand why, with connections.

Furthermore, as you do background work on an assignment, consider the following points:

1. *Suppose you are auditing an area with known concerns. In that case, you need to be wary of just validating this, where you might get the reaction, 'We already knew about that'.*

   So, for known risks, issues and action plans in progress, clarify whether management has considered the root causes for these gaps (using a recognised methodology) and whether their current action plans are just 'quick fixes' or really address underlying causes.

   That way, if an audit looks at known gaps, it can either (i) check any management RCA or (ii) examine the root causes of those issues as part of the assignment.

2. In relation to scope areas where no serious issues have been identified at first, consider: What kind of hairline cracks might arise that would result in an issue or a risk being out of tolerance?

Having ascertained these fundamentals about the context and the role of an internal audit, you can look at the eight commonplace root cause types and consider as appropriate:

(i) Are the goals relevant to the assignment scope clear? For example, has the risk appetite been established, and have the implications of this translated into relevant management key performance indicators (KPIs) and key risk indicators (KRIs)?

(ii) Is there a possibility that any relevant management information (and KPIs and KRIs) is missing, or is potentially misleading, or incorrect?

(iii) Is there any suggestion that roles, responsibilities, accountabilities and authorities (R2A2) for key risks or processes are unclear?

(iv) When was the design of any relevant process, policy, or procedure, or IT system last reviewed? For example, is each key control SMART?

(v) Are there enough key controls overall? For example, have controls been mapped against a Bowtie diagram (i.e. prevent, detect and recovery) and then checked the risk appetite (so you can do a design assessment)?

(vi) How have any relevant external factors or third parties been considered, monitored and managed?

(vii) Any questions about change or maintenance that may impact the area?

(viii) How have human factors relevant to the scope and objectives been appropriately considered by management?

(ix) Any signs of resource constraints, unclear priorities or dilemmas? How does the organisation prioritise tasks (related to objectives but also GRC issues)?

The important message is to 'start the ball rolling' with these RCA questions at the start of an assignment and on an ongoing basis so that:

1. You can be clear, using a boundary diagram (or 'audit' on one page), that the scope and objectives of the assignment will address some of the critical hairline cracks or opportunities for improvement and

2. As the assignment progresses, *you should already have a good idea, with some evidence, of what the causal factors for improvement might be.*

Thinking about RCA questions at the start will avoid slowing down an assignment at the end. In fact, RCA can accelerate audit assignments, which is what we found when I was the CAE of Astra-Zeneca and is explained in the book 'Lean Auditing'.

Incorporate RCA Thinking into the Audit/Inspection Methodology and Work Programmes

With audit teams I have worked with, we have moved beyond just bolting on RCA tools and techniques in the audit methodology to integrating key RCA points into the audit methodology and work programmes (e.g. risk control matrices [RCMs].) This can include how to align audit agile 'sprint' stages with RCA requirements.

The typical benefits you get are to 'prune and declutter' work programmes and make them a better platform for developing insights. Richard Taylor explains his experiences:

'Work programmes are useful to create a minimum standard for audit work as well as consistency between team members, and over time. But the danger is that auditors think doing a good audit is about filling in templates.

Sometimes you can slip into auditing in "robot mode"; have you ticked the box and completed all the templates? This can easily happen if you have huge work programmes with dozens of key controls and detailed audit tests. It all starts to turn into an exercise of "feeding the machine". But the important question is whether you have thought deeply about risks and control gaps and their causes, so you can find new angles of attack?

It sounds like a paradox because I am a great fan of discipline during audits, but you need work programmes to permit "out of the box" thinking. Staff need to be open-minded about the sometimes subtle but important things that others may have missed. And remember that sometimes these key weaknesses lie in-between departments or functions.'

This frame of mind encourages audit teams to recalibrate the way they think about risk appetite. Damian Finio explains:

'The quality of internal audit that I have seen in my career has varied greatly. I respect the focus on collecting facts and information in detail, but it's vital this effort is joined up with what matters. To take a simple example: anyone can tell me there is a minor, technical problem somewhere in the business, but *whether it really matters is the $64 000 question.*

I encourage all the internal auditors that I work with to calibrate their work to the risk appetite set by the board and executive. So, if we have decided that managers can authorise payments below $250 without significant extra checks, then the fact that it could be controlled more if the limit was $100 may be true but is it worth the extra effort? Audit always needs to recognise cost/benefit trade-offs. Unless there is a major problem they can foresee, they need to respect the tough choices the board and executive inevitably make to have a "fit for purpose" control framework. After all, if you controlled every organisation $1 at a time, you would have no business.'

An RCA perspective isn't just about highlighting gaps; it's about identifying whether adopting best practices would be helpful. Nancy Haig explains:

'If you have experience, or you have done the right research, you may be able to compare what your organisation is doing to a best practice. That way, if you make an observation, and a manager says, "Yes, but we are compliant," you can reply, "Yes, you may be compliant, but actually you have fallen behind good practice in this area, meaning you are encountering difficulties that others are not".

A classic example of this concerns the management of cyber security risks; when you are dealing with potentially criminal activity proactively seeking to find vulnerabilities in what you are doing on a real time basis, sometimes being "good" just isn't good enough.'

Use Root Causes to Consolidate Observations and Improve Action Plans

So, all going well, you will complete a work programme during an assignment and have:

(a) a series of interesting observations and

(b) a good understanding of the causal factors, already with some evidence to back this up.

In line with lean and agile auditing methodologies, you would be sharing these insights as you conduct the assignment. Then, you have a choice:

(I) highlight observations and propose actions at the level of symptoms and/or

(II) offer comments at the level of underlying causes and then propose actions at the level of root causes.

In an ideal world, proposing actions that address underlying actions is an obvious choice, but for IA teams, it can be more complicated than that in practice. Stephen Foster explains:

> 'When it comes to working with stakeholders around action plans, recognise that they are dealing with multiple issues and priorities of which an IA finding, or findings, is just one of many. Therefore, they may just want to be offered a red pill, green pill or blue pill that will solve the organisations' problems quickly.
>
> Usually, we know that addressing underlying causes can't be done through this sort of magic panacea, and care should be taken in suggesting it can. But you should also be pragmatic; it is not in any one's best interests for the opportunity to change and improve to be missed due to overwhelming decision-makers with the scale of organisational change needed all at once. So, where the situation or issue permits, look for the vital few, or smaller, easier steps to get the momentum going, to give a sense of progress being made, and that are contributing to the longer-term vision and goal. It is also important to remember that sometimes turning the tap off should be the first action before determining where and why a pipe is leaking.

They say management and senior executive attention spans can be as short as three weeks before they need to prioritise energies on the next major issue or opportunity. So, give senior management enough to keep them interested in investing in an area, keeping up the focus and energy. It's vital to remember IA work is about getting management to see the connection between GRC improvements and better business. This can be a multi-year task that needs the stamina and endurance of the whole organisation, so don't always ask for "gold-plated" perfect action plans to address all root causes the first time around; you can come back to some of those later; once the major risks are addressed, and people see the benefits of what has already been done.'

Richard Taylor offers a similar experience:

'As your RCA becomes more powerful, you need to be even more disciplined about the right influencing strategy. For example, you may find improvements in one department and have the confidence of 60% that there is also a system-wide change that could further help the situation. You might have been smart and engaged the IT department as part of the audit assignment and talked over your thoughts informally. If they are amenable to making changes, that is great, but sometimes budget and resource pressures will mean they can't yet make this a priority.

So, just because you can see that there might be room for improvement, that still doesn't mean that you are obliged to bring it up as an area for action, especially if (1) you don't have all the evidence you need to back up the causal connections and (2) you don't yet have a clear cost/benefit argument.

To my mind, it's best to think about the level of risk, the context and other work in progress in the business when you are proposing actions. And against this background, you can then think about the optimal way to build a persuasive case for action.

This is why thematic analysis of findings can be so powerful. After all, if the same factor comes up as a potential cause in several subsequent audits, you are building a stronger cost–benefit case for action.'

Diagram C.1 spells out the different levels of observation and action proposals an audit team can make at the end of an assignment. As you become experienced in incorporating RCA into audit assignments and management becomes more accustomed to hearing about root causes, it will be easier to focus on more systemic action plans. This normally results in a smaller number of action recommendations, and one CAE I know has a helpful motto: 'In our audit reports, we are aiming for *every finding only once*'.

Several audit teams I have worked with have started to share some of the RCA working templates with managers (such as the Bowtie and modified fishbone) to explain what they have found. Jerome Lobet explains:

> 'As a discussion tool towards the end of an audit assignment, the Bowtie appears to be working well. As we have adapted it, we can show both the hard and soft controls that are working well and less well.
>
> Most of all, the managers we work with seem to find it quite easy to follow and quite fair and balanced because it gives them credit for what's working well. At the same time, we can show some of the "hairline cracks" we have found, but in a neutral, non-attacking way, which is just what we hoped for.'

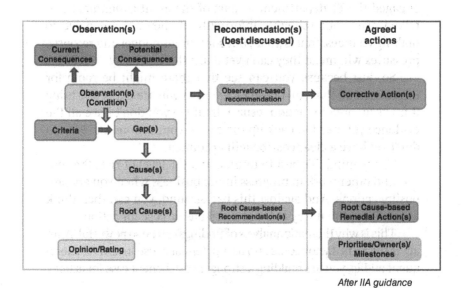

After IIA guidance

Diagram C.1 Some key ingredients of an internal audit report

Be Prepared to Look in the Mirror

On several occasions, I have discussed the 'boomerang' effect when doing an RCA. You look at an area, and you find it makes you ask questions about yourself. Audit teams are no exception to this. Reflecting on my practice as a CAE and working with IA teams for more than a decade, I could write a whole chapter on this topic. But let me offer a few brief pointers illustrating how easy it is for audit teams to miss their role in relation to organisational problems.

You Routinely Audit the Same Areas

Sometimes audit or inspection teams look at the same area every few years. This may be because there is an understanding a regulator would like this or because stakeholders have seen problems in an area, or fear problems in an area, and want extra assurance from audit.

But the danger with repeat auditing is that the audit team, and the organisation, can settle into a 'comfort zone' mode where everyone expects the audit to look at something. Still, little is changing or improving in the way the area is being managed. Supplement C1 provides an account of how a CAE refused to do a routine audit and, as a result, helped an organisation 'snap out of a trance' and start to make significant process improvements.

The Audit Team Is Reluctant to Question Its Own Culture and the Culture of the Organisation

Sometimes a CAE will explain that they are disappointed that some auditors are not writing reports how they would like and that they are not managing stakeholders as well as they could be. So, I will be asked if I could run a training even on report writing or stakeholder management. And my response is to ask: *if we train the team on these topics, how do we know whether we are working on the symptoms or the root causes?*

Here you can see that RCA isn't just something that applies to the audit process and observations about an organisation's performance. It can also be used to examine the way CAEs and audit management teams think about the problems their teams face.

It's not uncommon, when I am exploring the training needs for an audit team, to discover that the initial diagnosis of problems does not get to the heart of the underlying difficulties. To take the example of a lengthy and unclear audit report, is this a sign of:

(I)   a lack of auditor training? and/or
(II) a lack of auditor effort? and/or
(III) the personality and the mindset of the auditor? and
(IV) a more general problem of the process for formulating reports and how the audit team works together and with stakeholders?

In my experience, improving audit reports is often about points III and IV. This is one of the reasons why lean and agile ways of working encourage auditors to share initial observations with stakeholders. Assuming group dynamics can be managed, this process should 'calibrate' the thoughts of each auditor to give a more rounded and holistic assessment of what has been found.

The key message is: when was the last time you looked at an audit team challenge through the lens of a Bowtie or the modified fishbone to consider the reasons why?

Applying RCA to Day-to-Day Challenges the Audit Team Encounters

Let's take some other common challenge areas for IA teams and broaden our 'boundary' concerning root causes and cultural patterns. For example:

(a) A tug of war between local management, senior management and the audit committee wants in terms of an IA assignment (scope and timing);
(b) Questions about who the IA team should interview during an assignment;
(c) The audit team finds that disciplines around management monitoring and/or second-line checking (by risk or compliance) doesn't seem to have the rigour it needs;

(d) Delays in getting the organisation to provide the audit team with information on time (often a problem for some IA teams rather than regulators or external auditors).

(e) Questions about the importance of audit observations and any ratings;

(f) Questions concerning action owners and how quickly remediation should be completed;

(g) The IA team is disappointed that management doesn't seem to take the audit process and follow-up actions as seriously as they should.

In each case, there is usually more to these problems than meets the eye. To give two examples:

- Suppose there are delays in getting information (d). Is there any agreement on how quickly information should be provided to the audit team and what are the consequences if information is not provided on time?

  Many IA teams are now designing audit protocols to include turnaround times, and if there are delays in providing information, this is reported upwards as part of the audit process. In fact, many audit teams call out 'risk culture' or 'control environment' in their reports, starting with turnaround times, but also looking at management openness about risks and areas of concern, and the management attitude to understanding root causes, remediation tracking, etc.

- Do managers treat risk and control and audits in tick box way, only complaining if the audit rating is negative (i.e. points c. and e.)?

  Faced with such problems, some CAEs have changed their rating frameworks to make it clearer what might be reasonably expected and highlight that the goal should be to aim for leading or 'in control' behaviours where possible. Diagram C.2 illustrates how such a rating framework can work.

Where the design of ratings has been changed, line managers will often find they can no longer sit in a 'comfort zone' of doing the minimum to get by. In other words the design of ratings creates

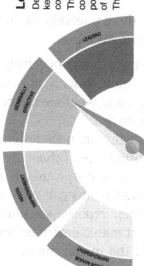

Needs improvement

Design and/or operation of risk identification and key controls requires enhancement to ensure that these are consistently in line with requirements

The unit management's awareness of risk and control requires enhancement to ensure that gaps are identified, understood and acted upon in a timely manner, and sustainability is ensured

Some oversight of remediation activities will normally be required

Needs major improvement

Design and/or operation of risk identification or key controls is not in line with requirements

The unit management's awareness of risk and control is not sufficient to ensure that gaps are recognized, to ensure that the unit can meet its business objectives and manage key risks

Careful oversight of remediation will be required in order to ensure effective remediation of the audit observations

Generally effective

Design and operation of risk identification and key controls are effective in the key areas, and the vast majority of key gaps are identified, reported and addressed

The unit management's awareness of risk and control is generally good; there are proactive efforts to identify and address gaps

The unit will generally be able to remediate audit observations with the current level of assistance and support

Leading*

Design and operation of risk identification and key controls is fully effective, and there is a continuous improvement cycle

The unit management's awareness of risk and control is highly proactive; they seek out potential gaps and act on these with a sense of urgency

The unit could act as a role model to others

* For example, where the risks is material and the organisation needs to avoid problems if at all possible.

Diagram C.2   Progressive approach to assignment ratings

new information for senior stakeholders that can highlight important priorities and as a result change management behaviour.

Other Materials That May Be of Use

While written primarily for a management and second-line audience (e.g. risk and compliance functions), Appendix B provides some helpful information concerning:

- Different RCA techniques to use, with their pros and cons.
- Thematic analysis and commonplace GRC improvement areas.

Concerning winning cost/benefit arguments to overcome a reluctance to act, Supplement C2 of this appendix provides two examples where audit teams have encountered resistance from management and then been able to overcome it by thinking in terms of human factors and cost/benefit.

Seeing RCA Improvement as a Journey and Remembering Mindset Change Takes Time

We are entering a time when RCA is (finally) coming of age, helped by greater stakeholder interest in getting insight and value from internal audits and an increasing focus on RCA by the IIA as well as various regulators/supervisors.

In parallel, many audit teams are developing their use of data analytics, but this becomes even more powerful when it is linked to RCA. For example:

- Looking at problems from new angles (e.g. end-to-end process work and thematic reviews).
- Focusing testing and analytics work in the right places (e.g. through working hypotheses of areas where they may be vulnerabilities).
- Consolidating observations into causal themes (explaining reasons why) and making the links to behaviour and culture.

- Highlighting why audit findings matter (e.g. by moving from current issues and consequences to potential future problems and consequences, etc.).

Embracing RCA does require a mindset shift for many auditors, but my experience with dozens of audit teams is that many things 'click into place' once they learn about RCA with a systems thinking overlay; for example, '*That's* why we are seeing a problem over and over again' and '*Now* I see why managers are not taking action the way I think they should be'.

For CAEs and senior members of audit teams, the more you learn to use the power of RCA and systems thinking and incorporate it into your audit activities, the more likely you are to be able to offer that 'something extra' that will either keep you at the top table or help you earn your place at the top table. This includes audit's ability to comment on behavioural risk and cultural problems, which becomes much easier when taking an RCA and systems analysis perspective.

As a rule, embedding effective RCA is usually a journey of months and sometimes 1–2 years for audit teams, depending on the level of practice that has built up. Here it is worth stating that if the current RCA practice has been built solely or primarily on the five whys technique, with just one root cause, etc., there can be a need to 'unlearn' and 'let go', which can be challenging for some. However, I cannot stress enough that it is just a matter of time before the 'one-trick pony' of the five whys will run into difficulty on one matter or another; so I would say it's better to embrace some of the richer RCA techniques that have been discussed, for the sake of the audit team and – most important – for the richer insights it will provide to senior management. This is not to say progress should not be 'step by step', but sometimes it is best to recognise that a step back is important before taking two steps forward. Needless to say, as much as is practical try to make links with risk, compliance and other critical functions so any RCA enhancements can be shared.

Finally, remember that good RCA will not overcome the inevitable stakeholder management and influencing challenges you will encounter when proposing actions on more fundamental topics. But it's worth noting that as you gain an appreciation for the systemic nature of some problems, you will, in fact, be more likely to 'see' why there is resistance to change and identify some of the politically savvy strategies that might be needed to make progress.

Supplement C1: Calling Out Unhelpful Patterns and Cultural Problems

During a discussion with a CAE, we examined the proposed audit plan and looked for resource headroom to enable them to look at some new areas. There was one audit, which took a considerable amount of time and was repeated year after year. The audit concerned various secure facilities that contained valuable and sensitive materials and therefore went beyond a straightforward check of basic security arrangements. I was advised that this had become an annual audit four years earlier because of significant audit committee and executive interest.

The CAE explained, 'I get kudos for doing the assignment, but many of the things we find are similar to what we have found in the past. The risk and control environment is only improving slowly. Still, *I could probably write 70% of the audit report without doing the audit*. They are making some fixes, but not really shifting their mindset about what it would take to make a step change in what is being done'.

I commented, 'It seems a bit like the organisation has become dependent on you to do its monitoring. It has become accustomed to "the same old" findings and – to some extent – so has the audit team. So, what about sharing the themes of what you have found in the past and your thoughts about the causes and suggesting that yet another audit is not going to add that much value'.

After various discussions, the CAE went to the Chief Executive (CEO) to talk about stopping doing the audit. The CEO was initially unhappy with the suggestion, saying, 'But you've got to look at it!'

However, after discussion, they conceded that there were funda-mental questions to consider, explaining why audit was essentially identifying 'the same old findings'. Finally, the CEO said, 'I want you to present your analysis of the key themes over the past years and – in discussion with the relevant managers – work through the underlying difficulties and constraints to establish how we can get this area working at a better level'.

The CAE did the analysis, worked with the relevant managers and presented some improvement action options, which were then discussed and agreed upon with the Executive Committee and the Audit Committee. Of course, there was a resource dimension to the changes agreed upon, but the result was that the CEO, relevant managers and the CAE got positive feedback from the board for initiating a step change in an important area.

And the CAE did not have to do the repeat audit for the next year, saving time to then work on some new areas. Henceforth, assignments on the secure facilities were much shorter, looking in depth at specific aspects from time to time, rather than just repeat-ing what had been done in the past.

This is not the only example I have encountered *where the brave thing has turned out to be to call out situations when audit is becoming an almost permanent substitute for things management should be doing.*

So, if you think an audit assignment is 'going through the motions' and are reasonably sure what you are going to find from year to year. In that case, it's almost certainly a sign that underlying causal factors have not yet been addressed.

Supplement C2 – Overcoming Resistance to Act: Joining the Dots

As discussed in Chapter 13 on action planning, it's important to cre-ate a solid cost/benefit case for actions that are proposed. However, it's still easy to encounter resistance to change, and not always be completely clear why it's happening.

Here are two examples I have been involved in that illustrate the need to 'put yourself in the shoes of the other person' and, as a result, find arguments that help to make audit findings more impactful.

Recruitment

For a UK national organisation, the audit team could see differing designs in relation to the recruitment process, resulting in inconsistencies in staff data and information that then needed adjustments when pulled together on a national basis.

The initial audit recommendation was that the recruitment process be standardised across the United Kingdom. It would allow for a more consistent data set to be collected without needing adjustments. But at first, the proposal to improve things got no traction from management because there would be a clear cost and disruption if the change was made, and the benefit seemed marginal.

After discussions with the audit team, we agreed that if there were greater standardisation, it would be possible to do recruitment on a cross-UK systems platform that would (i) improve data consistency, as mentioned, but (ii) reduce the number of recruitment systems in use (from three to one) and the administration overhead. When the details were analysed, an efficiency gain of many tens of thousands of pounds was identified, after which the organisation was keen to investigate standardisation and move onto one recruitment system.

Here, when audit found a problem with 'inconsistent data', management was not inclined to act. However, when the issue was represented as an opportunity for greater efficiency, with a clear savings benefit it became more interesting to senior managers.

Bond Issues

The audit team for a central bank established that issuing bonds took several weeks longer than similar organisations (where benchmark data was obtained). The audit team suggested that bottlenecks should be addressed to bring the turnaround time in line with others. Still, there was pushback from the bank governor because the bottleneck concerned the creation of legal paperwork. If it were to be done quicker, with a more prominent law firm, with more capacity, there would be a greater cost.

Various discussions had taken place using 'rational persuasion' tactics, but the governor was reluctant to make the changes for what he felt was no good reason, 'There's no problem as far as I can see, we don't have to do things at the same pace as other central banks, in other countries, we are different'.

On further consideration, during an RCA workshop, the audit team went on to analyse some data and established that while 80% of the time dealing with the bonds more quickly would make no appreciable difference, there was evidence that delays cost the bank hundreds of thousands in lost margin when certain market conditions arose. When this analysis was presented, the governor had it checked and once satisfied, authorised the use of the more prominent legal firm for bonds where the turnaround time was thought to be important.

So, a finding from audit that the bank was doing something slower than a peer group was not of interest, but when the delay was quantified, it became an important, value-adding insight the governor was happy to act on.

Both examples highlight the inevitable human factor that managers and staff may be reluctant to make changes when they sense 'nothing bad has happened yet'. So, unless audit can help them to 'join the dots', there will understandably be a reluctance to act. Making audit work more relevant and explaining the 'so what' is a hallmark of a progressive audit team.

Acknowledgements

CLOSING THANKS TO:

- All those I interviewed and have cited;
- The Arvon writers group that met in the summer of 2019, and Lois Pryce and Ian Marchant, for their encouragement that the Titanic story was worth retelling;
- Lance Bell, (at Visualise That) for turning my ideas into pictures;
- Clients and workshop participants near and far, for bringing your 'nuggets of gold' and helping me explore and refine many of the ideas here, and most of all, keeping things 'in the real world';
- The Four Musketeers: Sandeep Das, Stephen Foster (for 'What whys beneath'), Martin Falke-Hanson and Richard Taylor – for their interest in this book, time reading various drafts and helping me to find my way;
- Lynda McGill, for editorial oversight;
- Sarah Montrose, for being such a steadfast support;
- Associate Professor Dr Mohammad Farhad Peerally – for helping me see the bigger picture early on;

- Dr Mannie Sher, for finding the time and giving encouragement over more than a decade and always showing how to take things to the next level;
- Gemma Valler, for supporting the idea of a second book.

AND NOT FORGETTING:

- Julie Brown, Roger C, Nicola C, Paul G, Russell H, Professor Dr Erik Hollnagel (for his thoughts on the compatibility between FRAM and RCA), Tim Leech, Tim Maltin (Titanic expert extraordinaire), Professor Dr Henry Mintzberg (for expressing an interest in cause(s) and the excellent IMPM programme), Emma Norris (Institute for Government), Professor Dr Antony Pemberton and Kate Sibthorpe;
- Father Dr Anthony Cogliolo – for being such a fountain of knowledge and supportive friend to the family;
- The Cycling Amigos, Gordon and Fiona MacDonald, Nick and Sian Rudgard, Nigel and Susan Proctor, the Swim Team and the Slipper-men – for helping me maintain some balance during the COVID lockdowns.
- The Book Club – for continuing my education and keeping me as a member despite some lengthy absences;
- Joni Mitchell – for her foresight, courage to speak out and way with words and music.

Notes

Introduction

1. Douglas Adams, '*The Hitchhiker's Guide to the Galaxy*'.
2. The sinking and significant loss of life of the crew and passengers of SS/RMS *Titanic* in April 1912. The iceberg was the immediate cause as explained in Chapter 12.
3. Concerning Captain Edward Smith, the Board of Trade Titanic Inquiry concluded, 'He made a mistake, a very grievous mistake, but one in which, in the face of practice and past experience, negligence cannot be said to have had any part; and in the absence of negligence, it is, . . . impossible to fix Captain Smith with blame'.
4. In the film '*Groundhog Day*', the main character re-lives the same day repeatedly.
5. https://www.brainyquote.com/quotes/albert_einstein_385842

Chapter 1: Critical Points Concerning Root Cause Analysis (RCA)

1. Thinking in Systems: A Primer, by Donella H Meadows. Published by Chelsea Green Publishing Company.

2. There is a good discussion about the evolution of different root cause definitions here: https://www.taproot.com/definition-of-a-root-cause/. Note: one could devote pages to the topic of different cause types, but the scope of this overview book demands a 'common sense' approach in which types of cause should emerge during the course of the discussion, not least when we turn to the question of what action plans are likely to work.

3. There is a TED talk on causation vs. correlation: https://www.youtube.com/watch?v=8B271L3NtAw. A Manchester University link on causality language and types: https://www.phrasebank.manchester.ac.uk/explaining-cause-and-effect/

4. For more detail about the Bowtie, see https://www.caa.co.uk/safety-initiatives-and-resources/working-with-industry/bowtie/about-bowtie/where-did-bowtie-come-from/

5. Some call measures 'barriers', 'mitigations' or 'controls' – they are activities or steps undertaken to prevent, detect or recover from adverse impacts from relevant threats. Of course some measures are more appropriate and effective than others, which will become obvious during the course of this book.

6. News in 2023 about UK police data leaks and losses from the British Museum highlight the problem of limits to what has been done after an adverse event has occurred.

7. Some more illustrations here: https://risktec.tuv.com/risktec-knowledge-bank/bowtie-risk-management/lessons-learned-from-the-real-world-application-of-the-bow-tie-method/. In a medical context, see https://bmjopenquality.bmj.com/content/10/2/e001240 and https://journals.sagepub.com/doi/pdf/10.1177/0310057X1604400615. For a railway example, see https://www.rssb.co.uk/en/safety-and-health/guidance-and-good-practice/bowties/using-bowtie-analysis. For a project example, see http://wiki.doing-projects.org/index.php/Using_the_bowtie_method_to_evaluate_the_risks_in_a_construction_project

Chapter 1 (*Continued*)

8. As coined by Argyris and Schon: https://infed.org/chris-argyris-theories-of-action-double-loop-learning-and-organizational-learning/

9. See this overview of critical elements, etc. https://www.hse.gov.uk/research/rrpdf/rr899.pdf

10. See Heinrich's model for safety, an example of how near-miss reporting can be useful to head off major incidents or adverse events: https://www.skybrary.aero/articles/heinrich-pyramid; Further, there are a range of rather complex considerations in relation to quality-related root cause analysis in the Lean and Lean six sigma arena including O-PDCA and DMAIC as well as issues that potentially involve statistical analysis, where there are choices around One Variable at a Time (OVAT) and Multivariate at a Time (MVAT) approaches. It is out of the scope of this high-level overview to go into detail on these matters, but readers with a particular interest might want to consider this further by going to A Smalley's book 'Four types of problems': https://www.lean.org/store/book/four-types-of-problems/

11. HROs is a huge subject. See this McKinsey article: https://www.mckinsey.com/capabilities/operations/our-insights/what-high-reliability-organizations-get-right and also https://web.mhanet.com/media-library/high-reliability-organization-toolkit/

12. For example, https://www.taproot.com/is-there-just-one-root-cause-for-a-major-accident/; An article in a medical context that also highlights the problem of looking for a single cause: https://qualitysafety.bmj.com/content/26/5/417

13. https://www.goodreads.com/quotes/search?utf8=%E2%9C%93&q=Everything+should+be+made+as+simple+as+possible%2C+but+not+simpler&commit=Search There is some debate as to whether this quote originated from Albert Einstein, but the evidence points to him having a role in the form quoted.

Chapter 2: The Fishbone Diagram and Eight Ways of Understanding Why

1. http://scihi.org/egon-friedells-cutural-histories/

2. In relation to a given goal or objective, and assuming an incident has exceeded the limits for a setback that can be tolerated.

Chapter 2 (*Continued*)

3. McKinsey 7S: `https://www.mckinsey.com/capabilities/strategy-and-corporate-finance/our-insights/enduring-ideas-the-7-s-framework`

4. Galbraith Star Model: `https://www.jaygalbraith.com/component/rsfiles/download?path=StarModel.pdf`

5. COSO (ERM): `https://www.coso.org/Shared%20Documents/2017-COSO-ERM-Integrating-with-Strategy-and-Performance-Executive-Summary.pdf`

6. Often called a 'risk appetite'. So, a project might be budgeted at £5 million and be due to return £10 million. You might be reluctantly prepared to accept costs of £6 million and returns of £9 million, but you would not be happy with costs of £8 million and returns of £8 million.

   What you are and are not prepared to tolerate going wrong reflects the risk appetite.

Chapter 3: Systems Thinking and Eight Ways to Understand Why, with Connections

1. `https://deming.org/a-bad-system-will-beat-a-good-person-every-time/`

2. `https://ourhiddenworlds.com/facts/`

3. At MIT and the Sloan School of Management.

4. See `https://www.mckinsey.com/capabilities/strategy-and-corporate-finance/our-insights/the-beginning-of-system-dynamics#/`

5. The key idea was to recognise counterintuitive effects. A useful overview is contained at `https://systemdynamics.org/origin-of-system-dynamics/`

6. In my analysis, systems thinking has not become mainstream because (i) it hasn't seemed essential up to now and (ii) because of the way it disrupts some current paradigms. See also `https://www.researchgate.net/publication/341126538_Practical_Applications_of_Systems_Thinking_to_Business`. Other good systems thinking books include '*Stafford Beer's Cybernetics and Management*', Ralph Stacey's '*Strategic Management and organizational dynamics*', David Peter Stroh's '*Systems*

Chapter 3 (*Continued*)

Thinking for Social Change' and Mannie Sher and David Lawlor's '*An Introduction to Systems Psychodynamics*'.

7. Here a useful NASA example of systems analysis: https://ntrs.nasa.gov/api/citations/20050172128/downloads/20050172128.pdf

8. Thus, systems thinking questions a mindset that supposes that you can predict the future through simplistic trend analysis. As we saw with the financial crisis and the COVID-19 pandemic, disruptions and step changes can arise in a matter of days, weeks and a few months.

   A very topical feedback loop at the time of writing this book is the increase in CO_2 levels and the impact this has on climate. See this NASA overview of the Earth as a system: https://climate.nasa.gov/nasa_science/science/

9. This example illustrates why Tesla invested a great deal in dedicated car charging points at service stations.

10. '*Thinking in Systems: A Primer*' by Donella H Meadows. Published by Chelsea Green Publishing Company

11. The Malcolm Gladwell book '*The Tipping Point*' (Published by Little, Brown) is worthy of note, as are many of his books. He says: 'The tipping point is that . . . moment when an idea, trend, or social behaviour crosses a threshold, tips, and spreads like wildfire'.

12. Although some examples of inflation-related causal loop diagrams do exist, see https://www.bis.org/ifc/publ/ifcb57_22.pdf

13. There are various versions of this quote, for example, J Edwards Deming, Paul Batalden, and Arthur Jones, but I want to emphasise that it's more than just about the design of a system; *it's also about the operation*.

14. Other relevant systems may include stakeholder expectations or even our assumptions about what is possible. As the book will highlight, many things need to be 'in the mix' when looking systemically at why things are not going to plan.

15. For example, causal loop diagrams that include 'other systems that matter' can create new insights in problem-solving workshops.

16. The US Navy design motto KISS: 'Keep It Simple, Stupid'.

17. Adapted, with thanks, from Mikhael V. Oet's paper: 'Systemic Financial Feedbacks – Conceptual Framework and Modelling Implications'.

Chapter 3 (*Continued*)

18. From the 2023 book '*The Great Crashes*' by Linda Yueh, published by Penguin Random House.

19. https://www.ft.com/content/80e2987a-2e50-11dc-821c-0000779fd2ac

20. Not forgetting that many 'players' did foresee what was likely to happen and made a fortune as a result. (see Michael Lewis's book '*The Big Short*', published by Penguin books).

21. Changes in the US included: the Dodd–Frank wall street reform and consumer protection act, the Consumer Financial Protection Bureau, the Financial Stability oversight board (looking at systemically important institutions), and the Volker Rule, which looks at hedge fund investments, etc. Elsewhere there were other changes concerning senior manager accountabilities, capital adequacy, stress testing and the role of risk committees, etc.. It is also worth noting that some regulatory regimes were overhauled (e.g., in the UK). Still, elsewhere there are others who argue that there is more to be done to improve regulatory oversight, e.g., in the context of the collapse of the Silicon Valley Bank in 2023. See also https://blogs.lse.ac.uk/usappblog/2023/03/18/lessons-from-the-collapse-of-silicon-valley-bank/

22. See https://www.technologyreview.com/2011/02/22/196987/when-the-butterfly-effect-took-flight/

23. See https://onepetro.org/PS/article-abstract/61/05/48/33432/Root-Causal-Factors-Uncovering-the-Hows-amp-Whys?redirectedFrom=fulltext

24. The boundary may be implicit in an audit or inquiry scope or remit. FMEA builds on some of the ideas in Bowtie and is used extensively in the auto industry and Lean six sigma environments. For reference, see https://www.weibull.com/hotwire/issue165/fmeacorner165.htm. The boundary diagram in a systems and project context can be found here https://www.qualica.net/en/help/tools/project_management/boundary_diagram_sw/

25. Where I highlighted the financial crisis causal loop diagram was not looking at bonuses, etc. Considering Diagram 3.2, government policy may well influence the building of charging points, as would the availability of skilled technicians.

26. Thus, with the Titanic, 9/11, Enron, the 2007–2008 financial crisis, etc., the focus of inquiries was as much on how to manage the negative impacts on people, money, etc., as the specific immediate issue that arose.

Chapter 3 (*Continued*)

27. As an illustration of how to think about the 'actors' involved in a tragedy, see this list of companies involved, directly or indirectly, in Grenfell Tower: https://www.theguardian.com/uk-news/2017/jun/15/long-builder-chain-for-grenfell-a-safety-and-accountability-issue. See also this Grenfell 'web of blame' diagram shared by Richard Millett KC: https://www.constructionenquirer.com/2022/11/11/grenfell-firms-accused-of-spinning-a-web-of-blame/

28. Fortune article: 8th June 2023: https://fortune.com/2023/06/08/gm-tesla-ev-charging-network-us-standard/

29. See Forbes: https://www.forbes.com/sites/prakashdolsak/2021/05/05/the-lack-of-ev-charging-stations-could-limit-ev-growth/. See also The Atlantic: https://www.theatlantic.com/science/archive/2023/05/where-are-the-ev-charging-stations/674241/

Section 2: Eight Ways to Understand Why, with Connections

1. See https://www.goodreads.com/quotes/5382-history-doesn-t-repeat-itself-but-it-does-rhyme

2. This approach follows the Lean principle of paying attention to the 'Gemba' – i.e. what happens in practice rather than what happens in theory. See https://www.lean.org/lexicon-terms/gemba/

3. Author of '*Code Complete*', published by Microsoft Press. See https://softwarequotes.com/author/steve-c-mcconnell

Chapter 4: Setting Appropriate Strategies, Goals, and Understanding Risks

1. See https://www.goodreads.com/quotes/163904-the-best-laid-schemes-o-mice-an-men-gang-aft

2. For more information, see https://www.nps.gov/wrbr/learn/historyculture/thefirstflight.htm

Chapter 4 (*Continued*)

3. Otto Lilienthal is known in Germany and the glider community but deserves to be better known all over the world: `https://en.wikipedia.org/wiki/Otto_Lilienthal`

4. See this summary of the critical components of the flyer: `https://www.pbs.org/wgbh/nova/wright/flye-nf.html`

5. See `https://www.readthistwice.com/quotes/book/the-wright-brothers`

6. The article 'Of Strategies, Deliberate and Emergent', by Henry Mintzberg and James A. Waters (published by John Wiley & Sons), is a classic on the deliberate vs. emergent choice. The book '*Only the Paranoid Survive*', by Andrew S Grove (published by Profile Books), discusses the evolution of Intel towards the manufacture of computer chips. It is still a classic book for the detail, clarity and insight concerning what it takes to permit appropriate experimentation.

7. See `https://www.brainyquote.com/quotes/yogi_berra_124868`

8. Rudyard Kipling's classic poem 'If': `https://www.poetryfoundation.org/poems/46473/if---`

9. James Reason's book, '*Managing the Risk of Organizational Accidents*'. Published by Routledge.

10. For the BP Deepwater Horizon disaster, a Swiss cheese analysis can be found in the inquiry report on p. 32: `https://www.bp.com/content/dam/bp/business-sites/en/global/corporate/pdfs/sustainability/issue-briefings/deepwater-horizon-accident-investigation-report.pdf`

11. We need better metaphors for the way we run organisations because I have seen too much alignment be the cause of problems on numerous occasions.

12. Declaration: Alan Paterson is my brother.

13. The 2023 Police Service Nothern Ireland data leak in the process of responding to a freedom of information request may well involve workload factors.

14. '*The Icarus Paradox: How Exceptional Companies Bring About Their Own Downfall*' by Danny Miller. Published by Harper Business.

15. '*The Failure of Risk Management: Why It's Broken and How to Fix It*' by Douglas W. Hubbard. Published by Wiley.

16. '*The Black Swan: The Impact of the Highly Improbable*' by Nassim Nicholas Taleb. Published by Random House Publishing Group.

17. See `https://www.azquotes.com/quote/465361`

Chapter 5: Having Timely, Accurate Data, Information and Communications

1. See https://www.azquotes.com/author/4147-Peter_Drucker

2. 'Human Factors in Aviation (Cognition and Perception)' by Earl L. Wiener (Editor), David C. Nagel (Editor). Published by Academic Press.

3. See https://www.abbottaerospace.com/downloads/gama-publication-recommended-practices-and-guidelines-for-part-23-cockpit-and-flight-deck-design/

4. Some Human Factors and Ergonomics links: https://ergonomics.org.uk, https://iea.cc, https://www.hfes.org/

5. For more information concerning the evolution of financial accounting: https://online.maryville.edu/blog/history-of-accounting/

6. https://corporatefinanceinstitute.com/resources/esg/esg-disclosure/

7. This concerns how organisations account for what they are doing internally, which can involve 'looking through' the activities of different subsidiaries.

8. The Chartered Institute of Management Accountants (founded in 1919) has some helpful materials: https://www.cimaglobal.com/Documents/Thought_leadership_docs/Management%20and%20financial%20accounting/Academic-Research-Report-Strategic-Management-Process.pdf

9. Introduced by Robert S Kaplan and David P Norton in 1992, now championed by various organizations: https://balancedscorecard.org/bsc-basics-overview/

10. There is a good discussion on KPIs in 'Operational Risk Management' by Ariane Chapelle. Published by Wiley.

11. Sébastien Allaire (founding partner of Finaction & Associés and certification auditor for IFACI).

12. FMEA: Failure Mode and Effects Analysis, is also known as Failure Modes and Effects Analysis and is extensively used in the motor industry. It uses the 'boundary diagram' approach.

13. Low risks are rated 1–3/10, medium risks 4–6/10 and four high risks range from 7–10/10. The clever bit is that a 7/10 rating is for high risks; a 8/10 rating is for very high risks; a 9/10 rating is for extremely high risks, and a 10/10 rating is for dangerously high risks only.

Chapter 5 (*Continued*)

14. Sometimes senior executive and board involvement will make all the difference to how risk is managed because they may be able to (i) initiate cross-functional activities and (ii) make available extra resources or expertise to manage the risk better before anything goes wrong. And even if they can't do this, their early involvement will often result in much better crisis management preparations and more thought about managing press and stakeholder communications if something bad happens.

15. This framework seeks to align risk reporting with incident reporting. It is also 'asymmetrical'; in other words, a high-impact low probability issue is treated more seriously than a low-impact higher probability issue. Different variations are possible, adding urgency, etc., but it is out of the scope of this book to discuss this in more detail.

16. The Hurricane Katrina report: https://www.nrc.gov/docs/ML1209/ML12093A081.pdf, which has been followed by various reviews questioning whether all key lessons have been learned and implemented: https://theconversation.com/the-2021-hurricane-season-showed-us-isnt-prepared-as-climate-related-disasters-push-people-deeper-into-poverty-169075

17. Here, I am referring to whether a critical risk has been analysed into sub-risks and mitigations for each of these defined and then set to report in line with the appropriate 'risk appetite'.

18. Here, we are discussing the human tendency, if the criteria allow it, to give ourselves the benefit of the doubt when we report progress. The psychology concerns 'self-justification' and 'confirmation bias,' which will be discussed in the chapter concerning human factors.

19. Of course, other choices are possible such as 2250 m for days one and two, leaving 1500 m for day three, and some 'slack' if the team doesn't meet their goals on days one and two.

20. Let me stress that I recognise that many programmes and projects involve a number of things coming together at the end, but what I am highlighting is that without care about the way tasks are scheduled, *you can end up pushing even more things towards a deadline, which can exceed the bandwidth of what can be sensibly managed at that point.* There is some good material from McKinsey on this topic, under the title '*Beyond the Hockey Stick*': https://www.mckinsey.com/capabilities/strategy-and-corporate-finance/our-insights/the-strategy-and-corporate-finance-blog/hockey-stick-dreams-hairy-back-reality

Chapter 5 (*Continued*)

21. *'It Should Never Happen Again: The Failure of Inquiries and Commissions to Enhance Risk Governance'* by Mike Lauder. Published by Routledge.

22. The Columbia (shuttle) accident investigation report highlights the problem of weak signals becoming normalised: https://history.nasa.gov/columbia/reports/CAIBreportv1.pdf; an excellent short overview of some of the key points of note can be found in the book *'Aloft'*, by William Langewiesche. Published by Penguin Random House.

Chapter 6: Setting Appropriate Roles, Responsibilities, Accountabilities and Authorities

1. See https://quotefancy.com/quote/919778/Thomas-Paine-A-body-of-men-holding-themselves-accountable-to-nobody-ought-not-to-be

2. For a UK perspective on the role of an audit committee: https://www.frc.org.uk/getattachment/9ac07916-ea56-4027-864a-11ef9bfa24e4/Guidance-on-Audit-Committees-(September-2012).pdf

3. There are numerous detailed explanations of R2A2 available. For example: https://www.iso9001help.co.uk/5.3%20Roles%20Responsibility%20&%20Authority.html

    The importance of R2A2 in a root cause context was made prominent by various US Department of Energy root cause reports: https://www.nrc.gov/docs/ML0223/ML022340293.pdf

4. https://en.wikipedia.org/wiki/Separation_of_powers_under_the_United_States_Constitution

5. The research: 'No Body to Kick, No Soul to Damn: Responsibility and Accountability for the Financial Crisis (2007–2010)' by Olivia Nicol is just one example of many on the problem of accountability: https://psycnet.apa.org/record/2016-38247-001

6. Details of the UK SM&CR can be found at https://www.fca.org.uk/firms/senior-managers-certification-regime

7. For Australia, the BEAR requirements can be found at https://www.apra.gov.au/banking-executive-accountability-regime. Other regimes are available for different countries and organisations. The paper, 'With great power comes great responsibility', concerns banking supervisory roles: https://www.bis.org/fsi/fsibriefs14.pdf

Chapter 6 (*Continued*)

8. Quotes about this problem go back to Tacitus: 'This is an unfair thing about war: victory is claimed by all, failure to one alone'. This problem with the avoidance of accountability is closely linked to the tendency to scapegoat others: https://en.wikipedia.org/wiki/Scapegoating

9. Whilst there is a theoretical explanation of the 'correct' role of an internal audit function, concerning 'the three lines' model; in practice, this role is not always understood and agreed with business managers, which can create its own problems. And whilst the meaning of 'reasonable assurance' is quite well understood in external auditing, there is very little guidance regarding what this means in an internal audit context.

10. Or 'latent vulnerabilities': https://en.wikipedia.org/wiki/Swiss_cheese_model

11. RACI is one of the most used accountability mapping frameworks. More recently, McKinsey has started to propose the DARE framework: https://www.mckinsey.com/capabilities/people-and-organizational-performance/our-insights/the-organization-blog/the-limits-of-raci-and-a-better-way-to-make-decisions. DARE stands for Deciders, Advisors, Recommenders and Execution stakeholders.

    I have been using a specially modified RACI: RASCEIO – this includes support roles, execute roles (for third-party relationships) and oversight roles (for GRC matters such as policy owners, risk and compliance functions).

12. Bain & Company's RAPID is a tool to clarify decision accountability. It signifies: Recommend, Agree, Perform, Input and Decide. They emphasise the importance of connecting what needs to be addressed, who needs to be involved and how they are to be involved.

13. Swim lanes are often used for process mapping exercises. They are regularly used in Lean activities as part, inter alia, of a SIPOC analysis. For more information, see https://en.wikipedia.org/wiki/Swimlane

14. In my experience, some Internal Audit teams get used to unclear R2A2 and don't always see the connection between surprises and these problems.

15. This is often referred to as 'the bystander effect'. The excellent book '*Wilful Blindness*', by Margaret Heffernan, has a chapter called 'Bystanders'.

16. When it comes to a 'major incident' involving work between emergency services and local government, there is good guidance available in the United Kingdom: https://assets.publishing.service.gov.uk/government/uploads/system/uploads/attachment_data/file/62228/recovery-emergency-management-guide.

Chapter 6 (*Continued*)

pdf#:~:text=The%20graph%20shows%20the%20activity%20of%20
the%20police%2C,protracted%2C%20particularly%20where%20a%20
crime%20has%20been%20committed

Taking an organisational perspective, a useful book to look at is '*Requisite Organisation*' by Elliott Jacques, published by Routledge, in which he discusses, among other things, the fact that when you are looking at an organisation's strategy and goals, it is necessary to design an organisation that will match internally the level of complexity that the organisation will encounter externally and which should adapt as these challenges evolve.

17. Which can be a reason managers are reluctant to 'dig into' these problems.

18. Another framework to look at which puts culture, sub-culture, and behaviour in a proper systems perspective can be found in the Burke–Litwin model. An overview of the model can be found at this link: https://cio-wiki.org/wiki/File:Burke-Litwin_Model.jpg

19. One technique that is emerging is Organisational Role Analysis (ORA). This goes beyond accountability mapping and looks at how people take up (or don't) their roles in an organisation. It examines the fact that roles inevitably need to evolve and considers how individuals engage constructively in role ambiguity and resolve unhelpful differences when necessary. This is discussed in the '*Introduction to Systems Psychodynamics*' book by Mannie Sher & David Lawlor, published by Routledge, and also in this paper by John Newton: https://www.taylorfrancis.com/chapters/edit/10.4324/9780429480355-10/organisational-role-analysis-john-newton

R2A2 are especially challenging when you think look across a range of organisations, such as companies, regulators, charities, governments, NGOs and other international agencies.

20. Governance initiatives are a part of this story. Still, I want to emphasise the importance of broadening the focus of governance so that you can consider its operational implications not just see it as something detached from daily life in senior decision-making bodies.

Chapter 7: Ensuring a Suitable Design

1. See https://www.brainyquote.com/quotes/steve_jobs_169129

2. See https://www.wonders-of-the-world.net/Statue-of-Liberty/Construction-of-the-statue-of-liberty.php

Chapter 7 (*Continued*)

3. Essential details can be found here: https://www.toureiffel.paris/en/the-monument/key-figures

4. This webpage provides some useful links to images of the Eiffel Tower while it was being constructed: https://www.toureiffel.paris/en/the-monument/history

5. See https://theculturetrip.com/europe/france/paris/articles/gustave-eiffel-master-of-harmonious-design/

6. For reference, here are some links highlighting how important Clinical Trial design is: https://en.wikipedia.org/wiki/Clinical_study_design, https://www.ncbi.nlm.nih.gov/pmc/articles/PMC3083073/

7. See also https://designmuseum.org/discover-design/all-stories/what-is-good-design-a-quick-look-at-dieter-rams-ten-principles. A result is that we *will be making design decisions even when we are not consciously thinking about aspects of how something is being built.* And the question of what design means for new applications and AI, etc., is a new frontier that only a few fully understand.

8. A brief discussion about the different types of IT updates can be found in the attached link: https://www.microsoft.com/en-us/msrc/security-update-severity-rating-system. A more general overview can be found here: https://www.ncsc.gov.uk/collection/device-security-guidance/managing-deployed-devices/keeping-devices-and-software-up-to-date

9. This is an example of a design dilemma that I will discuss in Chapter 11.

10. Bruce Schneier regularly blogs about the security gaps that concern him: https://www.schneier.com/blog/archives/2008/03/the_security_mi_1.html

11. Some aviation checklists are provided here: https://www.skybrary.aero/articles/checklists-purpose-and-use. See also the award-winning book '*Complications*', by Atul Gawande (p. 44), which talks about the importance of computer algorithms in a medical context (and much more besides).

12. See https://www.hsj.co.uk/supplement-archive/clinical-care-protocols-when-safe-comes-as-standard/5072280.article

13. '*Lean Auditing*' book, by the author: https://www.wiley.com/en-us/Lean+Auditing%3A+Driving+Added+Value+and+Efficiency+in+Internal+Audit-p-9781118896884

14. Control activities are specific tasks that ensure the organisation is doing things correctly.

Chapter 7 (*Continued*)

15. John Bendermacher, RA, CIA and CRMA.

16. '*Skin in the Game: The Hidden Asymmetries in Daily Life*' by Nassim Nicholas Taleb. Published by Allen Lane.

17. GRC overview (IT links): `https://www.cioinsight.com/it-management/grc-framework/`. The UK Financial Report Council explains some minimum requirements for an Internal Controls framework here: `https://www.frc.org.uk/getattachment/d672c107-b1fb-4051-84b0-f5b83a1b93f6/Guidance-on-Risk-Management-Internal-Control-and-Related-Reporting.pdf`. This is a link to a PwC guide on GRC frameworks: `https://www.pwc.co.uk/services/risk/governance-risk-and-compliance/governance-risk-control-frameworks.html`; see a banking example: `https://www.bis.org/publ/bcbs40.pdf`

18. See `https://medium.com/productivity-revolution/20-inspiring-quotes-every-designer-should-know-b2777f1c3ff1`

Chapter 8: Understanding and Accommodating External Factors

1. See `https://www.goodreads.com/quotes/7687394-men-will-not-look-at-things-as-they-really-are`

2. If we consider the Bowtie diagram, external factors are threats, risks or uncertainties that must be recognised and factored into plans as much as possible.

3. See `https://www.brainyquote.com/quotes/carl_sagan_141336`

4. This is a simple illustration of a range of 'vertical' and 'horizontal' strategic moves an organisation might make to strengthen its position.

5. There are various sources of information in the public domain about fines and sanctions. Here is one US example: `https://fcpa.stanford.edu/index.html`

6. The Transparency International corruption index reminds us, if we need reminding, that many countries still have a significant problem with bribery, corruption, etc. `https://www.transparency.org/en/cpi/2022`. However, from the perspective of some in those countries, they might not regard all their business practices as corrupt (they might just argue it's 'different here'). And just because a country has a reasonably low corruption index does not mean there will be no corruption there.

Chapter 8 (*Continued*)

7. The use of the word 'business' appears on several occasions, but this does not mean to imply commercial business in all circumstances, rather the work/tasks of the relevant organisation.

8. If you follow the logic that you should never engage with a third party where there is even the remotest possibility of corruption risk, you could easily find you would not be able to operate with many third parties, especially in some environments. So, there is a dilemma here; take no risks and run a smaller business or take all reasonable steps and recognise that something adverse may happen nonetheless. The main message is that you can't just stop an explanation of getting caught out by blaming the external factor. And – all too often – signs can often be found (if you look) that something isn't right, but these may not be picked up and acted on quickly enough, with the right level of rigour.

9. Here is a helpful overview of critical points about SLAs in an IT context: `https://www.cio.com/article/274740/outsourcing-sla-definitions-and-solutions.html`

10. Of course, there are a range of reasons to choose consultants: for their specialist expertise or know-how, to provide extra resources if there is a shortage (e.g. be seconded to work on tasks under the direction of management) and to facilitate change workshops or – as will be discussed – to help validate a proposed course of action. A manager who says 'we don't need to get extra support', either to put on a brave face or for cost reasons, runs the risk of getting caught out.

11. Several inquiries have specifically called out the role consultants have played in relation to significant setbacks. For example, a discussion about consultants in the Fire Control project (covered in Chapter 9) identified they needed to be better managed (recognising that they require proper oversight to be effective). More recently, the role of consultants has been discussed in the BBC Radio 4 program '*Magic Consultants*' and in the book '*The Big Con*' by Mariana Mazzucato and Rosie Collington.

    As a consultant myself, my position is to say that there are many good reasons to use consultants; you just need to do this professionally, with your eyes open.

12. '*The Blunders of Our Governments*' by Anthony King and Ivor Crewe. Published by Oneworld Publications.

13. For example, there are many more interesting opportunities and threats to properly understand customers, shareholders or other investors, special interest groups, agents, partners, the media, legal and regulatory matters and other external factors of strategic importance.

Chapter 8 (*Continued*)

14. There is a considerable amount that could be and has been written about managing third parties. But my goal is to highlight that despite vetting processes, supplier management frameworks and ongoing efforts to monitor what is being done, it is still quite possible to get caught out. Sometimes this happens for 'obvious reasons' (such as poor vendor selection in the first place), but it can still occur when many good practices are in place. In my experience, the distinguishing feature between good and great practice can revolve around subtle points (which some call 'behavioural risks') that are easy to brush aside.

15. This takes us to an interesting, good practice that can tease out things that would otherwise be missed. Rather than relying on a third party's SLA compliance, pay attention to some softer, more intangible data about the third party (some refer to 'weak signals'). For example: How proactive are third parties about issues and setbacks? How often do they come up with process improvements that reduce their fees? Do they respond quickly to ad hoc requests? Are their good staff staying or leaving? How often are there additional charges to pay and why?

16. My late father became a policeman in his early twenties. By the time he left a dozen years later, he was a different man; some jobs and working conditions can change the way people are.

17. Once you have heard a few 'war stories' about what can happen in some countries, you realise how quickly, and how badly, things can go wrong in ways you can often not even imagine. It makes you realise, as well, how a 'tick-box' approach to compliance will open you up to problems in the long run.

Chapter 9: Effective Building, Maintenance and Change

1. See https://www.brainyquote.com/authors/arthur-bloch-quotes#:~:text=If%20your%20project%20doesn't,didn't%20think%20was%20important.&text=Every%20clarification%20breeds%20new%20questions.&text=If%20you%20improve%20or%20tinker,it%20will%20break%20or%20malfunction

2. Gannt charts: https://www.gantt.com

3. For an overview, see https://en.wikipedia.org/wiki/Manhattan_Project

Chapter 9 (*Continued*)

4. Those with a military background often had 'project management' skills that were useful in a range of business contexts.

5. Link to the Project Management Institute: https://www.pmi.org, Association for Project Management (UK): https://www.apm.org.uk/

6. For a Prince II overview: https://en.wikipedia.org/wiki/PRINCE2

7. See this useful overview of some of the key project management frameworks: https://thedigitalprojectmanager.com/projects/pm-methodology/project-management-methodologies-made-simple/

8. For an overview of Agile, see the attached: https://www.agilealliance.org/agile101/12-principles-behind-the-agile-manifesto/

9. MVP is also a Lean technique: https://www.indeed.com/career-advice/career-development/minimum-viable-product. Nowadays, there are other variants: Minimum Loveable Product, etc.

10. For more on Agile roles: https://monday.com/blog/project-management/agile-roles/

11. In other words, Agile working methods seek to address many of the 'eight ways to understand why' discussed in this book.

12. I see this quite often in other domains outside of Agile. Some managers get excited about something they have heard about in business literature or at a consultant's workshop and – buoyed on by success stories – push for the same thing, not fully understanding all the difficulties they may encounter.

13. Reliability-Centred Maintenance in overview: https://www.dnv.com/article/terminology-explained-what-is-reliability-centered-maintenance-rcm--207988

14. UK Public Accounts Committee Report on Fire Control: https://publications.parliament.uk/pa/cm201012/cmselect/cmpubacc/1397/1397.pdf

15. National Audit Office (UK) on Fire Control: https://www.nao.org.uk/wp-content/uploads/2011/07/10121272es.pdf

16. Charlie explained: 'If you run a workshop with mid-level and junior staff to ask them what they think about a new plan, they often look for "cues" whether the project, or plan, has already been decided or not. If they are in a workshop, they also look at one another or the boss, and they may sense the project is already a "fait accompli", so often they won't want to appear overly negative or disloyal. You can easily see group dynamics and

Chapter 9 (*Continued*)

groupthink. In the end, even the staff in the room, who don't believe in the plans, can persuade themselves: "We know we need to do something. This seems a rather ambitious plan, but maybe the senior folk know something we don't".'

17. There are only a handful of detailed pieces of work on adaptive accountability; here is one example from Australia: https://researchsystem .canberra.edu.au/ws/portalfiles/portal/33690626/file

18. 'Fact pattern' is a term you sometimes see in a legal context. However, it can be very helpful to think in these terms when you are exploring root causes and considering hypotheses for why things may not have gone to plan.

19. Because I am sharing a generic example, the causes and effects I show are necessarily simplified. Sometimes causes and effects can 'split' as you might see in a fault tree diagram. However, I am keeping this added complexity to one side for this overview discussion.

20. The project premortem appears in a September 2007 Harvard Business Review article: https://hbr.org/2007/09/performing-a-project-premortem. It should be stressed that there are better and worse ways of conducting a premortem. If you 'go through the motions' on a premortem there is every chance it will not be a huge help.

21. Megaprojects and Risk: An Anatomy of Ambition by Bent Flyvberg, written with Nils Bruzelius and Werner Rothengatter.

22. See https://www.goodreads.com/author/quotes/68024.Charlton_ Ogburn_Jr_

23. This topic will be discussed further in Chapter 11.

24. HBR article, September 2018, 'Too many projects': https://hbr. org/2018/09/too-many-projects

25. I have heard a range of quotes along these lines, this is a summary of several.

Chapter 10: Understanding and Adapting to 'Human Factors'

1. Act 1, Scene 2 of *Julius Caesar* by William Shakespeare.

2. As a former pilot, Sydney Dekker has written many interesting books, also considering hindsight bias.

Chapter 10 (*Continued*)

3. James Reason has written extensively about this in books and articles. Here is a link to a short article on the topic: https://www.ncbi.nlm.nih.gov/pmc/articles/PMC1117770/

4. The THERP technique provides some useful insights on this specific topic. Here is an overview paper: https://inldigitallibrary.inl.gov/sites/sti/sti/5680968.pdf. And another in the nuclear industry: https://inis.iaea.org/collection/NCLCollection-Store/_Public/40/103/40103869.pdf

5. When I write about human variation, this can cover a range of dimensions: physical variations, diversity-related differences (in gender, etc.), personality type, psychological makeup, etc. But in the context of this discussion, I am primarily referring to the way individuals might behave as they carry out their roles. This is part of a bigger picture. See the attached pack: https://ec.europa.eu/research/participants/documents/downloadPublic?documentIds=080166e5c1754eab&appId=PPGMS, where there is a good discussion from slide 16, with a discussion about variability on slide 57.

6. See this excellent Wikipedia overview of the Miracle on the Hudson, including links to NTSB reports. https://en.wikipedia.org/wiki/US_Airways_Flight_1549

7. Indeed, there was initially a concern that he had made the wrong decision because of the loss of the aircraft, which was not upheld in the end.

8. Daniel Kahneman's book '*Noise*' provides countless examples of how supposedly objective decisions are not decided objectively. For example, even court case decisions can depend on the time of the day. See also https://www.pnas.org/doi/10.1073/pnas.1018033108. Atul Gawande discusses this in a medical context in 'Complications' (p. 248) when he cites differences in treatment ratios depending on geographical factors.

9. The Human Factors definition is taken from https://www.hfes.org/About-HFES/What-is-Human-Factors-and-Ergonomics. This also lists several other definitions of Human Factors from different bodies. For this overview chapter, detailed differences will not be debated; suffice it to say that mostly the differences are associated with different contexts in which the terms will be used.

10. Flight simulators create realistic but unusual situations, sometimes involving dilemmas. But you still can't be sure what a flight crew will do on a given day.

11. Mr Spock is a Vulcan who approaches even the most difficult tasks in a cool, calm and logical way – created by Gene Roddenberry (with Gary Lockwood).

Chapter 10 (*Continued*)

12. The excellent book '*Safe Patients, Smart Hospitals*' by Dr Peter Pronovost and Eric Vohr gives some sobering examples of this happening in a hospital context, even during surgery.

13. Just culture simple overview: https://en.wikipedia.org/wiki/Just_culture. US article: https://www.ncbi.nlm.nih.gov/pmc/articles/PMC3776518/, UK NHS guide: https://www.england.nhs.uk/wp-content/uploads/2021/02/NHS_0932_JC_Poster_A3.pdf. Aviation in Europe: https://skybrary.aero/articles/just-culture.

14. Of course, 'just culture' links closely to the concept of psychological safety in the workplace. See this brief explanation: https://psychsafety.co.uk/psychological-safety-newsletter-36/

15. Restorative Justice: https://papers.ssrn.com/sol3/papers.cfm?abstract_id=1943422. Declaration; Dr Antony Pemberton is my cousin.

16. Concerning Barings collapse, see, for example, http://ifci.ch/135340.htm

17. What the 'bad apple' does might be an immediate or contributing cause, not a root cause.

18. https://www.jems.com/news/just-culture-high-reliability-buy-in-commitment-and-trust/

19. See the Bank of England report: https://www.bankofengland.co.uk/-/media/boe/files/working-paper/2021/organisational-culture-and-bank-risk.pdf?la=en&hash=81DD3E865BC0159475FD10A78AA2293F0379FB8E

20. In an ESG context, see https://www.esgthereport.com/what-is-tone-at-the-top-internal-control/

21. One discussion of culture as an emergent property and the reasons for this: https://academy.nobl.io/what-organizational-culture-means-especially-for-a-remote-workforce/

22. Which most behavioural scientists will understand.

23. See https://www.linkedin.com/pulse/94-rule-single-most-powerful-principle-every-leader-david-dibble#:~:text=Edwards%20Deming%2C%20the%20greatest%20quality,Not%20many

24. US 173 plane crash in 1978 in Oregon: https://en.wikipedia.org/wiki/United_Airlines_Flight_173.

Chapter 10 (*Continued*)

25. For example, (1) the robustness of capability assessments (i.e. do I have the right person for the job?) and performance management processes (i.e. have they done a good job?) or (2) training and development for senior managers on 'governance, risk and compliance' matters and other essential topics, such as financial management.

26. There are dozens of books and articles on psychology in the workplace: '*Predictably Irrational*' by Dan Ariely, '*Wilful Blindness*' by Margaret Heffernan, '*Moral Disengagement*' by Albert Bandura, '*Knowledge Resistance*' by M Klintman and '*Born Liars*' by Ian Leslie.

27. Some irrational forces in operation can be found in lists of cognitive biases: https://en.wikipedia.org/wiki/List_of_cognitive_biases. I often notice self-justification and confirmation bias featuring in RCA reviews. In the book '*Being Wrong*' (published by Granta Publications Ltd), Kathryn Schulz observes: 'Certainty and zealotry are not far removed from one another . . . If I believe unshakably in the rightness of my own convictions, it follows that those who hold opposing views are denying the truth and luring others into falsehood. From there, it is a short step to thinking I am entitled . . . to silence such people any way I can . . .' (p. 162).

28. Biases will exist even when staff has been trained on the biases and given checklists.

29. The topic of algorithm design and supervised vs. unsupervised learning for Artificial Intelligence are just two examples of how human factors impact play a role.

30. For example, Myers Briggs Type Indicators, where the book '*Do What You Are*' by Barbara Barron-Tieger explains how personality types are better or less well suited to specific roles.

31. This is a vast subject – here is a primer: https://en.wikipedia.org/wiki/Group_dynamics. The Tavistock Institute does excellent work in this field, including experiential 'group relations' conferences.

32. The Tavistock Institute also looks at board effectiveness questions and runs a board effectiveness practitioner programme: https://www.tavinstitute.org/news/new-book-on-the-dynamics-of-boards/#

33. See https://www.goodreads.com/quotes/9021237-leaders-who-don-t-listen-will-eventually-be-surrounded-by-people

34. You can find 'politics' everywhere there are people: in a hockey club, a women's group, universities and schools, charities, NGOs, trade bodies,

Chapter 10 (*Continued*)

in companies, and – of course – in local and national governments and international organisations.

35. See https://www.history.com/topics/renaissance/machiavelli

36. See this article on organisational politics by Baddeley and James: https://futureleadership10.files.wordpress.com/2010/02/political-skills-model.pdf

37. There are various versions of this sentiment, but I have been unable to find a direct source.

38. See Thomas Erikson's: *'Surrounded by Psychopaths: How to Protect Yourself from Being Manipulated and Exploited in Business (and in Life)'* or David Gillespie's *'Taming Toxic People: The Science of Identifying and Dealing with Psychopaths at Work and at Home'*. See also https://en.wikipedia.org/wiki/Psychopathy_in_the_workplace.

39. See the HBR article highlighting bullying as a significant factor in the workplace: https://hbr.org/2022/11/how-bullying-manifests-at-work-and-how-to-stop-it

40. Framework for the board oversight of Risks: https://www.cpacanada.ca/-/media/site/operational/rg-research-guidance-and-support/docs/02481-rg-framework-board-oversight-enterprise-risk.pdf

41. A summary of the Walker review is contained in this digest: https://www.iod.com/app/uploads/2022/02/IoD-The-Walker-Review-of-corporate-governance-an-assessment-61a2872e27b72eb26e247f816ab3700a.pdf. The full report includes an excellent annex on board dynamics.

42. See https://www.iia.org.uk/media/1691066/internal-audit-code-of-practice-report.pdf – section 11a. However, new Global Internal Auditing standards in draft as at 2023 have not picked this up at present. However, they have picked up the importance of better root cause analysis; see https://www.theiia.org/en/standards/ippf-evolution/

43. From *'Harry Potter and the Half-Blood Prince'* by JK Rowling. Published by Scholastic, Inc.

44. A root cause analysis on why this happens could be carried out but is outside the scope of this book.

45. See https://www.newyorkfed.org/governance-and-culture-reform and https://www.fca.org.uk/firms/culture-and-governance

Chapter 10 (*Continued*)

46. For example, diversity and inclusion statistics may be improving, but that does not mean all aspects of the culture have improved (e.g. creativity and innovation, the quality of decision-making, etc.). An illustration of the problems that the Metropolitan Police has had in changing its culture in various regards over 20+ years. https://www.instituteforgovernment.org.uk/article/comment/everard-inquiry-should-learn-macpherson-report-policing-culture

47. Recognising that foxes are masters in finding escape routes.

48. Chris Argyris' excellent book '*Overcoming Organizational Defences*' provides numerous case studies and practical examples of how organisations avoid painful truths.

Chapter 11: Addressing Resources, Priorities and Dilemmas

1. See https://www.azquotes.com/author/524-Aristotle/tag/goal

2. Crew resource management overview: https://skybrary.aero/articles/crew-resource-management-crm

3. Bridge resource management overview: https://en.wikipedia.org/wiki/Maritime_resource_management

4. 'To err is human' is a cornerstone report in healthcare safety, as it so nicely puts it; 'systems, not shame'; https://www.ncbi.nlm.nih.gov/books/NBK2673/

5. Safe staffing resources, this guide from Ontario, Canada, contains some excellent tools to think about staffing levels (see p. 21): https://rnao.ca/sites/rnao-ca/files/bpg/Staffing_and_Workload_Practices_WEB_2_-_FINAL_-_Jan_2017.pdf, Here is a UK NHS guide: https://www.england.nhs.uk/nursingmidwifery/safer-staffing-nursing-and-midwifery/

6. NICE red flags around staffing levels (note pp. 6, 7 in particular): https://www.england.nhs.uk/wp-content/uploads/2021/05/safe-staffing-adult-in-patient-appendices.pdf

7. Report on safe staffing challenges in the United Kingdom: https://committees.parliament.uk/committee/81/health-and-social-care-committee/news/172310/persistent-understaffing-of-nhs-a-serious-risk-to-patient-safety-warn-mps/. There are

Chapter 11 (*Continued*)

other emerging practices in safe staffing, ranging from qualitative considerations to quantitative considerations that need to be watched closely; if the design of safe staffing measures change then 'safe staffing' measures may not serve the preventative role they used to.

8. Lead times for recruitment are another external factor that needs to be understood and proactively managed.

9. TDODAR in more detail: https://pilot-network.com/news/decision-making-models

10. An Australian example of a Triage framework, from New South Wales: https://www.health.nsw.gov.au/Hospitals/Going_To_hospital/Pages/triage.aspx

11. One example of supplier categories: https://www.thefdagroup.com/blog/a-risk-based-approach-to-managing-supplier-quality

12. How to deliver good service with expedited actions: https://medium.com/@thorbjorn.sigberg/classes-of-service-940aa9056bf5

13. See this example of a financial controls framework guide: https://www.thecaq.org/wp-content/uploads/2019/05/caq_guide_internal_control_over_financial_reporting_2019-05.pdf

14. MITRE on Crown Jewels analysis: https://www.mitre.org/our-impact/intellectual-property/crown-jewels-analysis. Another useful three-page summary of what can be done: https://www.safie.hq.af.mil/Portals/78/documents/IEE/Energy/CJA_2021%20DAF%20fact%20sheet_final.pdf?ver=L5iwNjsgsHlxR8SPg710pw%3D%3D

15. Note the parallel with the 'Time' aspect of TDODAR.

16. Norman Marks: CPA and CRMA.

17. Ethical dilemmas training research: https://www.cambridge.org/core/journals/industrial-and-organizational-psychology/article/abs/applying-ethical-dilemmas-to-professional-ethics-training-and-education-practical-implications-and-future-directions/911DA226878E912A9FA9FDBD1CBF54F0. Note both regulators and organisations are in a difficult situation here; it has all the hallmarks of a 'Catch 22' situation either way.

18. Sometimes called the 'project management triangle', 'the iron triangle' and 'the triple constraint': https://en.wikipedia.org/wiki/Project_management_triangle

19. Discussions not recorded may just be a matter of the secretary's style to the meeting or they may be because of a 'foxy' intervention.

Chapter 11 (*Continued*)

20. 'Bad documents', brief discussion: https://www.lexology.com/ library/detail.aspx?g=aaf488bc-5f29-4c17-80d9-891 d953a9bcd

21. Freedom of Information in Australia: https://www.oaic.gov.au/ freedom-of-information, Freedom of information in Canada: https://en.wikipedia.org/wiki/Freedom_of_information_ in_Canada

22. See also the Eliyahu Goldratt 'Theory of constraints': https://www .tocinstitute.org/theory-of-constraints.html

23. While this was openly seen in India, similar impacts occurred in other countries but below the radar screen. In the United Kingdom, the advice to the public was to 'Save the NHS'.

24. See https://en.wikipedia.org/wiki/Pandora%27s_box#:~:text =From%20this%20story%20has%20grown%20the%20idiom%20 %22to,is%20%22to%20open%20a%20can%20of%20worms%20%22

25. Paul Krugman.

Chapter 12: The Titanic Tragedy and Parallels with Modern Disasters

1. See https://titanicfacts.net/titanic-quotes/

2. There is an added poignancy to having written the first draft of this chapter in March/April 2023 given the implosion of the Titan submersible and sad loss of the captain and passengers in June 2023.

3. Of course, many more details about the Titanic tragedy have attracted interest, including the question of the 'mystery' ship, etc.

4. In addition to the two inquiry transcripts, the recommended Titanic books include: '*A Night to Remember*', by Walter Lord, '*Unsinkable*', by Daniel Allen Butler, '*Lost Voices from the Titanic*', by Nick Barratt and '*Travelling to Tragedy*', by Dr Rudi Newton. In addition, there are several good National Geographic programmes, including '*Titanic: Case Closed*', with Tim Maltin.

5. What follows is my best effort and assessment of the 'fact pattern' and the resulting root causes on this basis. Conclusions have been tied back to the SOLAS enquiry results wherever possible.

Chapter 12 (*Continued*)

6. SS/RMS – Steamship/Royal Mail Ship.

7. Strictly speaking, the itinerary was Belfast, then an official departure from Southampton, then Cherbourg, France and finally Queenstown (Cobh, near Cork, Ireland).

8. Accounts vary about the exact number of passengers and crew: https:// titanicfacts.net/titanic-passengers/, *so I have kept to rounded numbers.*

9. Sources vary on the total capacity of the Titanic: https://en.wikipedia .org/wiki/Titanic

10. https://www.titanicinquiry.org/BOTInq/BOTReport/ botRepRoute.php

11. In 1912, there were around twice the number of icebergs entering the shipping lanes compared to the norm.

12. When you read the detailed accounts, you find a complexity to just about every aspect of what took place. It was, in fact, Sixth Officer Moody that answered the call from Frederick Fleet. Upon passing the message, First Officer Murdoch instructed the quartermaster and the engine room. Readers should recognise that there will be numerous instances where my summary glosses over all of the precise details, but my goal is to highlight the most material factors that influenced the final inquiry conclusions and the determinations of SOLAS.

13. The book '*Unsinkable*' suggests six watertight compartments were initially breached, but it has been said that the damage to the sixth was minimal. Most accounts state five watertight compartments were breached.

14. See, for example, https://www.history.com/this-day-in-history/ titanic-sinks. The best-known coordinates for the sinking location are 49.56W and 41.43N. However, this was uncertain until around 1985.

15. Details about the Lifeboats of the Titanic: https://en.wikipedia .org/wiki/Lifeboats_of_the_Titanic

16. The fact there was no ship-wide alarm must have been a factor, but some accounts say most people knew what was happening after an hour or so.

17. Around 710 crew and passengers were rescued by the SS *Carpathia*. Still, only a handful were rescued from the water. Hence, an estimate of 700 in the lifeboats immediately. Reliable evidence on this is very hard to get. And there is the added complication of what happened with some of the collapsible lifeboats. Again, it's not feasible to discuss all this in detail in this chapter.

Chapter 12 (*Continued*)

18. It is hard to give a precise account given the chaotic nature of what happened, but many passengers in the lifeboats testified that there were many people in the water from the sounds they could hear. Many bodies were recovered from the water over the next few days. It was freezing cold because of the Labrador Current from Greenland, which carried icebergs further south.

19. https://www.bbc.com/future/article/20120402-the-myth-of-the-unsinkable-ship

20. See https://www.encyclopedia-titanica.org/community/threads/imm-vice-president-phillip-franklin.2838/

21. The US Senate remit was inevitably developed at short notice. Still, its high-level scope gave considerable flexibility and led to the ability to 'dig into' the SS *Californian* question once it became known. Some say the inquiry primarily focused on what happened rather than why, and some have argued the questions of Senator William A Smith were somewhat naive (since he had little experience of maritime matters), but many now commend his forensic approach.

22. Within a few days of the tragedy, until 25 May 1912.

23. The US Senate inquiry transcript concerning the Titanic tragedy is available online: https://www.titanicinquiry.org/USInq/AmInq01header.php. The final report is also available online: https://www.senate.gov/artandhistory/history/resources/pdf/TitanicReport.pdf

24. https://www.titanicinquiry.org/BOTInq/BOTInq01Questions.php

25. British Wreck Commissioner inquiry transcript: https://www.titanicinquiry.org/BOTInq/BOTInq01Header.php

26. The questions you ask reflect the boundary of your inquiry.

27. Rather than with the support of black box data and voice recordings, you can sometimes find nowadays.

28. See '*Unsinkable*', p. 183 concerning third-class passengers.

29. There was no general alarm on the Titanic. However, it is worth noting that many crew members died at their posts, still doing their duty until the end.

30. For example, the exact site of the sinking, a compilation of all the passenger testimonies, and more work to properly understand the sea temperature and atmospheric conditions on the night of the sinking.

31. While the inquiry amounted to an organisation 'marking its own homework' to some extent, it does seem that many of the lessons the Board of Trade needed to learn were recognised.

Chapter 12 (*Continued*)

32. There are mixed judgments about Captain Edward Smith, most concluding that he did nothing different from what countless other captains would have done at that time. See '*Unsinkable*', Appendix III. The most critical judgment at the time fell on Captain Lord of the SS *Californian*. See '*Unsinkable*', Appendix II, but note these judgments (and earlier ones) have been called into question thanks to the efforts of Tim Maltin in his book '*A Very Deceiving Night*', published by Malt House Publishing. It provides an excellent analysis of why atmospheric scintillation most likely played a significant role in confounding the perspective of both the crew of the Titanic and the Californian.

33. Note that cost-cutting is a myth since the Titanic was built by Harland & Wolff on a 'cost plus' arrangement with the White Star Line. By all accounts, she was a well-built, technologically advanced ship. With 16 watertight compartments, it was conceivable that three parts of the Titanic could have floated independently.

34. See '*Unsinkable*', p. 73: 'It had been forty years since there had been a passenger ship sunk with serious loss of life, the last being The Atlantic, which struck a submerged rock and sank with the loss of 491 lives, in 1872'.

35. If you were being pedantic, you might say that the question of impact depends on whether you are thinking about the Titanic on its own or the White Star Line with its fleet of ships. To keep it simple, I am considering this question from the perspective of the captain and crew. The White Star Line continued another 20 years after the sinking of the Titanic, merging with Cunard in the 1930s.

36. Here are some of the Titanic's safety innovations: https://ultimatetitanic.com/titanics-safety-features/

37. Both during her design and construction at Harland & Wolff, Belfast, and during her sea trials: https://ultimatetitanic.com/sea-trials-launch/

38. Size expressed between 200 and 400 feet long, according to various testimonies: https://titanicfacts.net/how-big-was-the-iceberg/

39. Concerning the weather, it was exceptionally calm, which was paradoxically a problem for spotting an iceberg: https://www.theguardian.com/science/2000/jul/06/technology

40. Titanic inquiry (Board of Trade). Reginald Lee, who was aside Frederick Fleet, testified: 'It was a dark mass that came through that haze, and there was no white appearing until it was just close alongside the ship, and that was just a fringe at the top'. 'The haze' is most likely referring

Chapter 12 (*Continued*)

to the refractive effects that were happening that night (https://www.titanicinquiry.org/).

41. Optical effects caused by refraction. And the cold air in the vicinity of the Titanic that night also created very clear sparkling stars. The 'Titanic: Case Closed' documentary is excellent on this topic, but it primarily concentrates on contributing causes.

42. There is every indication the lookouts were on full alert. There is a good argument that binoculars might have made spotting the iceberg harder. The naked eye was customarily used to detect things in the sea, and binoculars were used to inspect them. Further, the optical effects that night may have had the effect of 'lifting the horizon', thus masking the profile of the iceberg.

43. Re-enforced by more recent research by Tim Maltin, see https://timmaltin.com/2021/01/05/thermal-inversion-titanic-disaster/

44. Travelled on the freezing cold Labrador current.

45. Board of Trade inquiry: Lightoller: 'I told Mr. Moody to ring up the crow's nest and tell the lookouts to keep a sharp lookout for ice, particularly small ice, and growlers. Mr. Moody rang them up, and I could hear quite distinctly what he was saying. He said, "Keep a sharp lookout for ice, particularly small ice," or something like that, and I told him, I think, to ring up again and tell them to keep a sharp lookout for ice, particularly small ice, and growlers. And he rang up the second time and gave the message correctly'. https://www.titanicinquiry.org/

46. Board of Trade inquiry: Lord Mersey: 'It was shown that for many years past, indeed, for a quarter of a century or more, the practice of liners using this track when in the vicinity of ice at night had been in clear weather to keep the course, to maintain the speed and to trust to a sharp lookout to enable them to avoid the danger. It was said this practice had been justified by experience, with no casualties resulting from it. I accept the evidence as to the practice and as to the immunity from casualties which is said to have accompanied it. But the event has proved the practice to be bad. Its root is probably to be found in competition and in the desire of the public for quick passages rather than in the judgment of navigators. But unfortunately, experience appeared to justify it'. https://www.titanicinquiry.org/

47. The Titanic was capable of manoeuvring well for a ship of that size, and she had started to move out of the way of the iceberg within the 40 seconds she had.

Chapter 12 (*Continued*)

48. Some argue if she had struck the iceberg directly, it might have been better because it might have impacted only the front four watertight compartments. Still, we cannot be sure, and in any event, it would certainly have meant the immediate death of those at the prow of the ship.

49. Passengers were already sending radio messages to Newfoundland, planning for their arrival.

50. The Titanic was planned to be a 'Wednesday' ship. Slightly slower than the Lusitania (a Tuesday ship) but more luxurious.

51. If it was the first four compartments. The design was to cope with up to two watertight compartments breached elsewhere along the hull.

52. Note that the Titanic's sister ship, the Olympic, collided with HMS *Hawke* in September 1911, where two watertight compartments were flooded, but her bulkheads served their purpose, and she could return to Southampton under her own power. This sort of lesser incident not resulting in a big problem can easily reinforce the (incorrect) impression that it is 'impossible' for something awful to happen.

53. Failure of Imagination: https://en.wikipedia.org/wiki/Failure_of_imagination. Bearing in mind the 800 metres stopping distance of the Titanic, it is clear, with the benefit of hindsight, that it was possible for the Titanic to scrape a significant portion of its entire length (of 230 metres) when trying to stop, potentially breaching many of its watertight compartments. In principle, this could have been seen in advance. Still, it would have required looking at something very unlikely and realising that there would be little chance of recovering from it if it occurred.

54. For a discussion about the reasonable worst-case damage that might arise and various flooding scenarios, see http://www.titanicology.com/FloodingByCompartment.html. For an engineering analysis, see https://www.simscale.com/blog/why-did-titanic-sink-engineer/

55. On bulkhead design (for watertight compartments), see, for example, the comments of Jack Grover: https://www.quora.com/Why-didnt-the-bulkheads-on-the-Titanic-run-all-the-way-up-What-were-the-engineering-challenges

56. Inquiry transcript: https://www.titanicinquiry.org/BOTInq/BOTInq20Carlisle01.php. This article highlights how the White Star Line relied on the regulator's view of what was needed: https://www.abc.net.au/news/2012-04-11/berg-regulatory-failure-of-titanic-proportions/3940980

Chapter 12 (*Continued*)

57. This highlights a dilemma that regulators can find themselves into this day. On the one hand, you want to create regulations that will address potential problems. On the other hand, you want to encourage safety to be 'built-in'. More generally, regulators will usually consult to understand how any new rules might be implemented. During this process, regulators often hear: 'Can we have more time before the new laws take effect' or 'Do we have to do all of those things, given we have these other safety measures in place?'. Thus, regulators can encounter dilemmas concerning: (i) how to untangle legitimate concerns versus exaggerated ones and (ii) implications for inward investment and competitiveness versus safety/compliance (another dilemma). This UK Government work contains its own fishbone explaining the reasons regulations can be fragmented and complex: https://www.gov.uk/government/publications/when-laws-become-too-complex/when-laws-become-too-complex

58. This short document contains a useful overview of the loading of all the lifeboats: http://www.castlefordacademy.com/wp-content/uploads/2020/12/Titanics_Lifeboats.pdf

59. But as a member of a 'Guarantee Committee' who was invited onto the maiden voyage.

60. Jack Philips bio: https://www.godalmingmuseum.org.uk/?page=jack-phillips-and-the-titanic. He was criticised for not passing on a message from Cyril Evans (SS *Californian*). Still, he had passed countless other messages of ice that day. He stayed at his post, sending distress messages to the end, despite being told he could evacuate.

61. Jack Philips's reply to Cyril Evans is infamous: 'Shut up, I am working Cape Race', but he was busy sending messages on behalf of first-class passengers concerning, among other things, their itineraries after landing. And there is every sign that other notices of ice were known to the crew.

62. See the article following the 1997 film *Titanic*, which highlights some of the problems of judging Cyril Evans and others on the Californian for not coming to the Titanic's aid: https://www.dailymail.co.uk/news/article-10426389/SS-Californian-wireless-operator-did-NOT-cost-lives-sleeping-Titanic-distress-call.html

63. According to the book '*Unsinkable*', there were eight white rockets (p. 159). The first rocket was launched around 12.50 (p. 162) and the last around 1.40 a.m. (p. 163).

64. Fourth Officer Joseph Boxhall and Captain Edward Smith on the RMS *Titanic* were convinced that a ship was close enough to be signalled by a Morse lamp. They signalled that the Titanic was sinking. Onboard the SS

Chapter 12 (*Continued*)

Californian, Apprentice James Gibson saw a flickering white light, thinking this might be a Morse lamp, but when trying to discern whether there was a message (using binoculars), he concluded it was the flickering light on the top of a mast and not a Morse lamp message. This is linked to the refraction point through a phenomenon called 'astronomical scintillation'. The atmospheric conditions that night may also have caused the significance of the flares to be confused as well.

65. This is a crucial detail. The crew thought they saw a smaller ship 5 miles away rather than the largest ship ever built 10 miles away. Miraging effects caused by the ice-cold air will likely be a reason for this. Tim Maltin's 'A most deceiving night' is helpful on this point. It is also thought to be a reason why the nature of the rockets was not correctly understood as well.

66. No charges pressed: https://www.quora.com/Why-wasnt-the-Captain-of-the-SS-Californian-charged-with-Negligence-or-manslaughter-for-refusing-to-help-The-RMS-Titanic-even-though-he-his-crew-could-see-distress-flares-being-fired. See this on the SS *Californian*: https://titanic.fandom.com/wiki/SS_Californian. Note also research suggesting the Californian was further away than many think. A PBS programme highlights the problem of seeking to blame Captain Lord: https://www.pbs.org/wnet/secrets/abandoning-titanic-promo/5432/. This research suggesting even if the Californian had tried to help, it would have made little difference: https://www.encyclopedia-titanica.org/californian-incident.html?utm_content=cmp-true

67. It is possible that the SS *Californian* could have, perhaps, done more. And the conduct of Captain Stanley Lord was not ideal in terms of coming forward at first to the inquiry, but both speak only to contributing factors in the whole story, *not the root causes of why so many died.*

68. See https://www.pressreader.com/uk/the-sunday-telegraph/20120325/286929586872559

69. '*Unsinkable*' book. Chapter 'The Lonely Sea' p. 140. Gertrude (Jean) Isabelle Hippach, who was on lifeboat 4, explained: 'You can't think what it felt out there alone by ourselves in the Atlantic. Do you know what they say when you see a shooting star, someone is dying? And we thought of that, for there were so many dying not far from us', from the TV programme 'Titanic: Case closed'.

Chapter 12 (*Continued*)

70. Article: https://clickamericana.com/topics/events/the-titanics-terrifying-last-moments-before-sinking-to-the-ocean-floor-1912

71. See Senator Rayner, in Senate, 28 May 1912. https://books.google.co.uk/books?id=fDkuAAAAYAAJ&pg=RA1-PA240&lpg=RA1-PA240&dq=We+must+change+the+admiralty+and+navigation+laws+of+this+country.+They+consist+of+an+incongruous+collection+of+antiquated+statutes+which+should+be+repealed+and+re-enacted+to+meet+the+necessities+..+of+the+present+day&source=bl&ots=YWo4COOw85&sig=ACfU3U2sFmtcIn-xHdkmwpfh5SLSQtwW4g&hl=en&sa=X&ved=2ahUKEwic_MDAopX9AhWUbsAKHd6KCi0Q6AF6BAgHEAM#v=onepage&q&f=false

    Clearly, rescuing passengers in the water is unlikely to have made a huge difference to the final death toll. But it is difficult to argue different actions from those in the lifeboats would have made no difference.

72. See https://www.titanicinquiry.org/BOTInq/BOTReport/botRepRec.php#a4

73. The first SOLAS meetings were in London in 1913: https://trid.trb.org/view/1148276

74. The start of the Great War (WW1) meant that its implementation took several years after its first publication.

75. 1914 SOLAS PDF: https://archive.org/details/textofconvention00inte/page/n5/mode/2up?view=theater

76. IMO latest SOLAS: https://www.imo.org/en/About/Conventions/Pages/International-Convention-for-the-Safety-of-Life-at-Sea-(SOLAS),-1974.aspx. But this is not to say that there are no issues with Maritime safety; see, for example, '*The Outlaw Sea*', by William Langewiesche. Published by North Point Press.

77. Often covering a number of the 'eight ways to understand why' topics discussed in this book.

78. New London Texas explosion 1937: https://lrl.texas.gov/scanned/interim/45/45_NewLondon.pdf

79. Exxon Valdez. https://en.wikipedia.org/wiki/Exxon_Valdez_oil_spill. Greenpeace also summed up the systemic nature of what happened, highlighting the problem of blaming the ship's Captain Joseph Hazelwood with the comment: 'It wasn't his driving that caused the Alaskan Oil spill. It was yours'.

Chapter 12 (*Continued*)

80. 9/11 Commission report: https://www.9-11commission.gov/report/911Report.pdf. The conclusions of the 9/11 report speak to many of the key root cause types I have discussed, for example, R2A2: 'Management should have ensured that . . . duties were clearly assigned across agencies . . .'; Design: 'AQ's new brand of terrorism presented challenges to US governmental institutions that they were *not well designed* to meet'; Human Factors: '. . . Capabilities were insufficient. Little was done to expand or reform them'; Resources, Priorities: 'There were broader management issues with respect to how . . . leaders set priorities and allocated resources'. Also of note is the way the report makes connections between some of these causes, e.g.: '. . . policy challenges were linked to the failure of imagination', highlighting, in my opinion, a systems-thinking mindset.

81. The unexpected benefits of Sarbanes Oxley, HBR article: https://hbr.org/2006/04/the-unexpected-benefits-of-sarbanes-oxley

82. NTSB involvement in investigations: https://www.ntsb.gov/investigations/process/pages/default.aspx. Medical investigation process (US): https://www.ncbi.nlm.nih.gov/pmc/articles/PMC1117773/

83. Of course, regulator investigations are a vast topic, which my comments only start to touch the surface of. A brief overview can be found at https://www.reuters.com/legal/legalindustry/regulatory-investigation-red-flags-that-signal-significant-risk-companies-2022-08-19/

84. You could apply this image to the superweapon Death Star, destroyed in the *Star Wars* movie because of this kind of problem.

85. Sometimes known as the 'Zone of Dread'.

86. Setting aside other causal conjunctions that arose for the sake of space/simplicity.

87. https://theconversation.com/lessons-from-lakanal-house-were-not-heeded-then-grenfell-happened-80051

88. This is why the book '*Skin in the Game*' by Nassim Nicholas Taleb is worthy of reading. He reminds his readers that when receiving, for example, investment advice, it's important to understand what the advisor might gain or lose and whether the advisor has personally invested in what they are suggesting.

Chapter 12 (*Continued*)

89. Here is an easy-to-follow Canadian example, written for financial institutions but applicable (with adaptations) for organisations in other sectors as well: https://www.osfi-bsif.gc.ca/eng/fi-if/rg-ro/gdn-ort/gl-ld/pages/e18.aspx

90. Which is why crisis management preparedness is so important.

91. The classic quote from Yogi Berra.

Chapter 13: The Challenges with Action Planning

1. Institute for Government, 'How public inquiries can lead to change': https://www.instituteforgovernment.org.uk/sites/default/files/publications/Public%20Inquiries%20%28final%29.pdf; UK National Audit Office, 'Investigation into government-funded inquiries': https://www.nao.org.uk/wp-content/uploads/2018/05/Investigation-into-government-funded-inquiries.pdf; The NAO has implemented an action tracking tool effective from 2019, but – at the time of writing – it has not picked up significant open actions from past reports. It is also not clear how delayed actions will be escalated for a resolution one way or the other.

2. This can be a common problem; e-learning training makes a brief reference to a topic, which someone like Mr Spock might think through and apply correctly in all contexts, but with most people, a more explicit discussion is needed to understand what this means in practice.

3. After all, the discussions with others who were not directly involved in what happened were outside the obvious boundary for the investigation. However, we were convinced this was a necessary issue to investigate, and it transpired it was very important.

4. That is, many departments or organisations within the boundary of the review.

Chapter 14: Where Are We Now and Looking Ahead

1. https://thedecisionlab.com/thinkers/philosophy/ludwig-wittgenstein

2. See https://practicalfounders.com/articles/the-future-is-already-here-but-its-not-evenly-distributed-william-gibson/

Chapter 14 (*Continued*)

3. This is a potentially challenging thought since a great deal of time and effort is invariably spent developing RCA and systems analysis tools and techniques, and learning how to use them effectively, so we have a 'sunk cost' that may make it hard to turn away from.

4. Starting with major infrastructure projects, but also including investments at scale on solutions that may not be all we hope for, e.g. EVs, wind farms, solar panels, nuclear and air source heat pumps, when other solutions (that are currently not so popular) may be more successful in the long run because they are not impacted by constraints such as the availability of rare earth metals for batteries, e.g. green hydrogen, hydro and tidal power, etc.

5. This certainly appears to be the case with the Bank of England: https://www.thetimes.co.uk/article/rampant-inflations-not-our-fault-governor-wx5rh979z. However, slowly, there appears to be some recognition by the Governor of the Bank of England that there are 'very big lessons to learn'. https://www.ft.com/content/b972f5e3-4f03-4986-890d-5443878424ac. It remains to be seen whether any review of the lessons to be learned will be independent of the Bank of England. Otherwise, there is a risk the results of the review will be subject to a conflict of interest, as discussed elsewhere.

6. Here, the problems with the Silicon Valley Bank in 2023 are in point.

7. Unsurprisingly, the decline in staffing levels for the UK NHS over a decade (doctors and nurses) has led, at the time of writing this book, to record waiting lists and industrial disputes as staff try to manage with fewer and fewer resources.

8. See https://www.thetimes.co.uk/article/english-reservoirs-wait-for-repairs-as-long-as-eight-years-f2v6cbh2v

9. You can link this point to 'Externality effects', see https://en.wikipedia.org/wiki/Externality

10. The book *The Scout Mindset* by Julia Galef (published by Piatkus): https://en.wikipedia.org/wiki/The_Scout_Mindset

11. I refer to 'conflicts of interest' in the broadest sense – e.g. an IT department leading an IT RCA or a Health and Safety department conducting a health and safety audit. On these terms, such conflicts are ubiquitous.

12. Let me remind readers that numerous books and manuals have been written on the basics of an effective RCA or inquiry. Here, there are cornerstones around evidence gathering, fact finding, the quality and experience of the investigation team, overcoming biases, how to demonstrate

Chapter 14 (*Continued*)

causality vs. correlation, etc. None of this should be forgotten in any of what I have said in this book.

13. The language we speak, the layout of roads, laws and regulations, how school curriculums are determined, how social media applications are configured, and in the future, how AI is designed and operated, etc.

14. George Washington's farewell address, 17 September 1796: https://www
.mountvernon.org/library/digitalhistory/past-projects/
quotes/article/however-political-parties-may-now-and-
then-answer-popular-ends-they-are-likely-in-the-course-
of-time-and-things-to-become-potent-engines-by-which-
cunning-ambitious-and-unprincipled-men-will-be-enabled-
to-subvert-the-power-of-the-people-and-to-usurp-for-th/

15. As an illustration, it seems likely that some countries immigration policies may be underestimating complex factors that mean people may still migrate towards peaceful and wealthy nations and seek to bypass border controls, no matter how many 'barriers' and sanctions are put in place. This is why comparisons between countries might be interesting. Although it will be complicated, there is a good chance that 'mindset' issues play a role.

16. Global risk report, World Economic Forum: https://www.weforum.
org/reports/global-risks-report-2023. UN: https://www.
undrr.org/gar2022-our-world-risk-gar. Work on existential risks in Stanford and Cambridge is worthy of note: https://seri.stan-
ford.edu, https://www.cser.ac.uk

17. https://news.harvard.edu/gazette/story/2021/09/our-own-
worst-enemy-looks-at-americans-lack-of-civic-virtue/ And there are a range of books and articles on the same theme.

18. See   https://www.mdpi.com/systems/systems-08-00020/arti-
cle_deploy/html/images/systems-08-00020-g001.png

19. https://www.ncbi.nlm.nih.gov/pmc/articles/PMC8371427/

20. https://data.gov.scot/child-poverty-system-map/images/
canvas-white-with-legend.png

21. OFSTED – Office for Standards in Education, Children's Services and Skills in the United Kingdom. https://www.theguardian.com/
education/2023/mar/17/headteacher-killed-herself-after-
news-of-low-ofsted-rating-family-says

Chapter 14 (*Continued*)

22. https://www.theguardian.com/education/2023/apr/05/ teachers-vote-to-abolish-ofsted-inspections-after-death-of-ruth-perry. With the amplification of these concerns through mainstream and social media.

23. The writer's workshop referred to in the 'Thanks' at the end of this book: https://www.arvon.org

24. As Sir Ken Robinson said in his much-watched TED Talk on the link between recognising and accepting mistakes and being creative (https://www.ted.com/talks/sir_ken_robinson_do_schools_kill_creativity/c): 'What we do know is, if you're not prepared to be wrong, you'll never come up with anything original. And by the time they get to be adults, most kids have lost that capacity. They have become frightened of being wrong. And we run our companies like this. We stigmatise mistakes. And we're now running national education systems where mistakes are the worst thing you can make. And the result is that we are educating people out of their creative capacities'. I regard creativity as a key ingredient to being able to solve problems effectively; likewise, the ability to admit shortcomings is central to an RCA and systems thinking mindset.

25. https://www.oreilly.com/library/view/the-art-of/ 9780857085399/c15.xhtml

Appendix A: Practical Advice on Action Planning

1. See https://www.azquotes.com/quote/1406679

2. https://www.lockheedmartin.com/content/dam/lockheed-martin/uk/documents/suppliers/RCCA-Problem-Solving-Guidebook.pdf

3. RCA squared and a useful hierarchy of actions:
   https://www.health.state.mn.us/facilities/patientsafety/ adverseevents/toolkit/docs/safetytoolkit_actionhierarchy .pdf

4. 8D framework: https://en.wikipedia.org/wiki/Eight_disciplines_problem_solving

5. https://www.forbes.com/advisor/business/smart-goals/

6. In line with KPIs and KRIs for other targets and action plans.

Appendix B: Practical Advice to Improve Rca in an Organisation

1. There are many manuals and frameworks to consider, for example:

   Canadian incident analysis framework, with some constellation diagrams:

   `https://www.patientsafetyinstitute.ca/en/toolsResources/`
   `IncidentAnalysis/Documents/Canadian%20Incident%20`
   `Analysis%20Framework.PDF`

   2006 framework with various excellent diagrams:

   `http://medicalstaff.fraserhealth.ca/getattachment/`
   `Quality-and-Safety/Strips/QIPS/Module-3/Links-of-Interest/`
   `Root-cause-analysis-framework.pdf.aspx/`

   CAA (Aviation) overview:

   `https://publicapps.caa.co.uk/docs/33/CAP1760%20Root%20`
   `Cause%20Identification%20Paper%20(Issue%2002%20April%20`
   `19).pdf`

2. This is one of the basic ways that you can spread good practice between centres of excellence, and it is also one of the ways that you can mitigate the risk of conflicts of interest, where a department may be reluctant to 'look in the mirror' concerning its own potential role in what happened.

3. First, it will highlight how important some 'cultural' problems are (e.g. problems with R2A2 or articulating resource requirements and dilemmas) across a range of areas, highlighting the need for change. Second, it may also make it clearer how areas that have implemented best practices (e.g. in training or process design) are less prone to problems. This is a way to leverage RCA to promote best practices across the organization – emphasizing the opportunity to use RCA proactively not just when an issue has occurred.

4. Neither this list nor the list in Supplement B1 is asserted to be a complete list. However, for many people starting on their RCA journey, this should be a reasonable starting point for study and further research as needed in a specialist domain.

5. Pros and cons are hard to provide in any definitive sense since this is based on the experiences of my clients and is not an exhaustive analysis. Apologies in advance to anyone who has a favourite technique they have mastered that they think is great. The more time and effort you put into any method, the more you can make it work. But as I have said, there are often limits to the time and resources you are prepared to invest that

Appendix B (*Continued*)

will impact the technique or tool you start to use. In all cases, I recommend readers do due diligence and form their own view, which will often depend on their specific needs.

6. The absence of five whys is not an accident. I would always avoid a 'pure' five whys approach, hence the title of the book ('*Beyond the Five Whys*') and the reference to the five whys two legs or three-way five whys.

7. Since these tools evolve, it must be recognised that precise functionality at one point in time may develop. Readers interested should check with relevant software providers.

8. Some clients use simple RCA techniques such as the fishbone or Bowtie in some situations and more exhaustive approaches (fault tree/systems approaches) when dealing with more significant and complex matters.

9. See https://www.lesswrong.com/tag/the-map-is-not-the-territory

10. If I had to give general advice on training and development programmes it would be to 'step up' the way things are made real – for example, at AstraZeneca we implemented a 'Managers driving licence' and 'Finance for non-Finance manager' training. With other clients I have overhauled risk training, making it much more focused on the business implications, rather than 'how to use the risk tool' and sometimes I have worked to implement senior level workshops on what seem to be basic points, but which are often problematic (e.g. committee dynamics and the hallmarks of an effective steering group).

11. During her career spanning 40+ years, Nancy Haig has held internal audit leadership roles in the financial and professional services, pharmaceutical and healthcare industries. Most recently, she was inducted into the American Hall of Distinguished Audit Practitioners, the highest honour given by the North American Board of the Institute of Internal Auditors (IIA) to those who have contributed significantly to the profession throughout their lifetime.

12. Norman Marks – CPA, CRMA.

13. Andrew Pal – CEng, FIMechE.

14. Dr Mohammad Farhad Peerally – MBChB, MRCP, PhD.

15. Providing a complete list of key resources is challenging, but I have endeavoured to set out a broad spread of useful materials. Readers should use the links provided as a 'starter for 10' and build from there.

Appendix B (*Continued*)

16. Some of these software providers do provide a significant amount of free-of-charge, easy-to-follow materials about root cause analysis, which is to be commended. They also offer webinars and training courses (inevitably highlighting, inter alia, how to use their software tools).

17. It would have been possible to provide links to materials concerning public inquiries as well, but often these are governed by the relevant laws of the countries in which they are carried out. Further, there can be different materials available outlining lessons learned. Here is a brief sample of materials:

    UK: https://www.legislation.gov.uk/ukpga/2005/12/contents

    Australia: https://www.aph.gov.au/Parliamentary_Business/Committees/Current_Inquiries

    Canada: https://www.canada.ca/en/privy-council/services/commissions-inquiry.html

    USA: https://www.senate.gov/about/powers-procedures/investigations.htm

Index